A TALE O[
CITIL

edited by
John Murray

*an anthology
of modern
world writing*

PANURGE PUBLISHING
Brampton, Cumbria
1994

A TALE OF TWO CITIES

first published 1994 by
Panurge Publishing
Crooked Holme Farm Cottage
Brampton, Cumbria CA8 2AT

EDITOR John Murray
PRODUCTION EDITOR Henry Swan
COVER DESIGN Andy Williams
Typeset at Union Lane Telecentre, Brampton, Cumbria CA8 1BX
Tel. 06977 - 41014
Printed by Peterson Printers, 12 Laygate, South Shields, Tyne and Wear NE33 5RP
Tel. 091-456-3493

ISBN 1 898984 00 X

All fiction submissions must be accompanied by
SAE or IRCs. Work is considered all the year
round, and talented new writers are
especially encouraged to submit.

British Library Cataloguing in Publication Data.
A catalogue record for this book is available from
the British Library.

PANURGE PUBLISHING
Crooked Holme Farm Cottage,
Brampton,
Cumbria CA8 2AT
Tel. 06977-41087

PANURGE PUBLISHING is
distributed to booksellers and libraries
by CENTRAL BOOKS, 99 Wallis Road,
London E9 5LN.
Tel. 081-986-4854

PANURGE

Kathy Janowitz

In The Mountains

It snowed thirty inches. The boys stuck their heads in it and had to be pulled out, the *eismeisters* swept the rink to glassy perfection with their long-handled brooms and the curlers appeared as if from nowhere to spin their fat tuffets across the frozen surface. In the lobby of the gracefully decaying old resort hotel where for the four odd decades since the last great war emigres had come back to roost and remember, the guests, some with small dogs asleep at their feet, sat drinking tea in the armchairs turned to face the great picture windows.

At Chantarella, out on the wooden terrace of one of the two restaurants, Irene struck up a conversation with Helen, a red-headed lady who was sitting alone reading in the erratic sunlight while her family ski-ed and she told Irene she was Scottish but lived in Brussels and her two daughters were grown and lived in Paris and London.

Helen ordered a bowl of soup and Irene asked for sherry, Helen addressing the waiter in French and Irene in her halting German - "Bitte, ein klein glas..." Helen said she and her husband were staying in the Bad next to the lake where you shared tables at meals, which she thought would be difficult but actually everyone was quite nice, and Irene said she was an only child and needed her privacy and Helen said she understood because being Scottish was the same as being an only child. The waiter came back with their orders - Helen was seated at the table behind her and Irene smiled at her and said, "I'll give you back your privacy," and she turned back to her book and her little glass of sherry which the waiter handed her with a sigh. "Are they driving you crazy?" she asked him, meaning the customers. "No, not them," he said, grinning. "Only my wife," and it was clear that he had sighed so she would ask and he could make his little joke.

And the walk up had been lovely too, her boots making soft hour-glass shapes in the snow, the warm breath of the big brown horses pulling the sleighs close to her neck and the pungent smell of their droppings in the cold, dry air.

Her cough had been bothering her at night. She slept with a cough drop in her mouth - Em-Eukal they were called, *hustenbonbons*, hard brown candies in pale green wrappers.

One night Irene visited her friend Claudia in the little weekend cottage she and Christoph rented from Claudia's parents. Claudia had cleared a narrow path to the door. The walls were yellow pine and the ceiling was very low. They ate pastries which Claudia brought from the city and Claudia talked about Mili Weber, the children's book illustrator and painter who had once lived alone in the house next door and showed her Mili's paintings of animals and beautiful children at play in moonlit forests and told Irene that she felt drawn to Mili's strangeness and her need for privacy. "She was always very kind," Claudia said. "I was never afraid of her."

Irene's night vision was poor. They carried flaming torches which made their shadows dance on the path ahead of them and Claudia held onto Irene's arm to keep her from slipping as they made their way to the little restaurant festooned with holiday lights.

She woke up one night, coughing, to a darkness damasked with light and, putting a cough candy into her mouth, she remembered the train ride through the mountains, speeding through the lace-white curtains of snow and into the heart of the earth.

It was the holidays and Claudia fed her pastries and the black birds came in droves to dive for crumbs in the snow. A pyramid of logs blazed in the lobby fireplace. The big shaggy horses heated her back as she walked uphill thinking every time has its music and she imagined the snow as it had come, crystal by crystal.

In a bookstore she found a German picturebook set in Prague, the story of Peppo the carp, carried home in a shopping bag filled with water and ultimately saved, returned to the river known as the Vltava in Czech and in German the Moldau. She went to the movie house with the smoke-filled lounge and the dark red ladies room and when she began coughing Irene put a cough candy in her mouth and sat on the ledge of an open window and a young man down in the street looked up at her and smiled.

She woke up coughing one night and, putting a cough candy into her mouth, she felt tired, as if she could sleep, and then she slept and in her dream she found herself at the threshold of Mili Weber's little house and Mili was standing in the doorway, her hair around her like a cloak of flames.

Subscriptions and Resubscriptions

PANURGE RAFFLE TERMINATION

We're sorry to say that the Panurge Raffle has been discontinued! It was an attractive idea, to reward prompt subscribers with raffle prizes but it turned out to cost us more in revenue than it gained us. We hope that the new bigger Panurge will be enough in itself to encourage lapsed subscribers to resubscribe promptly.

WHAT A SUBSCRIPTION MEANS

Remember that Panurge comes out every April and October promptly. *Remember also that a subscription does not represent twelve calendar months but two consecutive issues of the magazine.* New subscribers often have to resubscribe within months of their first cheque, and this is because they have had the current and next issues, and their subscription has consequently lapsed.

Prizewinners for Panurge Raffle drawn 1.12.93
1. £55 Book Token won by Miss B. Taylor of Glossop, Derbys. **2.** £30 Book Token won by Ms S. Rose of ESCAP, Bangkok, Thailand **3.** A £15 Book Token won by N. Baker of Saltash, Cornwall. **4.** A £20 Wine Token won by David Watson of Holland Gardens, Belfast. This was kindly donated by **Ulverston Writers Group**. **5.** J.C. Spence of Sutton Coldfield won *Dai Vaughan's* first novel *The Cloud Chamber* plus a year's subscription to Sunk Island Review. **6.** Pat Jackson of Henfield, Sussex won one year's subscription to Sunk Island Review. **7.** Vicky Grut of London SW16 won a complete set of Panurge back issues including all those out of print. **8.** Julia Clarkson of Morden, Surrey won £30 worth of books kindly donated by **Fourth Estate**. **9.** A. Calder of York won £50 of books kindly donated by **Faber**. **10.** G.L.Ward of Irthlingborough, Northants won 5 years free subscription to Panurge.

STANDARD SUBSCRIPTION / RESUBSCRIPTION

☐£10 UK   ☐IR£15   ☐£12/ $15 overseas   ☐£18/ $25 Air Mail

Cheques to: **Panurge, Crooked Holme Farm Cottage, Brampton, Cumbria CA8 2AT United Kingdom** Tel 06977 - 41087.

Name..................................

Address..............................

....

....

Panurge Tale of Two Cities Fiction Competition 1993 - 1994

WINNERS
First Prize: **Richard C. Zimler** of Oporto, Portugal with *Personal Fulcrums.* Worth £500 plus standard publication fee.

Joint Second Prize: **Mairead Irish** of Waterford, Eire with *Ships Passing.* Worth £100 plus free subscription to Panurge until 2000 A.D. Also standard publication fee.

Joint Second Prize: **Julia Darling** of Newcastle-on-Tyne with *Bloodlines.* Worth £100 plus six years' free subscription and fee as above.

Third Prize: **John Cunningham** of Glasgow with *Beady Eyes.* Worth £50 plus free subscription until 2000 A.D. plus standard publication fee.

A few comments
1. There were **297** entries over an eight month period. The very last eligible day yielded **42** entries!
2. There were **28** stories shortlisted. Thus the percentage of entries of approximate publication standard (i.e. deemed worth shortlisting) was about 10%. This is a very high rate and probably relates to the fact that the competition was a *set theme.* Thus the writers had to sit down and write the story to order as it were.

Shortlisted writers in chronological order of listing
James Cressey of Torriano Avenue, London
Julia Darling of Newcastle-on-Tyne
John Cunningham of Glasgow
Helen Kitson of Worcester
R. Morris of Jerusalem
G. Swain of Ilminster, Somerset
Daithidh Mac Eochaidh of York
Audrey Hopkins of Lytham St Annes, Lancashire

Clive Murphy of Brick Lane, London
D.C. Couch of Plymouth
Scott Kleager of Cologne, Germany
Menzies McKillop of Glasgow
Elizabeth Morse of New York
Nigel Jarrett of Newport, Gwent
Aisling Maguire of County Dublin
Sam Garrett of Amsterdam
Derek Gregory of Middlesborough, Cleveland
Jean Pickering of Fresno, California
Crysse Morrison of Frome, Somerset
Alan Dunn of Penrith, Cumbria
James Waddington of Huddersfield
Richard C. Zimler of Oporto, Portugal
David Rose of Ashford, Middlesex
Ulf Goebel of London SW12
Iain Richardson of Brighton
Mairead Irish of Waterford, Eire
Sandra Staas of Pennsylvania, USA
Norah Hill of Middlesborough

3. Gender

Two male judges shortlisted 12 women writers and 16 men writers. The original 297 entries were split almost equally between men and women.

4. Locations

There were 35 entries from outside the UK i.e. about 12%. Of these 9 were shortlisted. Thus 12% of the entries constitute 35% of the shortlist. Possibly foreign competitors tried that much harder as they felt so remote from where the action was?

5. Favouritism?

9 of the shortlist have either been in Panurge or will appear in future issues irrespective of the competition. This looks a bit fishy, but bear in mind that all of 21 writers who have appeared or will appear in the magazine did *not* have their entries shortlisted!

6. General Comments

Quite a lot of half-good stories and three-quarters good stories, which didn't make the shortlist. Very few of the stories made much of the cities themselves in the way of vigorous depiction or attempting to make the cities, as it were, characters in the stories. Mairead Irish's story was a fine example of one that did. There was no requirement to do so in the rules, but it would have been nice to have had a few of the entries showing some intensity of feeling towards particular places. We also hoped for some good stories with strong contemporary concerns (e.g. about Sarajevo and Belgrade; Dublin and Belfast) but the ones that arrived tended to be some of the weakest. There were one or two brave shots at allegorical and imaginary cities but they again tended to have more ambition than basic accomplishment. Mick North enjoyed being a judge as did I. We hope you enjoy the winning stories and let us know what you think of them whether or no ...

7. *Presentation Ceremony*

Cheques to the winners were presented by **D.J. Taylor** the distinguished novelist and critic on Saturday 19th March 1994 at the White Lion Hotel, Brampton, Cumbria. Present at the ceremony were: Lancaster University Creative Writing Department (David Craig, Anne Spillard, Alan Burns, Linda Anderson); Panurge editorial past and present in the shape of John Murray, David Almond, Sara Jane Palmer, Clare Crossman, Frederick Lightfoot; publishers Rachel Taylor and M.J. Thorpe; Union Lane Centre, Brampton in the shape of Gerard Edwards, Sue Lurz, Henry Swan; Cumbrian and North-East literary editors and administrators and authors such as Lorna Tracy, Sharon Gould, Kitty Fitzgerald, Peter Mortimer (Stand and Iron respectively), Graeme Rigby (The Page), Jenny Attala and John Bradshaw and Chrissie Glazebrook (Northern Arts), Martin Wheeler (Startext Publishing, Cockermouth), Peter and Margaret Lewis (Flambard Press); writers Marian McCraith, Janni Howker, Alan Hankinson; graphic designer Andy Williams. Partners of the above were also present in some instances.

8. *Sponsorship*

We gratefully acknowledge sponsorship from The Union Lane Centre, Brampton; Sponsors Club, Newcastle-on-Tyne; Border TV plc.; and Human Resource Development of West Hall, Brampton.

9. *Publication of Winners*

Across Panurge 20 and Panurge 21 (October 1994).

10. *Thanks*

To all who helped with the competition, especially the energetic and scrupulous judge Mick North. Also to everyone who entered, who took up the challenge and tried. Also to Charles Dickens who gave John Murray the idea in the first place. Dickens once stayed overnight in The Howard Arms, Brampton, upon the outside of which a plaque commemorates the fact. So there you are.

John Murray, Spring 1994

JOINT 2ND PRIZE

Ships Passing

Mairead Irish

Cork then was the sweep of the wind down Dean Street, and the special leaves that blew in front of it over the dry road. There was a little gold angel on the back of St. Finbarre's and she said that was medieval, the day I told her a corner of my garden was Greek. If anything ever happens to that angel it will be the end for Cork, so they say. I used to stand there in the presence of the angel, watching the leaves swirl on the steps of the big houses or nestle against the wall of the church. I used to love that street in every little detail, even the surface of the road, worn down by years of wheels and feet.

That was Cork, then. But I don't live there anymore.

I arrived in the coastal town a stranger; at seventeen I had never seen the sea. Where I came from was just flat plain and bogland and sluggish canals. She was a native of the place, but had left home and moved around constantly, with flats and rooms everywhere, little pockets of the city that she slid in and out of. I lived in the same house all the time I was there, a damp old place in Glasheen where the enormous rooms had been divided up with thin partitions, and that usually housed half a dozen people. Wherever she was there was always a piano. She'd bring it with her every time, even moving every few weeks like she sometimes did. She'd have it levered in through windows, raised with ropes, hauled up stairs and squeezed sideways through doors. Of course I thought it must be special to her, until right after one move I found she had it sold and replaced with another. She called it the 'cargo'. Sometimes there wasn't much else in her room - a bed and maybe a table, none of the things I thought women would have.

I first saw her on the North Main Street, an autumn morning when I was delivering the bread. I brought bread every morning from the bakery on the South Main Street to the cafes on the North, and she told me later that that route, between the two arms of the river, was the span of the medieval town. The morning light in October is the clearest you can ever see things, and I was stopped in my tracks by the way it seemed to shine through her skin. I knew she must have crossed the river from the northside, because the light

11

is different there. That's all I can remember - waves of hair, the cold, her pale face with the sun on it. I had flour in my hair and a bag of Vienna loaves over my shoulder.

I had worked in the bakery for nearly a year and lived in the city of Cork for that long. At the start I used to love the sticky stretching dough in my hands, but I got so used to that I hardly noticed it. People would come in and say the smell was so good, and leave with six loaves when they had come for one. I couldn't smell the baking bread anymore, couldn't hear the clock in the shop although they say it ticks all the time. You lose everything in the heat and the ovens go all day, blasting a thunder of heat out when you open them, ten loaves out, ten loaves in, always against the clock, flour in the eyes, flour in the brain, every day from five until closing.

I asked everyone who she was. No-one knew exactly, but some people had seen her playing piano in clubs or hotel bars. The other lads laughed when I brushed my hair going out and dawdled over my deliveries, but she never reappeared on the North Main Street. Then I learned about the pub on the far side of the river, down at the bottom of an alley, where she sometimes drank in the early evenings.

I began to keep watch on it. Sometimes from a bridge opposite I could see people come out of the narrow laneway or disappear down it. After a few days I managed to walk past slowly, with a casual glance down the covered alley hung with lanterns. Wind blew off the river and the lanterns swayed wildly, throwing patchy light right down to the bottom, to the panelled doors of the pub. She went there alone I was told, and had long solitary drinks before the evening sessions in piano bars.

It was weeks before I went down. I bought the evening paper and held it tightly under my arm while I eased the door open. It was so dark inside I couldn't see how big it was or how many people were there, but I could sense that there were figures sitting very still in the shadows. I sat in a corner and drank thick dark coffee with the paper half-open on my lap. I looked up casually every time the door opened, and tried to pick people out in the gloom. Ten evenings I went there as soon as I had finished in the bakery; ten nights I lay awake because of the coffee.

She came on the eleventh day. I'd always been sure she would come, so I was very calm when I recognised her, reading my paper and not even looking to see where she sat. But the cup shook when I lifted it from the saucer.

After that I used to watch her, sitting directly across from me every evening. She drank a glass of beer, sometimes two. Her face in profile had a rough outdoor look, not at all a handsome face. She was older than me, twenty at least. Sometimes she asked the barman for the morning paper, sometimes she sat and stared straight ahead. I could see the raised blue veins on her wrist, just where the pale skin disappeared under the white cuff. Her voice when she ordered her drink or asked to borrow my paper was a disappointment, thin and flat. I started wondering why the light on her face on a certain day of the year should make me want to sit there every evening like a fool.

She borrowed my paper and said a few words. Over the weeks we started talking, about what was in the papers, about disasters at sea, the weather, what ships were in the harbour and what they had brought. She spoke about foreign ports, which she seemed to know a lot about - Valparaiso, Lisbon, Constantinople. We seemed to talk for longer each day, until once she drank a third glass of beer and I had a second cup of coffee. I lay awake all night and made resolutions.

The next evening while I listened to her I watched the dull shine of her hair under the lamp and felt the tightening in my throat. As she was standing up to go I asked if I could walk with her. She was going home, she said, and we stepped down the alley and out onto the street. The light was just fading, leaving stark trees and black buildings behind it. When we walked together up the hill to Sunday's Well, the streets where I had loitered for so long seemed unfamiliar, and the leaves rustled in a different way. Out of the side of my eye I watched her walking with me.

We left the pub at the same time every evening to walk to wherever she lived, sometimes taking detours through the park and over the shaky bridge, and stopping on the bridge to feel the vibrations of the passing feet on the boards. We'd go over the whole of Cork she said, street by street. She'd show me ship's chandlers down by the harbour where they sold heavy rope and brass lanterns and flat-bottomed decanters for the captain's table. I'd see the crooked spire of the church in Glanmire Road and the two black swans on the Lough. She'd show me the gold angel at the back of the cathedral that held the fate of the city of Cork in its wings.

On the seventh evening we stopped for a long time on the shaky bridge. The river was sleek and glassy, trees on each side dipped down to the water to drink. We leaned on the railings and felt the bridge shaking under us when people crossed, then the silence and the smoothness of the water until they came again. Once I saw my hand tremble even though the bridge was still. Darkness drifted slowly into the trees and the water. She took my hands from the railings and we kissed long deep kisses while the shuddering feet came and went and the bridge swayed from its suspensions. Later on we walked, crossing the full width of the city. From St. Luke's we saw it all spread out, the lights, cathedral spires, a red cross shining on a hill opposite. She left me in Glasheen and went on alone.

*

When I woke I thought I was in a strange town or a strange room. It was very still, not a breath of wind outside. Through the silence I could hear the slow drip of water off trees in the garden, the tiny rustle of beetles scurrying for cover under leaves. I lay in bed listening for a long time.

When I went to wash there were roses, roses bulging through the air, roses lilting round the room while I filled the basin and splashed my face with clear rosewater. I could hardly bear the heavy sweet spongy scent that hung in the air, too strong. It seemed to be everywhere, in the beaded moisture of the bathroom, swamping my lungs with every breath. I passed the soap over my face and stepped into the bath, rolling the wet splurge of roses down my arms. The cloying sweetness was overpowering. I wrapped myself in a towel and grasped at the window and a wave of cold stinging air. I stepped into my clothes with the cold rosepetal air still wisping over me.

It was Sunday and I could hear no-one else in the house, so I made myself a pot of tea and looked for something to eat. There was nothing in the cupboard except bread. I never eat bread, I can't stand it. I grasped the thick warm handle of the teapot and poured, and what came out was not the light fresh scent as normal, but a heavy tannin smell of tea. I raised the cup to my lips, a sweet hot burning, and the smell was still the thick brown heaviness of tea. But it had hardly any taste when I gulped it down. Only smells, it seemed, had tripled in strength - the pot of rotted roses in the bathroom, the rose-scented soap, and now the tea unbearably strong.

There were three chocolates in an open box on the sideboard. They smelled of sweet fat butter, bitter cocoa, sickly toffee. Picking one up was like drowning in chocolate. I ate them one by one, sinking my teeth into the fudge, the slippery cream, smelling deep sweet fondants under brittle cocoa shells. In the garden I could smell the soil, the damp grass, woody mouldy smells from under the ground, light herbal scents, and the air, soft, moist, plump with further rain. I wondered suddenly how the city would smell, and

14

decided to visit her.

Out on the streets I choked with fumes and smoke and dust. On the Mardyke I could smell the elms, the stench of the river at low tide, the brewery's roasting grain and yeast, and behind it all the rough salt of the sea. She was sitting up in bed, and called to me that the door was open.

Valparaiso, she said, is a jewel of a city, just in the shadow of the Andes, almost in the sea, a city built of washed-up white gold. In Cork they build with red brick and coral limestone, the whole lot jumbled up together in the one wall, and they call it streaky bacon. She said something odd had just happened. A bird had come in through the open window and flown wildly round the room and couldn't seem to spot the way out again. She was lying in bed, it was very early and she didn't want to wake up. The thing was bashing itself off the walls and against the glass and chirping away in great distress and she'd eventually got up and lowered the window as far as it would go. Some little songbird type thing it was she said, that had detached itself from the dawn chorus for a solo in her room. And still it wouldn't find the top half of the window that was open but kept crashing into the bottom half and looking like it had knocked itself out. Then off it'd go careering around the room again. It landed on the piano keys once, but was too light to play itself a note. In the end it perched up on top of the wardrobe and stayed there, sizing her up. She got back into bed. The two of them stared each other out. Would you go out the window you stupid bird, she thought. And it did.

Her room smelled cosy, of stale air and night sweat and warm dreams and dust. When I drew close her skin was musk and tobacco. Fresh sweat rose to the surface. I lay down beside her and was dizzy with smells, the oily feathers in the pillow and the faint must of the bedclothes, and the various smells of her, salty, yeasty, once a wave of sweetness like ripe fruit. I could smell the years of dampness coming through the walls, and the lives of all the people who had lived in these rooms before, rank chamber pots under beds, charred dust from their bedroom fires, the wicks of their wax candles. Later we went to the park and rolled in the dead leaves, with brittle shards sticking to the twists of her hair. She was wearing a vivid purple dress and she sat on one of the covered tin boxes painted bright colours which were supposed to serve as litter bins. The box she sat on was painted scarlet and the next one up was purple, the same mad purple as her dress. We sat on the swings and soared over the trees, we took our shoes off and ran in the grass with freezing feet.

A beautiful city, she said, the grey-green Pacific, the blue-dark mountains, the white harbour gleaming in the sun. The Incas knew there was gold in the mountains. Have you every seen platinum? The most precious metal, white silver buried deep in the rock. There are earthquakes. At any time the city could be buried. It was buried once, hidden for centuries under the mud until the next tremor came and it rose again out of the sea, sparkling white.

-Where did you get this Valparaiso? Was it a song?

-A ship.

Sometimes I walked through Cork alone now, in the evenings after I had left her to her piano. I got to know every tree on the streets and had my own names for them. On Donovan's Road I had the flurry tree, all twisty little twigs dripping into the air, all fronds and tendrils. I know none of the proper names for things, but I knew that tree. Sometimes I'd have to catch my breath when I saw it with a weak sun behind it, covered with spider threads and glittery drops of rain. Through the college railings I could watch the students. I used to watch them standing at the edge of the river skimming stones and think, I could do that. The Queen's college had tall gates and a wide avenue, and they owned a part of the river that ran through the grounds. But only while it ran through. I watched a leaf fall onto the water, and sail out under the bridge to freedom. I spoke to the students eventually. They had strange voices. I asked them where was Valparaiso.

She talked about it more and more. She wanted to go there. She was homesick in her own country, lonely for places she'd never been.

-Are there hills, like Cork?

-The Andes.

-Does it have a river that divides in two?

Cork is one city in sunlight and another in rain, so they say. Sometimes a damp, sad city like Lisbon. In the sun it's an old European port, with stone warehouses for spices and wine and gold. Salt fish and sides of beef wait there for Alexandria, damp sawdust and mouldering grain, hogsheads of claret and gold for making angels. There are alleys in Cork where the sun never goes. Time has not made it through the narrowest of them, where you can still find an old tavern where a stooped figure tends a char-grill, women in lace bonnets carry food to tables and brandy is drunk from greasy bottles that were smuggled in hidden in firkins of butter. There are no windows there, no clocks, and the gaslights burn all day.

Women from Santo Domingo slums

Philip Wolmuth

-What do you think of the political situation in Chile?
-I'm going when the wind is fair. I have a boat.
I didn't believe that. I looked up at the gold angel on St. Finbarre's playing her twin trumpets and thought, nothing will ever happen to her. She could dance on the head of a pin. It hardly matters what type a tree is, because they all stand out black and spidery in the dark. And the angel wasn't medieval either, she was a Victorian, gold leaf with a soul of cast iron, and on top of everything else she was probably male, a boy angel. If you looked down the alleys to that century you'd know that they would never have let a girl angel dance on top of their cathedral. I walked and walked. It was winter, and the smoke and coal dust clogged the air. But it didn't overpower me now.

I dreamed we were out walking at night, over coals, over rough boggy country towards a palace we could see shining in the distance, which we desperately wanted to get to. We trudged along and the ground became rougher and the palace seemed as far away as ever. And now we were climbing over boulders and hills and still it looked so beautiful blazing in the dark and we knew we could not live without it. Then I stumbled and looked down and saw that we were walking on ramparts, on the heads of the citizens and the walls of the palace, even though it shimmered still on the horizon. The walls were dark and crazy, half-knocked like ruins but this was the palace itself we were stumbling over, walking on the skulls of the people, crushing them in their sunken city clotted with silt and weed.

You might find it disappointing, I said. She took me down to the quays and showed me the boat. I can't say what type it was, I know nothing of boats. But I was glad to see it looked so sickly and unseaworthy. She'd barely be able to get out of the harbour in that.

She knew all my secrets by then. She knew about the Greek bit at the bottom of the rented garden, full of temples and urns and ships full of corn with three banks of oars poised to sail. I had my gods there. But the wild oceans were different. Suppose she went, suppose she took off in that little boat and nobody stopped her? I tried to imagine her out on the sea alone, days beyond land, miles away from me. Ships sail past each other out there, in the dark without so much as an embrace. And yet they recognise each other, with horns, lights, signals exchanged. They manage to slide past without colliding, their huge silent hulks cutting through the water like magic, greeting with such massive restraint, moving on. They have hoards of stories stored tight in the hulls: cities, storms, scurvy and sickenings for home, shipwrecks and deaths and canvas-wrapped bodies slung over the side, the howlings of men dying miles from land, homecomings with fat catches, barrels of gold. But they say nothing. They cut through the black air, saying nothing.

-You can't go anywhere now, in the middle of winter.

-It's summer there.

-How far are you going to get in that thing?

-The stars are different there. The world is upside down when you look up.

-Maybe we're upside down.

-Maybe.

From the mast of the boat to the harbour wall I could see a thin silver thread, as thin as the ones spun by spiders. Then I noticed another one, running from the edge of the boat to her shoulder where she sat with her feet dangling over the side. They billowed in the breeze, disappearing and reappearing in the light, looking so fragile against the force of the wind, but holding. Then I saw that the boat was covered in them, that threads ran from every protruding part to every other, a whole misty filigree swathing the boat. It hovered round the rough surfaces like a ghost, blotting out the rust and cracks and rotting wood. When she climbed aboard she broke through it and all the severed threads wound round her. She clambered about getting covered in wisps of this net, until everything, her hair and face and limbs and feet were threaded with filmy silver.

She worked away on the boat, preoccupied. I watched the stupid bend in her hair that wasn't even a curl, her feet sticking expertly to the little ledges, the ugly gurgle of the water slapping against the painted sides.

I walked every night now. I don't know why Dean Street became the place I always ended up in, by a variety of routes. There is nothing special about it. It has a coal yard at one end and a cathedral at the other. There are tall gaunt houses from the eighteenth century, with rows of squat terraces just round the corner. The church is just the latest shelter - people have prayed in that place for a thousand years, the legend goes. So she said. I started to cherish that street with all its blowing leaves, the dust in the gutters, every crack in the stone that had sprouted a weed.

You can see the angel up close from there. But then you can see the angel from nearly every part of the city. No-one else much bothers with the angel. They rave instead about the church of Shandon, which looks out over the city four ways, which has bells and four clock faces that all tell different times. People say there is something wrong with the mechanism. The truth of course is that they are all correct.

We used to go night after night to the Lough in the hope of seeing the black swans. We'd get ourselves bags of chips and walk twice round the lake, and sit on the bench watching for a long time. We counted stars and made up names for them. She knew how they were all arranged up there, but not what they were called. I told her there were never any black swans, that she had just dreamed them up. She said now that I'd said that they would definitely come. Maybe we just can't see them in the dark, I said once. They were nesting on the island in the middle of the lake, she said. She crouched at the edge of the water, staring out towards the bushes. From across the lake a pair of standard white swans turned tail to swim towards her, while from the bushes came a slight movement disturbing the water, and in a straight line five small downy birds came floating, black-brown. Larger forms moved in the shadows. She turned to me in wonderment.

-The five little goblets, she whispered, first-born to the black swans!

*

It means 'Valley of Paradise'. It is formed of two halves, the part that rose from the sea, and the part that grew from the rock. Between the two parts are spirals of roads, steps, bridges, tunnels, zigzag lanes, mechanical lifts, trains that can climb hills. The higher up you go the poorer it gets. On the lower slopes are the villas, then the smaller houses, then the huts, and further up the tiny shacks. But the poorest people have the finest view.

She said the wind was looking favourable now, and the tide was right and the stars. I knelt in my Greek temple and prayed.

-Are women supposed to go away to sea leaving men behind?

-No, they're not.

I started walking the evening she left, knowing that to cover every route we'd ever taken and visit every pub we'd been to would take me a long time. I worked my way slowly across town, taking in Dean Street, and the park and the bridge and the Lough. I sat by the Lough in the dead of night with no sound from man or bird. I saw her churning with sickness, writhing on deck under the freezing stars. I saw her docking in some stinking seaport, trailing through the foreign streets and slumping down on some strange quay to sleep. When I looked up there were millions of stars, and I was very far down under them.

I was down by the docks by the time the sun came up and trailed round all the bars that open at that hour for the sailors and the men coming off night shifts. She'd left on a ship, they told me. I never asked them where it was going, just wondered to myself if there'd be a piano on board for her. I went to every building where she'd had a flat and every cafe where we'd stopped, and when evening came I took in the remaining pubs, and finally the alley. It was nearly closing time and the place was thick with people, all giving me strange looks. I remembered that I had been walking for two days when I saw them part to let me pass, to let me sit in a corner and drink strong black coffee. I took the sips reluctantly, as slowly as I could, knowing that every drop brought me closer to the end I couldn't face. I knew too if I could only drink it slowly enough I could slow down the passage of time.

That evening lasted forever. I kept all those people there with their glasses half-full or half-empty, glancing uselessly at their watches, helplessly intending to put on their coats. I kept the barman smiling, pouring drinks he'd never poured before, rattling the same coins in the till. I inhaled the smell of muggy beer and coal smoke and the cool damp air outside. And all the time I watched her sitting under the lamp, borrowing my copy of the *Evening Echo* and smiling over at me.

I'm the kind of person who will stay, cherishing the homely stones I see every day that have become like friends. But every time I knead another dream into a loaf, or chop it up into plots to grow vegetables on, or break it with an axe to light the winter fires, I will think about her, swaggering down towards the harbour.

In time I did drain the cup, and the people slapped each other heartily on the back and left, and I lingered on for as long as I could. When they finally persuaded me to leave that corner I stood outside in the alley and smelt the tang of the river blowing down it. Then I lay down on the cobbles, halfway between two pools of lantern light, with my back against the wall in the most heavenly comfort. I slept soundly on the stones, on the bare Cork earth, the last night I ever spent there.

You cannot live in Byzantium. I will never visit Cork again.

Success

Patrick McCabe

They say success changes you and they are 100% right. I know - because it did it to me. The year was 1966 and it was looking like Eusebio was going to win the World Cup all on his own. That was why I wanted to be him. I said to the other boys on the team: "Right. From now on I am Eusebio and you have to pass it to me." They looked at me with their mouths open. Then they said: *"All* the time?" I said: "Of course. Are you stupid? Do you not see it on the telly? They *always* pass it to Eusebio. How is he supposed to score the goals if they don't? I don't want to start laying down the law for you boys but unless you pull your socks up we've lost that cup. We've lost it. We can forget about it." They looked at me again and then looked at their feet. They exchanged sad looks and said: "OK Pat. You're right." I bounced the ball and said: "Oh - and that's another thing. My name isn't Pat anymore." They bit at their lips. I could see they were wondering what I was talking about. Eventually one of them said, sort of half-hoarse: "Well if it's not Pat, then what is it - Fred or something? Ha ha." When he said the 'ha ha' part, the others laughed too. They thought it was funny the way he said it. I ran my hands over the plastic surface of the ball. It had black pentagons all over it. And my old name, written in faded felt pen. Faded because the rain had got at it when we were playing Paraguay. "I'm glad you think it's funny," I said. My eyes went sort of dead. "It was just a joke really," one of them said. "It wasn't meant to be serious or anything." "I see," I said. "A joke." They flushed a little and started staring up at the birds on the wires and the odd few clouds that happened to be going past. I cleared my throat and said: "There'll be plenty of time for jokes when the tournament's over." They could see where I was coming from now OK and said: "OK, Pat. There'll be no more jokes until it's all over - OK?" I stood in front of them and fixed them with a steely, ball-bearing-type gaze. "I said," I said, "I said my name's Eusebio." When they replied "OK Eusebio," they were doing impersonations of very hoarse frogs in the depths of Winter. That very evening Eusebio scored two beauties and put Portugal into the semi-final. The following day I buried three in the back of the net and Railway

Rovers were on their way to Wembley. They all said to me: "Pat - that was fantastic!" I shrieked at them: "I said my name was Eusebio!" "Eusebio," they croaked. That night I put a little bit of boot polish on my face and said: "Hey gringo pass ze ball to me" into the mirror. I had plenty of time to practise Eusebio talk all week because we weren't playing until the next Saturday. The new rules were that one of the boys was to carry my boots and the other my socks and togs. I needed all my energies to plan strategy and all that type of thing. I knew we couldn't lose. I could feel it in my bones. And we would have only they wouldn't pass to me. As a result of their greed we lost 6-0. I couldn't believe it. "You see!" I screamed, "I told you! Now you see what you did!" They looked at me. But this time they weren't looks of fear or reverence. As I soon found out when they said: "Ah would you shut your mouth now you see what you did! Now you see what *you* did you big bollocks you, pass it to me pass it to me. If you hadn't of been standing there with your mouth open like a hen shiting thinking I'm Eusebio we might have won. Ah fuck this. Fuck this for a World Cup. And fuck you and Portugal and everything for we're going home and we don't care if we ever see any more football matches. It's cricket for us from now on!" I ran after them and shouted as they turned the hotel corner: "No! Come back boys, please! I won't be Eusebio anymore! I'll be Nobby Stiles! I'll be Lev Yashin! Whoever you say boys - I'll be it!"

But it was too late. They were gone and all that remained was a Malteser wrapper flapping idly across the square and the white, pentagon-painted sphere stuck in between the bars of the railway gate-goalmouth resembling nothing so much as a bloated, living full stop that was as some poignant metaphor for the swelled heads of history the world over, those sad and deluded despots and toppled monarchs who would have deemed themselves superior to their fellow human beings.

I must confess that that night I wept copiously and begged forgiveness for my repugnant vanity. But I soon forgot all about that when some weeks later I received a letter in the post to the effect that my joke had won the 'Captain Mac Tell a Joke' competition in the Irish Press. I just could not believe my eyes. My joke was, as discerning readers will note, that fascinating little anecdote which was to surface many years later in my acclaimed novel of sausages and psychosis, *The Butcher Boy*, namely "What does one flea say to the other - will we walk or take a dog?" No sooner than I was finished reading that letter, I had my mind made up. I was going to become a writer. Without further deliberation, I took all my Charles Buchan Football Monthlies, Goals and Free Only With The Hotspur Wallets which were full of grinning carrot-headed idiots whose only function in life appeared to be booting recycled heifers up and down the length of whitewashed fields. My patience with them and the sad, grey world they represented was at an end and I put a match to the lot. One of the boys happened along, obviously eager to ingratiate himself with me, having conveniently forgotten the abrasive antics of himself and his colleagues some weeks earlier. "What are you doing Pat?" he said. I frowned. "If you don't mind!" I said, "I'm busy. I'm trying to think up some jokes for Captain Mac." He thought I didn't hear him. But it is not a writer's job to hear these things. Neither was it of any consequence to me that he was of the opinion that I was an Effing auld cunt! or whatever equally pejorative declaration escaped his sour lips on that smoky day of revelation at the bottom of our garden.

Little did I know it then but I was to remain successful for the rest of my life. Little did anyone else know it either, and never would. In particular Captain Mac, who never accepted any more of my jokes, and after receiving the seventy-fifth, which was 'What do you get if you cross a sheep with a kangaroo?', the answer to which is 'A woolly jumper', he wrote to me and said: "We are not accepting any more jokes for the foreseeable future."

Undaunted by these cruel blows, I applied myself with vigour to the writing of an assortment of funny stories, anecdotes and epigrams, which are now in the Pat McCabe Collection in Boston University or would be, if my father, after a particularly hard night on the stout, had not cut them up into small squares and hung them up on a nail on the toilet door.

I have to admit however that I didn't become seriously famous until 1979 when David Marcus published my story 'The Call' in The Irish Press and for which I won a Hennessy Award, no brandy and £150. From then on, it was dark glasses, taxis everywhere and a Havana the size of an orang utan's mickey, if an orang utan has a mickey. I waited for the phone to ring because I knew Universal would want me to do sushi and talk turkey to them about the film rights. When they eventually did call, it wasn't them at all but a man called 'Eamon Shedwell' looking for 'Patsy', whoever he was. I never did find out.

What I did find out though was that after you are famous the first time you have to wait ten years before you are famous the second time. And believe it or not readers, the second time starts right here - in this very magazine!

I realise of course that there will be readers who will say: 'It's not true - he made it all up' but with all the breathless enthusiasm which Jack Palance displays for flesh-eating sandwiches in Inner Ecuador and the like, all I can do is assure them that it is indeed true, as true as Maggie Thatcher is the best fiction writer in Britain. When my story *Together* was accepted by the prestigious Panurge, which of course had sumptuous, air-conditioned offices, a bursting drinks cabinet and enough contracts available to make a fleet of paper planes, it was all I could do not to run into the nearest 'Boats for Sale' shop and say: "One yacht, please."

But sadly it was not to be, and so ended another era as I once more packed away my ivory fag-holder and smoking jacket, digging in for another ten years.

When next we see our hero he is writing a novel on a Remington portable that looks like it has been kicked stupid by a platoon of jealous poets but that doesn't deter him because he knows for sure that this book *Music On Clinton Street* is going to be the literary equivalent of a bushfire. It certainly is. Total sales - 200 copies. The round of literary parties was exhausting. One bottle of Paul Masson, a box of styrofoam cups and "What did you say your book was called? Clapton Street? Clipper Street? I'm sorry. My wife reads though."

As the old saying goes: 'When all fruit fails try haws' so exile it had to be and off we went with the brown paper parcel, two biros and a copy of *The Essential James*, just in case we got stuck and didn't know what to do when we were sitting in the pavement cafes chewing pencil stubs. Around that time as it happens word processors were invented. Did you ever see the like of them? What I wanted to know was could you buy a separate one for poetry, another for short stories, a good big one for novels and so on. When I asked in Dixons they all laughed at me and I felt 800 years of oppression bearing down on me once more. I gave them the fingers under my coat and left round by the televisions. On an Amstrad 8256 I wrote *Carn* which paid for the house in which I now live, a beautiful cardboard semi with Kelloggs written on the outside.

Having submitted a draft of my follow-up novel, then entitled *Baby Pig,* to the same publisher, who said with extreme politeness, goodbye now, I discovered William Faulkner's door. It is the door that slams between the author and the world of publishing and the sound it makes is the most valuable noise a writer will ever hear. With this door firmly shut, ironically I wrote my only commercially successful work.

When John Murray, editor of this wonderful magazine which ought to be force-fed to every sushi-munching, deal-closing, lotus-eating publisher in the land, asked me to write this article, I thought to myself: "What do I think of success? I don't think anything about it. I don't even know anything about it." Now I realise that that was wrong or certainly inaccurate. I do think something about it. And I know something also. I know that every so often the Faulkner door creaks open and lets in a little light. And there's a shadow there too. I don't know whose it is. Whoever they are, they might have with them a bottle of wine. Or a fat cigar. Or something to say about *The Butcher Boy.* Or - mirabile dictu - *Music '200 copies' on Clapperham Street.* Or maybe they have nothing at all to say. Maybe they are just looking. I mean no harm, no harm at all - but all I want to say to them is - close the door. Close it softly now won't you? I'm writing.

FIRST PRIZE

Personal Fulcrums

Richard C. Zimler

I was looking at magazines at the San Francisco Public Library a couple of weeks ago and happened upon a contributor's note in which the author said that all his stories were about an innocent paralyzed when confronted with trauma. In my memory, I saw a seven-year-old boy with long blond bangs standing frozen in front of a skinny man in blue pyjamas sitting on a hospital bed. The man had gaunt cheeks and sad eyes. His skeletal hands were sticking out of wrists wrapped with gauze and bandages.

The little kid was me. The withered guy on the bed was my father. My mother says that he got that way after losing two quarts of blood. Most of it soaked into the bathtub, and by the time paramedics reached him, the water was clouded pink. She also says that I was found trying to pull him out. I'd called 911, then gone back to him. I don't remember any of it.

I wasn't supposed to be at home, of course. But my Little League baseball game had been called in the second inning. It was only a drizzle, but home plate was a little lower than the rest of the field and had become a puddle.

My mother never even tried to get the blood off my uniform. And we never bothered ordering another one. She was able to find work again as a saleswoman at Magnin's, and we were able to keep the house, but we really didn't have extra money for hobbies. I suppose if I'd begged... But playing shortstop for the Giants was no longer a dream.

Dahlias bloom in September in the San Francisco Bay Area. Each year, on my father's birthday, the 27th, I put some big violet ones like pompoms from my garden into a vase and sit it on my mantel. I suppose this ritual is insane, but what do you do for a father who simply got into his Rover one fine day in May and disappeared without a trace?

One of my earliest memories is of him clipping a flame-colored bud from a rosebush in the backyard of our house in the San Jose Hills and asking me to bring it inside to my mother. "Tell her I'll be in for lunch in a minute," he added.

Why do I remember that simple line and not anything whispered

27

to me at the last minute? All my life it has seemed that I never got the secret advice or password from him which I'd need to make me a man.

After the wounds on his wrists had healed, he came home. I remember meeting him at the door, standing with one foot on each of his, then walking together into the kitchen. He had great black boats for shoes. Two days later, he was gone. No note. No clues. He left while I was at school and while my mother was shopping at Safeway.

The morning after our first night without him, my mother said, "He'll be back, don't you worry." The ash was curling at the end of her cigarette. She was sitting on her bed in her nightgown, nursing a brandy in her mouthwash cup. Years later, when I was in junior high school, I asked for a possible explanation. My mother shrugged. She said he was simply a car mechanic who liked to cultivate flowers. A normal guy. He watched Giants' games on Channel 2, bought a Rover because he'd seen Laurence Harvey driving one in some English movie. His favorite foods were pot roast and shish kebab. On Sundays, he liked to read the *San Jose Mercury* in bed, then take a long shower. She didn't know if he'd been unhappy. He certainly never said anything.

"Didn't you ever discuss his suicide attempt with him?" I asked.

It was then that she lost control and screamed: "Goddammit Charlie, he ordered seeds from a hundred different fucking seed catalogues!"

This must have meant something special to her, but I never found out exactly what. As a teenager, you think your parents are weird and inexplicable, even the ones who don't abandon you. Too late, I realized that you'd better ask questions like this while you've still got time.

My mother died four years ago this June, occupies one half of a dual plot she reserved in the Hillcrest Cemetery in Los Gatos. I suppose she still believed right up to the end that he'd come back. But I don't think that the other half of the plot is ever going to have a body. He's just not going to call and warn me that he's on his deathbed. Or make some pilgrimage home like a lost elephant to its ancestral burial ground. Even so, you'd have thought in the thirty-two years he's been gone that he'd have sent me at least a postcard saying that he was fine and working at a botanical garden in South Carolina or a tropical nursery in Maui or wherever it is that gardeners who are also car mechanics go to really get lost.

Each year, at Christmas, I send the Filipino family who bought our old house a card and remind them to forward to me any letters my mother or I might get. They must think I'm some lovelorn nut hoping to get a letter from the girl who got away.

When I can get beyond my white-hot anger, I confess to myself that he might have been an interesting person. *He ordered seeds from a hundred different seed catalogues.* I would have liked to have known him.

*

After I read the contributor's note about innocents paralyzed by trauma, and after I thought, *this poor guy must write about schmucks like me,* I remembered a time several years back when Lana, my wife, and I were walking on Castro near 18th Street. It was spring, sunny. All the Victorian houses seemed to possess the proud and colorful promise of homes in a naive landscape. We were happy, had just bought scones at the Cheese Board and an autographed copy of *Flaubert's Parrot* at the Walt Whitman Bookstore. As we passed the Elephant Walk bar, we saw a pregnant woman panhandling under the awning. She must've been at least seven months along, looked haggard and hopeless, like one of those dirt-poor Appalachian mothers photographed during the Great Depression. My heart leapt against my chest as we passed, and I felt as if I'd swallowed poison. Tears started as soon as we got into our car. Lana got pissed. "So instead of sitting there and balling like you always do, why don't you *do* something!" she yelled.

I just looked at her. I mean, what was there to do? This was 1987 in Ronald Reagan's America, and if a pregnant woman was homeless and begging, then that's the way people obviously wanted it.

Lana has large brown eyes so dark and stunning that that's all you see when you first meet her. She was staring at me with them then like I was her enemy, was making me feel impossibly heavy - like a huge boulder that won't be moved no matter what.

"I'm going to call the cops," she said. "They have an obligation to do something for her, to take her to a shelter or something."

Lana called the San Francisco Police from our house, a stucco cottage on the southern slope of the hill separating the Castro District from Noe Valley. Then she tried three shelters. When she reported back to me, she said, "The cops won't go help her and the shelters can't send anyone to pick her up. She has to present herself

29

at one of their doors and ask for a bed." Lana was livid. "It's fucking unbelievable," she kept whispering to herself.

I was feeling kind of justified knowing that there was nothing you could do even if you tried. I patted the couch next to me, but Lana wouldn't sit. She ran her hands back and forth across her short brown hair, mussed it up into a tangle. Then she started pacing. I stayed put where I was; she's petite and lean, but you don't want to get in front of her when she's angry.

When I met Lana I didn't know anything about this rage of hers. I thought she was reserved. You only find out about people's wounds a few months after you begin sleeping with them. She had long hair back then, wore only jeans and loose-fitting sweaters, was studying for her master's degree in gerontology at U.C Berkeley. I'd just gotten back to San Jose after four years in New York. I'd earned a bachelor's in classical guitar from the Manhattan School of Music.

Lana always had a lot of interest in elderly people because her Grandma Winky, her mother's mother, was the bright spot in her life. Winky was from Oxford, Mississippi, and when Lana was a kid she used to sit her on her lap and tell her stories embroidered with antiquated words and people. One in particular I remember was about an elegant octoroon from New Orleans who worked as a butler for cousins of William Faulkner. One day this 'gentleman of impeccable manners who spoke French better than any French ambassador' just up and disappeared without a trace. The other I always remember was about an eighteen-year-old white girl named Irene 'with curls in her hair like Mary Pickford' who'd had a baby out of wedlock by the first black paediatrician in Lafayette County. Irene had been sent off to live with her father's sister Harriet in Little Rock. She never saw her lover again. Her baby boy, called Isaac, was given up for adoption in Memphis. Irene's heart had been broken.

Winky told us that she and her parents left Mississippi during the Depression and found migrant labor work in the peach orchards which then covered San Jose. Only much later on did we figure out that that was a lie. Eight years ago, when she died, we found a canvas suitcase at the bottom of the linen closet of her apartment in Menlo Park, and in it was a photograph of a wrinkled old woman wearing a dark, high-collared dress. On the back was written in Winky's scrawl: Aunt Harriet, March 1933. We also found a couple of dozen letters written to Winky from her parents, all with Oxford postmarks and all addressed to 722 Clarion Way in San Jose. Obviously, her family didn't move out with her to California. As for Aunt Harriet, she was undoubtedly Winky's aunt, not some relative of any Irene. In fact, there never was any Irene. Or rather, we figured that Irene was Winky, that she'd been exiled to California after having a child by a black man to whom she wasn't married. None of the letters from her parents made mention of any of this, but, of course, any 'proper' Southern family would have done its best to forget that such events ever took place.

We confirmed one part of this story by checking in a 1940 San Jose phone book that had been put on microfilm by the public library. Morgan was the last name Winky had had before she married Grandpa Don, the father of Lana's mother. On the microfilm, we discovered the name Harriet Morgan. That must have been Aunt Harriet, because the address given was the same as on the letters, 722 Clarion Way. We drove down the forty miles from San Francisco to San Jose, got lost on a ghastly strip of car dealerships and gas stations, and eventually found a tiny old clapboard house with hydrangeas out front, smack dab in the center of a run-down Chicano neighbourhood. It was here, and not in Little Rock, that Winky as Irene 'had spent years staring out the window, always facing east, toward Oxford and the life from which she'd been severed.'

We wrote to the Memphis police and some hospitals in the area, but we never learned what happened to Winky's baby. Maybe he wasn't given up for adoption in Memphis. Maybe his name wasn't even Isaac. But somewhere near Oxford, Lana must have a great-uncle and maybe some second cousins we'll never find.

Lana's mother and father claimed that they'd never heard anything about Winky's life before she'd married Grandpa Don. We didn't believe them, but we weren't going to press the issue.

I suppose I take these things too personally, but all these discoveries about Winky really upset me. Not, of course, because she'd had a baby out of wedlock. Or because she fell in love with a black man. It was that she had to give up both him and the baby and move clear across the country to escape her past. And I admit that I was hurt that she had lied to us about it. Lana wasn't. "You really thought all of Winky's stories were the whole truth and nothing but the truth?" she asked, so much disbelief in her voice that I didn't even bother answering.

Personal Fulcrums

When I first met her, Lana wasn't just studying gerontology in Berkeley, but also waitressing in San Francisco three nights a week at Paprikas Villa in Ghirardelli Square and doing stand-up comedy on Friday and Saturday nights. In May of 1977, we decided to rent the cottage together in San Francisco which we ended up buying three years later when the owner died. An incredibly busy girl, Lana was at the time. We hardly had time for lovemaking. But it was exciting, too. She opened a few times for Robin Williams at the Holy City Zoo, did improvisations with Dana Carvey at Fanny's. Later, when she realised she wasn't interested in putting in the decade of club work it took to make it to the Tonight Show, she began working on a screenplay. Then, after she got her master's, she bought a video camera and editing machine and started making videos of weddings and bar-mitzvahs. "Nobody realizes it, but I make Andy Warhol movies," she used to tell me. "Avant-garde oral histories." At first I wasn't convinced, but it's really true. Because along with the usual shots, she interviews the close relatives of the bride and groom or bar-mitzvah boy so that people watching learn something about the history of families involved. She's got an Italian grandmother singing threshing songs she learned back in the hills of Calabria; a ninety-year- old Jewish tailor giving an eyewitness account of the Warsaw ghetto uprising; Irish old buggers talking about garment industry strikes in New York when they were beaten by their cousins on the police force. We've been married seventeen years now, and I'm her biggest fan. I like it most when the people in her videos talk about the events around which their lives turned. That's the information she really tries to get. I dream that someday she'll be discovered and that they'll do a retrospective of her films at the Pacific Film Archive. I've already come up with the title for it: *Personal Fulcrums: The Videos of Lana Salgueiro Sanderson.*

Lana likes classical guitar music on her productions. So she records me in her editing room playing Bach suites or Villa-Lobos preludes or whatever it is she wants, then transfers the music to the videos. Other than that, all my income comes from teaching individual guitar classes at U.C. Berkeley and San Francisco State. I garden on the weekends, cook Thai food at least once a week, watch the Giants on Channel 2. I love living near Castro Street and being able to sit outside at the Café Flore. From the wooden patio there, I watch things that are unusual elsewhere in America - gay men kissing in public, college students with pink-tipped hair sipping espresso, fog ribboning through the Twin Peaks in the late afternoon. I enjoy browsing in bookstores and walking downtown amongst the businessmen. I like looking at skyscrapers. I'm happy. In all the years Lana and I have been married, I haven't once been tempted to take a razor to my wrists or off myself some other way. So maybe we can downplay the possibility of a genetic cause for my father's suicide attempt and disappearance. Maybe he just got sick of us. Once, on the Phil Donahue Show, I heard a father who'd abandoned his wife and kids say just that. It sounds absurd, but it's got to happen sometimes.

I've been thinking about my dad and Lana and my past a lot more than I like of late, not so much because of the contributor's note I read at the San Francisco Public Library, but because Lana's baby brother, Denny, was kicked out of their parents' house a week ago and disappeared for a few days. I don't think I've slept more than four hours a night since then. I get too hot under the covers, then too cold. And then the muscles in my legs begin to stiffen and ache. Pretty soon, all I'm doing is thinking about my father.

Apparently, Denny robbed a corner grocery store. The owner didn't press charges for some reason, so he didn't have to worry about prison. But Mr. Salgueiro, Denny and Lana's father, decided he didn't want to risk any more visits from the San Jose police to his house and told his son to clear out. The boy only disappeared for a few days. The parents never called to tell Lana. When she telephoned them as she does every other Sunday, her mother explained the situation and said, "He's seventeen. We've done what we can. It's his life."

Denny returned still barred from his parents' house and began sleeping in the garage. Lana drove down to San Jose to speak to him and try to broker a compromise with her parents. When she asked him where he'd left to, her brother said, "I just went away," and wouldn't say more.

Negotiations never really got started. Mr. Salgueiro said, "I don't want that *filho da puta,* in my house", took himself a beer from the refrigerator, dropped down in front of the TV and that was that. He lapses into his first language, Portuguese, when he's pissed or drunk. Lana tells me that *filho da puta* literally means 'son of a whore', but is equivalent to our 'son of a bitch'.

I suppose my father would also be vague about where he left to if I could find him. Though by now he might be pushing imported tulips or antique roses in some finely landscaped cemetery in La Jolla reserved for gardening mechanics. Apparently, such cemeteries for specific kinds of people are the new thing; the last time I was at the Gaia bookstore I saw an advertisement in *American Yoga* magazine for a cemetery in Orange County for New Age worshippers of the Goddess and another one in *Vegetarian Lifestyles* for a cemetery outside Austin, Texas reserved for people who'd been vegetarians and non-smokers. Stuff like this makes me think sometimes that things are more than a little wrong with America these days. Like we've all just snapped under the pressure. Though maybe my father is an exception, is married with three lovely children and a collie, living a Leave-it-to-Beaver life in some Midwestern town where people still leave their front doors open at night. Maybe the problem was us, after all - me and my mother, I mean. She implied that to me once. We were over at my Aunt Liz's house for dinner, and the two of them had gotten smashed on gin and tonics. I must have been about sixteen, was trying to watch a Warriors game on TV. "Before we were married, Charles was great," my mother said, talking to Aunt Liz about my father, loud enough so that I was sure to hear. "We used to bum around together. Go dancing in North Beach. Eat burritos in the Mission. He was fun. Really fun! Then we got married and suddenly I'm living with an impostor. Angry all the time. Mean. Doesn't like all the things about me he used to like. Even started saying my tits were too big! When we had Charlie, it was all over. He wouldn't touch me. It was like he realized only then that you got a kid from fucking."

One night just before she died, my mother was staying with us and came into our bedroom crying. Lana was in her editing room. I was alone with my guitar, reading through a new piece by Leo Brouwer. She stood before me, tears streaming down her cheeks. By then she had jowls, brittle gray hair which she let down at night. "I feel so cheated," she whimpered. "I was a virgin when I married your dad. Look what he did to me."

I was about to say, "You think *you* feel cheated..." But I shut my mouth and went to her. Lana says she can't believe I didn't tell her anything about my feelings. But what would've been the point? I mean, once my dad left, my mother couldn't see or hear me any more.

*

Three days ago, the night after Denny moved into his parents' garage, Lana woke me up at two in the morning and said, "We've got to do something."

"About what?"

"My brother."

The clanging sound of the raccoons trying their best to knock over our garbage cans reached me. I got up. The back yard was real dark, but I could see the white spathes of the calla lilies sticking up from behind the lawn like so many ears listening for my response. "Those little bastards want our garbage again," I said. "There'll be coffee grinds everywhere."

"Charlie," she said, "we've got to help him."

"What can we do? He's seventeen. He lives with your parents. And we've got Caroline."

Caroline was an old friend of mine from my days as a music student in New York. She'd been staying with us for a week and would be with us for another five days. I love her dearly, but she requires a lot of attention. I didn't need one more responsibility.

"We still have to do something," Lana insisted.

"Such as?"

"We could take him in."

"Oh no, this is between him and your parents. I'm not getting caught in the middle."

"In the middle of what?"

"Your family."

She knew what I meant by that only too well. A long time ago we decided that if her parents had been born as plants, they'd be thorny old weeds putting burrs in everything that passes. I could tell from the way her jaw was throbbing, however, that she was about to start screaming, so I said, "Look, when Caroline leaves, we'll talk about it. We'll go down and visit your parents and talk it all out like adults."

"It's just that Denny's all alone," she said.

"We'll figure something out. I promise."

But I was lying. I didn't intend to figure anything out. I figured that after a few more days, the parents would let him back in, or he'd run away or something would happen to take us off the hook. It was a mistake; Lana can always tell when I'm lying. I don't think she's got any special radar. I just think I'm no good at it. My voice must change or something. So she started yelling after all, accusing me of being a coward and not wanting to confront her parents. It's an

35

argument we've had before. Usually I just sulk. But this time I told her the honest truth. I suppose it was my lack of sleep. "You're the one who's the coward," I said. "For the last twenty years you've been avoiding telling them what you really think."

Lana looked out the window for a long time at the calla lilies. After a while, I crept up behind her and together we listened to the raccoons jumping against the garbage cans.

*

The next day I woke up and found the oven top cleaned. It's aluminium. It was shining like a newly-minted coin.

"I cleaned it with this solution I make out of baking soda and vinegar," Caroline explained.

"Looks great," I said.

Caroline has a lot of extra energy these days for cleaning because she's recovering from bulimia. She used to vomit as much as eight times a day and spend a good deal of the rest of her time thinking about her illness. How she managed to keep giving a full load of viola classes I'll never know. Anyway, now she's down to twice a day. And she *is* looking better. Goat-ribbed, she was. Now she's got some gentler contours. Though she's still got that gaunt face, those bug eyes. Her closely cropped gray hair doesn't help, seems to accent all her boney angles. The new hobbies she's taken up to fill up her spare time are knitting and pottery making. The red vest she started making for me three days ago has a front already. As for her cleaning, all the cans in our pantry have had their tops washed; our steak knives are newly sharpened; and our bathroom looks like something in a TV commercial. She even bleached the shower curtain and ironed the fluffy throw rugs on the floor. I didn't even know you could iron them. You want a hygienic house, Caroline and I decided, then hire a recovering bulimic. I've already asked her to paint the outside of the house next year. Free room and board for as long as it takes.

Lana and I are the only two people Caroline has told about her bulimia. Aside from her shrink and the members of her help group, that is. I don't remember exactly when she told me. She thought I'd be horrified, but those kinds of things don't horrify me. I don't think I'm very judgmental about people. Except for my father, of course. Maybe all my judgment focused on him, and there isn't any left for anybody else. So once Caroline knew she was safe with me and Lana, details of her life started coming out. She tells us more each yearly visit she makes. First, there were stories about her abusive grandmother who raised her. Caroline's father had been killed in World War II. And her mother, I suppose she was working all day. Caroline speaks English perfectly, so I tend to forget that she's actually German, from a small town outside Bonn. She came to the United States thirty-four years ago on a scholarship when she was just twenty-one. Went to the University of Virginia of all places and did a bachelor's in History, only later started taking her viola playing seriously. I suppose because her family was German, I always picture her grandmother like the witch in Hansel and Gretel. She used to beat Caroline black and blue. With wet towels because they don't leave permanent marks. The biggest villain, though, was her stepfather. He forced her to suck his cock. That's the terminology Caroline uses. Just this year we learned that he was the town doctor, *Herr Doktor,* a well-respected man. It was just after World War II in Germany and people were living on turnips. The family got meat and sugar through the good doctor and he got Caroline in exchange. From age twelve to nineteen, he forced her to suck his cock while the family fattened up on veal and *apfel strudel.* Two days ago, Caroline confessed to us that when the bastard died, she sobbed. I asked why, of course, and she said, "I guess I loved him." But she said it as if it were a question.

Apparently, the relationship between abusers and the abused is more complicated than I ever thought. I suppose I'm pretty innocent about that sort of thing. I was spanked a few times, yelled at frequently, but never treated roughly. So I think I'm pretty naive about people's shadow lives. Like when Lana told me that her brother Denny must have had a different father than her. I was floored. Then it made sense, of course; he's twenty-one years younger than she is, and I don't believe for a moment that her parents were still having relations by then. So my mother-in-law must have had an affair when she was about forty, probably thought she could never get pregnant. Though I can't imagine who would want to touch her. When I told Lana that, she said it was probably the guy who was their mailman at the time. Apparently, she was only half joking; she says he had Denny's shade of red hair.

Lana and I didn't speak about it, but we both know that her mother's affair was the real reason Mr. Salgueiro called Denny a *filho da puta* when Lana went down to San Jose to try to broker a truce. What he was really saying is that he thinks his wife is indeed a *puta*, a whore.

Caroline told us a few days ago that before she vomits she feels like her skin is crawling with bugs. She wishes she could shed it and step out all nice and new. She meets in a group with other bulimics once a week at North Shore Hospital on Long Island. All of them want to have new skin.

*

I've been thinking about all this tonight because I've been unable to sleep. From about two to four in the morning I just listened to the raccoons in the backyard and lost myself in thought.

When I look over at Lana on nights like this, I realize how lucky I've been. For so many years I never thought I'd be capable of loving anyone. People always said I was a cold person. A guitar teacher I had in high school told me that I had no passion. My mother told me once she thought I was dead inside.

There have been many times when I've broken out into a cold sweat thinking that they might be right about me. That maybe I've ruined Lana's life. After all, she wanted to have kids and I never agreed. She's thirty-eight now. In another two or three years it'll be too late. She says that she has no regrets, but sometimes I'm not sure.

This sort of guilt began to invade my thoughts at about four in the morning. It must have been the power of suggestion, but I felt a little like Caroline, like my skin was too confining. So I dressed real quietly and crept downstairs. When I closed the front door behind me, it felt right. The air was fresh and cool. Castro Street was empty. I got into my Honda and started driving.

I drove down Market Street to Highway 101 and headed south. My parents' old house is just off Lafayette Street in San Jose, right near the airport. I thought I'd take a look at it, but when I reached the exit about forty-five minutes later, I just kept on going. That felt good, like I was released from a servitude I'd never really agreed to. I wondered if my father had felt like this.

*

All of San Jose's peach orchards are gone now, and the city has sprawled into a tangled mess of fast-food strips and residential neighborhoods - like Los Angeles without UCLA or the County Museum or the beaches to redeem it. I've absolutely refused to orient myself on the visits Lana and I make to her parents' house in one of the new 'suburban dream' neighbourhoods down by the Los

Gatos hills. So I wandered around for an extra half hour before I found Alpendra Drive. When I parked in front of Hell House, as Lana, Denny and I call her family home, I still didn't know what I was up to. I thought I wanted to tell Mr. and Mrs. Salgueiro that they were assholes who had no right having children and then not loving them. But that wasn't it.

I found the garage door closed. I gripped the handle and lifted it up. "Who's there?" came Denny's voice, all rushed and frightened.

"Your idiot brother-in-law."

"Charlie?"

"You got another one?"

I heard the sound of feet on cloth, then the light came on. Denny was in his underwear, standing on his sleeping bag. He's a skinny kid. Too pale for California. True, he has beautiful green eyes, but he does everything he can to make himself look awkward. Like his hair; it's dyed black as can be, clipped close around the sides but left bushy on top. And he's got a quarter-sized enamel earring shaped like a garlic bulb in his right ear. Bought it last summer in Gilroy when me, Lana and him went to the Garlic Festival.

"What are you doing here?" he asked in a hushed voice.

"You can't keep sleeping in a garage."

"Whisper, you'll wake my parents," he told me.

"You think I care? I haven't slept well in a week. Why should *they?*"

"You mean you haven't slept well because of me?"

"Because of you and Lana. And my own past. Sometimes with me everything gets all mixed together."

He looked down, considering his options. "Did she send you?" he asked.

"Nope. I take responsibility for this. So put your clothes on. I'm tired."

"I can't go with you."

"Why not?"

"School. I've still got two months of school left."

"You can go to school in San Francisco."

"I can't transfer at this point in the year. And I'll have to repeat the year if I quit now. I won't be able to start college in the fall."

"We'll worry about that later."

"No, I can't go," he said definitively.

Mr. Salgueiro's old black Pontiac was parked in the garage.

39

"That is one *ugly* car," I said to Denny. He smiled. He's got a nice smile. He's a good kid, a little lost and lonely, but who wouldn't be in his position? I realized for the first time how much I loved him. Strange how you can live for years not really knowing things like that. I said, "Listen, have you got your driver's licence yet?"

"Why?"

"Have you got it or not?"

"Yeah, I got it."

"Good, then you can get up a bit earlier than usual and drive to your regular school from San Francisco. It'll take you less than an hour."

"Using whose car?"

"Mine or Lana's."

"How will you get to work?"

"Denny, we can stand here thinking up questions all night long. Just put on your damn clothes and come with me. Seventeen years of this is enough. I'm not saying you have to give up on your parents. But Lana's got a good heart. And she loves you. I can't say either of those things about the occupants of Hell House. Can you?"

"I think they love me," he said.

"Maybe. Maybe I don't understand love. I don't know. I don't even care. The point is, you're locked out of your house, and your father isn't going to let you back in. You want to live your life like a refugee you can. You want to come home with me now, you can do that too. Your choice."

Kids will put up with too much from their parents, and I could tell he was about to refuse my offer. So I told him to just try it with us for a week and see if it works. In the car, we talked about his robbery. Turns out, things were a lot more complicated than I thought.

He said, "You'll be the first person I've ever really told about it."

Sometimes I wonder why it is that people will open up to me. Caroline says that it's because I never show surprise on my face. When she's in one of her esoteric moods, she says I'm the reincarnation of a very old being who has seen everything. When she's like that she calls me 'The Watcher.' I suppose I should be flattered, but I don't particularly like it.

"Go ahead," I told Denny. "It can't be that bad."

He shook his head. "It's worse."

"So...what is it?"

"You can't tell my parents. Or even Lana." His voice was imploring.

"I won't say a thing to your parents. As for Lana, I can't promise. When we lie in bed at night I say things I..."

Before I could finish my sentence, he said, "I'm...I'm gay."

He squeezed it out of him like he expected me to slam on the brakes or start pulling out my hair. I can't say I'd ever suspected it, but on the other hand I wasn't floored. I said, "Denny, you live in the Bay Area you stop thinking that being gay or straight is any big deal."

"You're wrong. It's still a big deal in San Jose. It's not like San Francisco." Denny's hands had formed fists. "People here...it's like San Francisco's an island with pretty houses and cafés and bookstores and a thousand fucking Chinese restaurants. San Jose... San Jose, man, it's... it's got people who watch Monday Night Football and drink beer and just want to get through their days without having too many hassles from their kids. It's all people who would hate Lana's videos."

I knew that what Denny was saying was mostly true, but that he was talking more than anything else about his father. I said, "Just tell me what being gay has to do with you robbing a grocery store."

"It's not just a grocery store. It's got a section where people can rent videos. It's a weird little place."

"Go on."

"I don't know," he said. "I just did it."

"Not good enough."

"It's the new manager. He's a Turkish immigrant. Maybe thirty. I was buying cigarettes there one day..."

"You've started smoking?"

"They were for my father."

"And what happened?"

"And we started talking. It was during the day, but nobody was there. We were talking about Turkey because I noticed his accent. He said he had some photographs of Istanbul on the wall of the stock room. He locked the front door and we went back there. Then he just sort of reached down and held my cock in his hand. I mean, he felt me through my jeans."

"And then?"

"Well, he sort of gave me a blow job. It was the first time... the

41

only..."

His voice was choking up. To put him at ease, I asked if it had been any good.

He laughed like people do who've been close to crying. "Not really. I was too nervous. Afterward, I figured I wasn't really gay because I didn't really enjoy it."

"My first one was awful, too," I said. "I think you can still see the teeth marks on my cock if you look closely."

Denny didn't laugh this time. He asked, "Charlie, do you think I'm really weird?"

"No."

He was biting his thumbnail and staring out the windshield.

"Look," I said, "You want to make being gay a big deal, you can. I'm just glad you discovered it now and not later when..."

I was about to say, "... when you're married and have a seven-year-old kid." I surprised myself with that. But being gay suddenly seemed like a possibility for my father. Maybe he left us out of guilt. Maybe it wasn't me and my mom, after all. Maybe he thought that *he* was the one at fault, that he was ruining our lives, was going to make me gay if he stayed. *He ordered seeds from a hundred different seed catalogues. He began to say my tits were too big.* Was that my mother's crazy way of saying...? Was it possible?

"When what?" Denny asked me.

I was disoriented and didn't answer, so he said, "Why are you glad I discovered it now? I want to know."

"It's just that the sooner you understand that sort of thing the better. Cuts down on the complications."

"I'm not sure what you mean by complications," he said. "It seems pretty complicated to me."

"Doesn't matter for now. We'll talk about it later. Anyway, you went back to see the Turkish guy."

"Yeah, a few days later. And he did it again."

"And this time you liked it."

He smiled shyly. "But on the way out of the store, I don't know why, I was angry at the guy, stole some videos from the shelf. And ran. It was like I had to get back at him. He called the police to get his videos back. But he didn't press charges. I suppose he didn't want the story about us coming out."

*

The sun was just coming up over the Bay when we got home to San

Francisco. Lana and Caroline were already at the kitchen table. Coffee had been served, was steaming out of the ceramic mugs which Caroline had made for us this year. They're tawny-colored, with purple irises glazed on the outside.

Caroline was wearing her pink kimono, was stirring in a bowl the mixture of yoghurt, yeast and powdered vitamins which she eats each morning to make up for the nutrition she loses into the toilet twice a day. Lana was in her sweat pants and one of my Giants baseball shirts. When she saw Denny, she jumped up and hugged him. While she danced him around the kitchen, I told Caroline a bit of what had been happening. Then we sat around talking about Lana and Denny's parents. While I was starting on my second piece of toast, Caroline tilted her head like she does when she's about to spring a real direct question on you and said, "What made you go down now and get Denny?"

So I told them all about the contributor's note I'd read at the library. I said, "Apparently, this author writes about people like me - who cry now and then when faced with bad situations, but who don't *do* anything. So I finally decided to go ahead and do something."

"That's bullshit," Caroline said.

"What is?" I asked.

"Are you blind? Who do you think got a scholarship to music school, who plays like an angel, who scraped together enough money to put a down payment down on a cute little house? And who made your marriage work? Your mother...? Your father...? And why do you think I'm here? Because you're some passive asshole?"

What she said upset me. I guess I never thought of myself as so responsible for the way my life had gone. I made believe I was tired in order to escape the pressure of her stare. I stood up and said, "I'm going back up to bed."

"You're not angry with me?" Caroline asked in a hesitant voice. Her shoulders were hunched, and she looked like she might cry.

I was gripped then by a really strange sensation - that I'd brought her, Lana and Denny together that morning for a reason that went far beyond Denny's trouble with his parents. It felt as if I were in need of their protection. "No, I'm not angry," I replied. "A little confused, I suppose. I guess I'll have to think about all this when I'm more awake. Maybe it'll make sense then."

Lana took my hand and led me to the stairs. We left Denny with Caroline. She was explaining about why she puts yeast in her yoghurt. Then Denny called my name. "Thanks for coming to get me - for rescuing me from San Jose," he smiled.

I didn't respond with words, just nodded. Looking back at him made me lose my voice. Because it was then that I realized that what hurt most is that my father never said anything to me about calling 911 and saving his life, never even thanked me. It was like I'd made some sort of mistake I was going to pay for for the rest of my life. And that I would pay for it by never being able to have a family of my own.

Conrad Williams

Other Skins

Through my window at bedtime I'd watch the tree and the faces it made at me. When the streetlight next to it was working, soft shafts of orange thrust out of its clutch of leaves as though in a slow explosion. If my parents weren't arguing, its shushing was the last thing I heard every day.

Winter it would become just another famished thing, along with the exposed bones of more demolished houses on our dwindling street. The wrapping of night turned the diggers into still monsters cocking their heads for the slightest sound. These brittle days flogged the life from me. The tree was a dead thing - a totem which everything around tried to mirror. The ground turned black and white save for the people it cradled and quietly sucked the colour from. My friends, my family, we were all grey things dying with the town. Skies at the year's arse-end were birdless and stained with the breath of the detergent factory. Any grass was bleached by exhaust fumes; any snow that might have prettified the place was streaked with filth. When we met by the tree - me, Rob and Dave - it was as if the lethargy of the wood had crept up through its roots into us. Our playtimes were morbid affairs. We dug in the soil for life and mashed or torched it. We threw stones at trains as they passed behind the hospital and pissed into empty crisp packets which we flung at pensioners by the bus stop. On the days we made it into school (of which we only had another six months till we left), we behaved so badly we were forced to stand in the corridor. Often we just buggered off home again.

It became so cold I had trouble sleeping. On nights like that I would look out for my Dad returning from the pub at the end of our street. The murmuring wireless downstairs told me what Mum was doing. Sometimes, with a lull in the music, I'd hear the clack of needles as she knitted something she never seemed to finish. More often than not, when Dad appeared Mum would be in bed and he'd stroll down to the house with a woman linking him. The branches of the tree appeared to become more lively then, as though in welcome of someone it knew - a fantasy I liked to entertain. Standing beneath the tree, they'd smoke and chat and I'd sometimes see his face rippling beneath the tree's restless shadow. Their bodies might sag against each other and his eyes would roll till I saw whites embedded in the orange of his skin, his teeth clenched like a yellow bar as her hand briskly rubbed a dark area between them. After a while he'd kiss her goodbye, slipping into the house while I watched her lurch towards the main road, the tree's long black fingers falling upon her. I'd hear Dad getting into bed, Mum's laughter and the tired song of their mattress for a few minutes, till silence returned and I lay clenched in my blankets thinking of Dad's eyes rolling deep into his head beneath the tree.

Weekends, when he wasn't working, he spent at the allotments. Sometimes I went along to help. It was good to walk down there on my own. You could see the chimney (God's cigar, Rob called it) behind the hospital and the great blue gasometers on the horizon of roofs. I liked to look at huge buildings, they reminded me of pictures I'd seen of cities, of places that were away from here. I heard the men in the allotments before I saw them, shouting and laughing, or if it was too chilly for that, the gritty noise of spades as they broke through soil. Approaching from the top of the hill I'd see them hunched like black commas over cold, dull blades as they hacked at the earth, smoke rising from them like empty thought-bubbles. The sight both cheered and demoralized me. The allotments were nestled in a valley on the town's edge and winter frequently brought day-long mists which, like batting, tucked itself into the gaps between thin garden sheds. More men would loom out of the white like ill-sketched figures or you could see pulses of orange in the shed windows as they tried to get warm with cigarettes or candles.

I'd help him turn the ground or plant seeds and he'd share his sandwich with me, let me have a swig from his bottle of brown ale. At times like those I felt a raw affinity with him, though I knew better that to assume the distance between us had been reduced. Had I asked him about the woman he'd have clocked me and sent me home. Later they'd have a fire at the centre of the allotment and pass round a flask. All those pale eyes staring into the flame plucked at something within me and I watched their interest in this brief flicker of warmth and colour as an almost holy thing. For a while the mist was pushed back and the black creases of their faces softened, let through moments, or at least memories, of innocence. All their poison: the hatred and resentment and frustration building up inside them was forgotten. The fire touched something ancient and pure, something unquestionably male. A community had brought them closer than any huddle could possibly manage. It was all there, in the spark of fire in their eyes. For my part it rescued me from thoughts of the tree which, I then realised, I latched on to all the time. It was the bolt to which all my plans and actions were fastened. Still, I didn't perceive that as any great threat. Not then anyway.

Eventually, the frosts that trapped the rubble like fossils in amber melted, though the weather still contained enough of a pinch to bruise the skin blue. People died. Men and women I'd seen the previous week, or month, were now gone. The coffins ferried through town worried me. I wanted to stop each one to check someone was inside, to reassure me that Mrs Harris, Mr Ollier and the rest of them hadn't just disappeared.

Thoughts of hollowness, of shells haunted me. Every night for a week I watched the tree. In its sinuous tangle of arms I saw their faces. Sometimes I'd swear blind the tree was breathing. Its bark writhed as though it wanted to shed it like a coat. My dreams were filled with glistening flashes of what moved underneath but, thank God, I forgot on waking. The knowledge that a tree can look healthy while its insides spoiled and died from disease worried me deeply. It was a symbol I could see everywhere.

Mum died, not from the cold but because of it; killed by a rogue patch of ice by the market. This time I got to see someone lying in a silk-lined box though it did nothing for my phobia. The cold seemed to have followed her to this final bed, whitening her cheeks. Though pallid, she looked perfect. Dad cuffed me when I kissed her waxen mouth; I cried even harder when he gathered me in his arms and whispered sorry.

I saw less and less of Rob and Dave; ironically, the absence of my mother proved more of a check on my behaviour. Perhaps a more acute guilt was involved. Anyway, I stopped playing cruel games and took to drawing the tree. From a new angle, looking at it with my back to the demolished terrace, it seemed fatter and its trunk was curved and knotted like a spine wrenched out of true. As much as I strived for a likeness, my tree didn't contain the faces I glimpsed in its bark or branches. Come spring, and its leaves, there would be even more.

The thought I'd be leaving Mum behind as we crossed the threshold of the coming New Year filled me with a profound despair that lasted for weeks. Christmas was an empty time - I was growing to see it as a tawdry bit of glitz meant to relieve winter of its dour persistence, but which was unable to pierce a cynical shell I was retreating into.

Towards the middle of February, Dad brought Helen into the house for the first time. He was spending every day in the pub (having lost his job on Twelfth Night). I didn't mind her being there but Dad felt he had to go overboard to make sure it was okay by me. As if that mattered. I started picking through the rubble. Here and there, shoots were pushing through the chaos of brick and plaster, cheering me. Of all the seasons, Mum liked spring best. It was easy to picture her smile; it was good to feel close to her in the sprouting of these bits of green.

On the night before the first warm sun of the year, a squall tore across the town as though angry that winter was over, or in preparation for milder days. For an instant, when I heard the laughter, the rhythm of their bed, I thought she was back, that winter had been a hoax played by my mind. The tree was a glossy piece of tar teased into a shock of lines. Its branches whipped and struggled with the wind as if it were a tangible stuff. Slates lifted from roofs and smashed silently on the ground. In the uppermost reaches of the tree - level with my window - I saw Mum's face. I thought it was a reflection in the glass but when I turned round only the tussle between light and shadow on the wall greeted me.

"You'll come visit me soon love?"

"Yes Mum," I said, natural as you like, looking back into the black core of the tree where darkness nested. Gradually the storm passed on, unlike my fear, which thickened as I brooded upon what I'd heard.

In the morning, leaves peeked from the swollen joints of the tree and the memory of Mum's voice was more a comfort than cause for panic.

Coming back from the allotments one afternoon in that week (the weather brightening every day; at one point I was able to dispense with my sweater as I trowelled a shallow trench) I felt a compulsion to alter my route. By the time I reached the cemetery that need had dissolved into a warm band of rightness, of expediency. Rather than feeling honour bound to be near her, a gentler more natural yearning had taken me, for which I was glad. Immaculate as it was, I fussed her grave, briefly disturbed when I imagined that raised mound as thick blanket stifling her. Of course I was tensed for her voice which didn't come and I didn't know whether I was grateful or disappointed.

Maybe Dad noticed how subdued I'd become that evening so he slapped a little aftershave on my furring cheeks and took me down to the pub with him. It was a still night, the houses seemed coiled in expectation of some kind of event. Though the calm was a pleasant change it only made my nervousness more noticeable. I was grateful Dad didn't chide me about it. The pub was a mass of yellowed windows: my shadow cowered as Dad pushed open the door and people roared his name. We entered a fug of smoke and sweat. Women I didn't know ruffled my hair and winked at Dad while he bought drinks. Anonymous hands patted my backside. When Dad returned, pushing a big glass of foam into my chest, his forehead bore a brown lipstick smear. In the second before recognising it as such it looked like he'd opened a third eye. I wondered what my Dad's true constitution was like. It seemed as though I'd only ever seen him as this fleeting harlequin figure in guises of drunkenness and deceit. Beneath the cologne and bravado he was as much a stranger to me as the other faces in this bar. In that clenched knot of people I felt a moment of abject panic: the one genuine person I knew was gone, and I couldn't associate my own identity with anything more solid than the tree outside my window. In a slow swooping vision I saw myself ten years on, resigned to the crude safety of parochial life and playing a rake's role within the beery cocoon of this pub.

Predictably, my pessimism faded as the bitter took hold and I was swept into the bawdy cameraderie of it all. Comments that I was 'the spit' of my Dad made me feel proud, not threatened. A haze fell, when everybody's faces melted into gently shaded rumours and I couldn't distinguish between one person and another. I slurred my goodnights and barged my way outside, vaguely registering a volley of protests at my departure. The soapy air dilated the disharmony in my head so that the lights became great glassy shards I couldn't see beyond.

"It's this way, lover," came the voice at my ear and what I'd assumed to be a bloated sensation in my guts proved to be the arms of a girl encircling me from behind. She frogmarched me home; I could just make out the tree, jarred with each footstep into a dim beast, arms outstretched to greet me, its many faces lost in the blaze of orange flame. I began to flay my arms when she manoeuvred me into its shadow as though I was a sacrifice but she spun me round just as I saw its brackish maw become discernible in the pattern of bark. Pressed up against me, her mouth trying to draw some kind of orderly movement from my own, I felt the runnels at my back squirm, as though, like a slowly feeding thing, it was trying to subsume me. Trapped, I rolled my eyes in desperation, struggling to voice my distress, and, seeing my vacant window, understanding what I was becoming, struck out against the girl, who was working her leg between mine. Off balance, she fell on her backside; I couldn't decode the babble of filth she spat at me: my mind wasn't working that quickly. As she hobbled away, I let myself into the house, imagining the tree straining against its concrete base to recapture my warmth, to suck me into itself. I slept shallowly, dreaming of disease. I imagined pink, smiling faces collapsing from corruption eating people inside out. When I woke up, my head thudding, I was afraid to move lest parts of me caved in. I lay still for hours that day, smelling the grimy sky drift through our house, listening to the hushing outside.

These things I remember well.

And here I stand again, on the street I finally managed to escape so long ago. The pub's still standing though it doesn't look as busy as it once was. All the houses are new: our terrace must have been knocked down shortly after I left. Dad's well and still living in the area. I'll visit him in a while. The tree. I can see the tree. I'm brave enough to touch it - momentarily it feels spongy as skin, but that's just moss on the bark. 'Hug a tree,' my old English teacher used to say. 'They're extraordinary things, beautiful things. Show you appreciate them.'

It's with some surprise that I realise I never climbed the tree or tied a rope to its branches and swung like a monkey. Why was that? I'm asking though I know full well.

With my penknife I carve the first letter of Mum's name but it's too much like cutting myself. I have to turn away, to go *now*, before I see the sap: I'm not sure it will be the colour I expect.

God, the way you whisper to me as I hurry down the street. And were I to take one last look back, at the faces shifting in your branches, might I see my own somewhere?

Michael Zadoorian

War Marks

The stain could have been blood, long dried and brushed away, or it could have been just one of those stains that appear on things you keep in the closet for many years, usually on something white, like a favorite dinner jacket or a wedding dress.

It had been so long I couldn't remember how the flag had originally looked. I know it wasn't clean. How could it have been, with everything I carried it through? All the mud on Leyte, the jump on Tagaytay Ridge, Luzon.

I still have a few friends from that time. I've been to the 'D' Company 511th Parachute Infantry Regiment (PIR) reunions, each year someplace new. One year Texas, the next Arkansas, the next California. I'm still waiting for them to have one in Michigan. Just as well. Detroit is a strange place to be when you've fought the Japanese.

I talk to these ex-soldiers every year. Some of them I barely knew at the time, or even disliked. But now we are friends by necessity. Every year, there are fewer men than the year before. But there are always a few who have just discovered the reunions. They always have new stories, new details, new things you realize you haven't thought of in decades, all of it sparking new-old memories.

When I saw Johanovich, I went right up to him and started talking. I recognized him, even as an old man, from the photos we had tacked up. Sure as hell, he had no idea who I was, until I told him. It was his first reunion. He brought his second wife, five Japanese flags and three swords. That's Johanovich. Evidently, the swords are supposed to be worth big money. I think he thought there would be someone buying them there at the reunion. He had already looked into selling the flags back at his home in Oregon. "They aren't really worth that much," he said. "But I thought maybe we could hang them up somewhere."

I knew about the souvenirs gathered during the war. My first glimpse of the enemy was of their dead. Jap soldiers lying in impossible positions; shirts ripped open, pants half off, slain and bare-assed in the mud. The flags and swords now hanging in rec-rooms and workshops and finished basements and war rooms.

Johanovich is the one that told me about the symbols written on the flags. They contain information about the soldier. As soon as I

Blind 85 year-old President Balaguer　　　　　　　　　　　　*Philip Wolmuth*

got home from the reunion, I started looking for the flag I took from the body of my first Jap. When I finally found the thing, it looked different. I looked at the symbols smeared on it, and at the stain, and suddenly I didn't want to put it up in our basement. It felt like something I had misplaced for forty-five years. Something that didn't belong to me.

*

The Speak Easy Translation Bureau is located in one of those small gray or tan office buildings you can pass every day of your life and never notice. It is about five miles from the house I live at with my wife. One of their specialities, according to the phone book, is Japanese.

When I walked in, the woman behind the desk startled me. Her hair was ratted and teased and sticking out in big shocks, black at the roots, then bleached almost white at the ends. There was make-up caked on her face, with slashes of rouge at her cheekbones. She had painted bright red polish on her fingernails, cuticles and the skin all around them, almost down to the first knuckle. Her mascara was black and thick, two eyes staring from the dark. She asked what I wanted and I didn't know for a few seconds.

I unfolded the flag finally and kept my eyes on it while I told her what I needed done. They were not very busy today, she said, I could probably just wait. She slipped into the back for a moment. It looked to me like they hadn't been busy in a long time. The place was deserted. I sat down and read the newspaper and tried to avoid looking at the woman when she came back out. I read a story about a fire in Bad Axe. A boy killed on his nineteenth birthday while making french fries.

After about ten minutes, a Japanese kid came out of the back. He looked like a college student: khaki pants and a pink shirt. The woman at the desk turned to him and said, "This man wants the characters on this flag translated."

The kid looked at the bleached-out symbols on the flag, then at me, and said, "Okay, I'll do the best I can." He said it like he wasn't sure of something.

I read more of the paper (car accidents and more fires) until he came back, about an hour and a quarter later. He walked up to me, sort of cocky and said, "Where did you get this flag?"

I looked up from my paper. "What do you care where I got it?" I said.

That flustered him a little. These kids see an old man and think they can say anything they want to him. He started to fumble with his words then. My son did the same thing at that age.

"I was just wondering if it was from World War Two?"

"It is," I said.

"How did you get it? It's a Japanese flag." His voice was getting higher as he spoke.

I looked at him square and said, "I took it off a dead soldier's body." I was damned if I was going to lie. I did what I did. Fuck 'em all but six, we used to say. The ones that carry you out.

The kid looked at me almost frightened, then shoved the flag and a big envelope into my hands. Taped to the envelope was a bill for thirty-five dollars. I paid the crazy girl and walked out to my car, where I opened the envelope.

After I read the translation, I drove to McDonald's for lunch.

*

I have had people ask me what it was like to jump from an airplane. I always say the best part about it was getting it over with. To me, the whole thing was nothing but a series of shocks to the system. The first one being when you jump. Then there's a hell of a jolt when you come to the end of the suspension lines, and your chute opens, and then when you see the ground coming up very fast. You realize that a piece of silk is the only thing there to save you, to let you float back down on to the world, maybe not gently, but there all the same. Then it happens and you find the ground and are down hard and roll and get out of your chute and the earth seems like a friend who has been missing, and things are like the way they were. But then you look around and find you're in an entirely different place.

The soldier's name was Katsuhiro Miyazaki. He was from the town of Mugi, located on Shikoku, the smallest of the four major islands of Japan. According to my atlas, roughly 1900 miles from where I killed him outside of Mahonag, on the island of Leyte in the Philippines. It was strange to find all this out about someone whose life you ended forty-odd years ago. Of course, if I hadn't killed him, I would be dead. I know that. Probably some of my friends as well. My children would never have been born. As for that Jap soldier, whatever his name was, I have no memories of his face. There was a uniform. There was a gun.

After I killed him, I felt only relief, hope that maybe I was strong enough or lucky enough to make it out of there and get back home. I may have felt something for an instant, but there was no time for it. More were coming and we had to kill them.

I had to call long distance to the Japanese Consulate to get the address for the City Hall of the town of Mugi. I wanted to write to see if anyone from the Miyazaki family was still there. The chances of this were decent, according to the woman I spoke to. It was a fairly small town. I had told her that I was trying to return a lost item.

My letter went like this:

To whom it may concern:

I am writing to inquire if the Miyazaki family still resides in Mugi. This family has lived there for at least the past forty-five years. A son named Katsuhiro died during the Second World War. If this family is still living in Mugi, I would appreciate it if their address could be sent to me.

Thank you,

Carl Downhour

I enclosed a stamped, self-addressed envelope with the letter and had the whole thing sealed up when I realized it was all in English.

*

The same girl was at the desk as before. I don't think she recognized me, even though it had only been two days since the last time. She was a nutty one. She looked about the same, only this time she wore a light blue blouse with spots on it, from what I guessed was lunch. Told me I couldn't wait for the letter to be translated. I mentioned that I had waited last time for the flag.

"It'll be ready after noon tomorrow," she said.

*

The next morning, the Free Press had a story about a farmer who accidently slips into his manure pit and is overcome by methane fumes from the manure. His son goes in to rescue him and is also overcome, then a cousin. Finally, a young friend of the family goes in as well. Ages nineteen to sixty-three, all of them collapse into about eleven inches of manure. None of them get out in time. In the paper, it said methane is fast-acting, odorless and colorless. An invisible enemy.

I pointed the story out to my wife. "What a horrible shame!" is what she said.

By the time I got to the translation place, it was five past noon.

Crazy girl didn't say anything to me at all, she just handed me a big envelope. I didn't see the Japanese kid anywhere, but there was an invoice for thirty-five dollars taped to the envelope that was just like the other one.

Out in the car, I looked at the letter. There was a lot of symbols like the ones on the flag, only more distinct. They were linked snug across the page. Some of them looked graceful, others dangerous, like something ninjas from the movies might throw. I sent it out airmail that afternoon.

*

Eight days passed and I got a call from Cass Wojack, an 11th Airborne buddy from California who hadn't made it to the reunion that year. He asked me how it had been. His voice was scratchy over the phone. I told him there were a few new guys from 'D' Company, but that was about it. I told him about Johanovich, still peddling his flags and swords, just like during the war.

"Once a hustler, always a hustler," Cass said. We both laughed at that. He asked about the food.

"Better than last year," I said. "They had 'Make your own sandwich night', then 'Fiesta night', then the banquet on the last night. Everything was good," I said. "It must have been. Johanovich ate like a pig." Cass got a kick out of that one.

Then for some reason, I told Cass about what I was doing with the flag, that I was going to try to send it back to the guy's family in Japan. Cass' exact words were: "What the hell are you doing that for?"

"I don't know. I don't want it anymore," I said. "I can't throw it out. It's made of silk."

"Well then, damn. Give it to me," Cass said. Then there was some quiet on the other end of the line. "You're not getting chicken-shit in your old age, are you?"

"Fuck no," I said. "I still got my jump boots and my go-to-hell attitude."

"Well, hang on to those."

There wasn't much to say after that. I told him with any luck, I'd see him next year.

*

On the nights during a reunion, I sometimes dream about the Philippines. Not the fighting so much. I buried all that a long time ago. So deep, those memories only came back in my middle age, and

56

then as war stories, with the same tone of action and adventure as the Doc Savage pulp books I read as a teenager. It felt good not to make them so real.

No, in my dreams are all the friends I had during the war. They are mostly in the same places as the snapshots I took at the time, the ones we now put up in the 'Hospitality Room' at the reunions. They are doing the same things as in the pictures, only moving. Standing around, holding M-1's or Thompsons or squirt guns, looking tough, cigarettes dangling from their mouths; shirts off, digging trenches; holding up souvenir flags. Behind them is mud or canvas or straw. They are all still alive. Some of the men were killed days or even hours after I took the pictures, way before I could pass the roll off to get developed. I remember thinking at the time, 'They are still there on the film.'

I'm never in the dreams. I only watch, listen to them talk, think to myself during the dream, 'Is that how his voice sounded?' or 'Where was I when this was happening?' When I wake up I feel all right, I feel good, just not sure who it is inside this worn body. Sometimes I will even see one of the guys I dreamt about that next day at the reunion. I never mention anything.

*

After another three weeks, I got mail from Japan. It was just my envelope with a card in it, in both Japanese and English, with the name and address of someone named Kazuo Miyazaki. I had been waiting till then to figure out what I would say in my note. It had to be worded carefully, it seemed to me, if I wanted to get rid of the flag.

Mr. Miyazaki:

I am an American who served in World War II. I have in my possession a flag that was once owned by Katsuhiro Miyazaki, who I believe was a member of your family. It was retrieved in the jungle on the island of Leyte in the year 1944. Please contact me by mail if you are the correct person to send it to.

Thank you,

Carl Downhour

*

They were beginning to know me at the Speak Easy Translation Bureau. When I walked in, crazy girl was just sitting there, staring at the blotter on the top of her desk. Without even glancing at me with those blacked-out eyes, she said, "You want Ken? I'll have to check

57

to see how busy he is. I think he can do it for you right now, if it's short." She spoke very fast then disappeared into the back. I started to open the newspaper.

The Japanese kid was behind her when she came out. Crazy girl pointed at me and said, "He's the one!" That sort of put me off. It was pretty damn silly considering I was the only one sitting there. The kid looked at me and when I met his eye, he looked away. I looked away myself, a second later.

I stood up. "I have a short note that needs translating." I held it out toward him.

"I'm afraid you'll have to wait until tomorrow," he said.

My hand just hung there. The paper was starting to wilt in it. "Fine," I said, putting it on the desk.

The kid walked out of the room without another word. Crazy girl just shrugged her shoulders at me.

I drove home and took a shower. It was bingo night for my wife and movie night for me. I was in the mood for something with some action in it.

*

I slept in the next day, made it to McDonald's just before they stopped serving breakfast. I got my English muffin and decaf and sat down to read the newspaper. On the second front page, there was a story about a man in Detroit, a guy in his mid-fifties, who drives to the medical clinic where he goes for back and heart problems. His car is covered with Nazi flags and swastikas, his face has paint streaked all over it. He's holding a rifle when he walks into the place. The receptionist knows him. She's nervous because of the rifle, but she knows the guy, she's kidded around with him. She says, "You know you're not supposed to bring a rifle in here. What's the matter with you?"

"I'm at war," he says to her.

"Who are you fighting?" she says.

He looks around and whispers, "It's personal."

Pretty soon there are police all over the place. The guy drops his rifle and tries to run out to his car. The police tackle him. There's a scuffle and suddenly this guy stops moving. He has a heart attack and dies right there in the parking lot.

I can't think of a worse place to die.

I didn't even get my free refill. I threw the paper away and just drove around till I could pick up the translation. When I got there, it was all waiting for me in a manila envelope. I paid crazy girl the thirty-five dollars and left.

After I mailed the letter, I forgot about it for a while. I was busy at home. Somewhere, my wife got a notion to re-do the bathroom for the first time in fifteen years. I had been given orders to wallpaper. I worked in the bathroom while my wife washed down the walls in the dining room.

When I steamed off the wallpaper, I realized something must have gone wrong a long time ago. A problem when the house was built, when the wet plaster was applied, some sort of moisture that had seeped through. On the wall of our bathroom, there were huge blotches, damp spots right on the surface. Then I remembered painting the wall a few times, trying to cover the spots, with the spots always returning, always bleeding through the new paint. I wasn't sure if I had just dreamed it up.

When I showed the blotches to my wife, she said, "Of course those are there. They've always been there. That's why we've always papered in the bathroom. Don't you remember?" I agreed with her just to quiet her down.

I re-papered the wall and assumed I would forget again.

*

During that time, I received a new copy of *Airborne Gazette,* a little newspaper published by the same fellas from the old division who organize the reunions. It has photos from other companies' reunions, news about new members, obituaries, and usually some articles about the war.

There was a story about a place where 'D' Company was stranded, late in the Leyte campaign. The guy in the story called it 'Hungry Hill' but I'd never heard that. Ten days in the rain with no food, living in our ponchos. Most of us sick with dysentery and breakbone fever. So wet there, I kept a rubber over the muzzle of my M-1.

Finally, when the cloud cover broke for a short time, C-47's managed to fly low enough to drop boxes of rations. Us standing behind trees watching those crates slice into the mud. What the article had mentioned, what I had forgotten about, were the two men who were killed by falling 'C' rations. I wondered what they told the families in the telegrams home.

*

Word from Japan caught me by surprise. It was a strange square envelope in the mail. My name was written on it in a scraggly, stick-figure printing style that I still sometimes see on old steamer trunks in junk shops. Opening the letter, the paper felt different to me, coarse.

Mr. Downhour:

Please forgive language of this message.

A friend is giving translation. I would be pleased to receive flag of Katsuhiro Miyazaki. He was uncle of mine I have never met. Please how did you receive his flag? Why are you returning?

With thanks,

Kazuo Miyazaki

I read the note a few times. It was clumsy, but I knew what it was saying. At that point, it had been well over two months since I had started the whole thing. Part of me had gotten real tired of it. Not to mention the expense. My wife was asking questions. How was I going through my house allowance so quickly? I told her it was for something I was working on down in my shop. It was costing more than I thought to finish.

*

Mr. Miyazaki:

I regret to inform you that I am responsible for your uncle's death in December 1944 near Mahonag on the island of Leyte in the Philippines. I took the flag from his body. I am returning it because it belongs to your family. The flag is enclosed.

Respectfully,

Carl Downhour

*

There was a new girl at the Speak Easy Translation Bureau, a little brunette who looked like she might have been just out of college. She was on the phone when I came in. When I spoke to her, she tilted the receiver away from her face and clasped her hand over the mouthpiece. I told her that I wanted a letter translated. She said she was just a temporary, handling the phones. Had I been there before? Could I just do it myself?

"If I could do it myself, I wouldn't be here," I said. She giggled. "Sure, I'll take care of it," I said. I walked toward the room where I had seen the Japanese kid come from during my other visits.

He was in there, eating his lunch. His back was to me, but I knew it was a peanut butter and jelly sandwich. I've made enough of them in my life to recognize the smell.

"I'd like you to translate this for me," I said. His head went erect. I could tell I'd startled him. He must have put his sandwich down before turning around because he took a while to face me. When he did, he looked right at me like he had been getting ready for it. He wiped his fingers with a wadded-up paper napkin before taking the letter from me.

"I probably won't be able to get to this until late in the afternoon, or even tomorrow," he said, in a hurry to get it out.

I was about to say fine, when I saw him start to read the letter. I should have left then and there, but I didn't. I watched him read it. When he was done, he looked back up at me and said, "I'll do this for you right now. You can wait in the other room."

I stood there without saying anything, then wandered back to the waiting room. The new girl was there, still on the phone, jabbering away at someone. I took off my hat and sat down. Since I had forgotten my newspaper, there was nothing to look at except for an old *Reader's Digest*. The only interesting story was about a man who was revived after receiving a prolonged electrical shock from a household appliance.

About forty-five minutes later, the kid came out and handed me everything. It wasn't all neat in an envelope like before. "It's all set," he said. There was the start of a smile on his face.

"Thank you," I said. I was having a problem meeting his eyes. Then I met them and that was that.

"I think what you're doing is good," he said.

I stood, picked up my hat. "You don't know a thing about it," I said. "And even if you did, it would be none of your business."

He maybe was going to say something else, but then he just turned and went into the other room. I noticed he hadn't given me a bill.

I looked at the translated letter, at the tiny smear of peanut butter on the margin. Finally, I turned around myself, got the girl's attention, and paid my thirty-five dollars.

Lorna Tracy

The Tears of the Unicorn from 'The Famous Writers School'

1.   EXTERIOR.   SWIMMING POOL.   1967.   AN HOUR BEFORE   DAWN. LATE SPRING.

Florence Green's Westport, Connecticut, estate.   The huge oval pool, glowing with concealed underwater lighting, is a transparent lens of aquamarine in a surround of cypresses, columns, statuary and Roman pavements of tesselated marble.   The water lies motionless as a mineral in the warm, still air.

Long Shot: the guest house beside the pool where gentle red-gold light shows through louvred shutters.   We are zooming in slowly to an open louvre.   Sound of a single cricket.

Close Shot: through the open space of the louvre showing a blank crimson wall.   A beat.   A blurred shadow crosses the wall from left to right.   Two beats.   The open space of the louvre is filled with two staring eyes. *Freeze.*

2.   GUEST HOUSE. INTERIOR. NIGHT.

A great divan spread with an Anatolian kilim is centered against a crimson wall where a Bokhara carpet hangs.   On the opposite wall is a Venetian mirror and an ebony chair inlaid with mother-of-pearl.   On the parquet floor someone has constructed a considerable ziggurat out of empty Coors beer tins.   A lamp on a carved chest beside the divan lights the room flickeringly as if it were a fire.

Reginald Purge, forty-three, wearing pyjama bottoms, turns away from the shuttered window and sits down on the divan next to a packed suitcase standing open to receive the pyjama bottoms.   He is a famous English dramatist holed up on Florence's estate, hiding from his wife while he finishes a play for television.   He has a round head, a flat face, and a gracile figure just under six feet tall.   His flat brown hair is combed forward into a fringe.   His pugged nose seems made to root and not averse to stenches.   Close-up shots show hints of silver stubble on his jaws and throat at this hour.

He stares at the floor.

Close shot: Purge probes his lower left jaw first with his tongue, then with the little finger of his left hand.

Close-up: Hand opens chest beside the divan; it is a mini-bar and empty except for one can of Coors.   The hand does not find it at first.

Purge falls to his knees and urgently peers in.

On Venetian mirror: We see Purge walking up and down the room drinking from the can. Purge approaches himself in the mirror, halts.

PURGE: [Reflectively.] In America happiness is compulsory. What a depressing thought.

3. SWIMMING POOL. NIGHT.

Slow pan around pool. Fade up on sound of a single cricket.

Long Shot: The tower and upper storeys of an Italianate mansion at the top of three garden terraces. The house is dark.

4. GUEST HOUSE. NIGHT.

The man who is Purge in real life too is stretched out on the divan in his pyjama bottoms. He delves in the open suitcase for an electronic note-taker. He lies down again and turns out the light. The room is immediately dim, as if lit by a few pale tubers.

PLAYWRIGHT: [Speaking into the note-taker.] INTERIOR. 1967. AN HOUR BEFORE SUNRISE. BIRDSONG.

The Playwright suddenly springs up and throws open the guest house door. Listens intently. Silence. Not even a cricket. The sky is still dark.

PLAYWRIGHT: [Yelling.] Let's hear it from you *birds.*

5. POOLSIDE. NIGHT.

A woman, forty, lies on a chaise-longue at the opposite end of the pool from the guest house. A small suitcase stands beside chaise, with a large handbag. The woman has a bland Ginger Rogers-ish face and wears a smart trouser-suit. Her hands are clasped behind her head as she stares at the sky. Where she's just come from it's already mid-morning.

Long shot: The guest house.

Point of view: The occupied chaise-longue.

The Playwright in the door hears a brief call from a hermit thrush.

PLAYWRIGHT: Right. *Thank* you. Thank you, Mr Chickadee. [Speaking into his note-taker.] To Florence every bird is a chickadee. A rooster is a chickadee. So is a swan, a bustard, a buzzard, a crow. The dark chanting goshawk is a chickadee as far as Florence is concerned.

6. GUEST HOUSE. NIGHT.

The playwright is again lying on the divan in the dim room.
PLAYWRIGHT: [Speaking into the note-taker] INTERIOR. 1967.
AN HOUR BEFORE SUNRISE. BIRDSONG.
Close up: The Playwright's face staring into the middle distance.
PLAYWRIGHT: The alcoholic, lonely, insomniac Famous
Playwright composes a note for his hostess's char... My lovely Peg -
if Peg is not your name, forgive me; we've never been introduced...
My play is finished. My hostess is laid. And last night I was finally
asked up to the mansion. Florence gave dinner to three hundred of
her closest friends and me. You probably know this. Now I am
spending the night, its minute coins a kind of foreign currency, on
much wakefulness. I have not wasted these coins, dear Peg. I have
composed a new lyric for my daughter's rock band, whose several
members are collectively known as The Human Predicament.
Perhaps you have seen them on TV. You might care to tell me
sometime, Peg, how the lyric strikes you. I myself have reservations
about one or two lines, but the basic requirements of the form, which
you will recognize as the triolet, seem to me to have been fulfilled. I
am not a poet, Peg, but the triolet is within my compass. It's called
'Blue Letter Home' and has been composed in the accents of your
native land.

> *Yeah, he was somethin' to write home about, sure enuf*
> *Till come the night he said he's signin' out*
> *Now I've sent him on his way, but it's been ruff*
> *He was somethin' to write home about, sure enuf*
> *He's all the news there is, folks. Makes writin' mighty tuff*
> *From the 'Dear Mom' down to 'Love' I'm all wrung out*
> *He was somethin' to write home about, sure enuf*
> *Till come the night he said he's signin' out*

... So, Peg, what do you think? Top Twenty? I'm a bit unsure about
the way it ends... The way it ends. The way it - hey - HEY! *There's*
the name of the song, Peg! 'The Way It Ends'. Better, don't you
think? ... Mind you, I quite like 'Blue Letter Home' for its suggestion of
melancholy and scatalogical content as well as the hint of foreign
origins. You are familiar with those aerograms for sending
messages from one country to another? Ah, look there, Peg. The
subtle treachery of language. You and I, Peg, are not two foreign
governments. Our messages are not from one sovereign nation to
another, but from person to person. Eternal vigilance, Peg, or else
the bloody words will have us saying what we never intended. Like

that directive the other day from your president, Mr Johnson, to the Peace Corps volunteers. Did you read about that, Peg? He warned them not to identify themselves as Peace Corps volunteers when they protest against the war in Vietnam. Did you hear what the White House spokesman said? This is the beauty part, Peg. Here is what the spokesman said. The spokesman said: 'President Johnson wants his soldiers to fight this war in peace.' Isn't that marvelous? Who could top that? Only another politician, Peg. Only Bobby Kennedy complaining about some book about JFK's assassination. Remember what Bobby said? 'Nobody's going to make a killing out of my brother's death.' Words, Peg. Double agents... Good. That's sorted out, then... Long, long ago when I first arrived here from The Old Country... when was it? Six weeks ago? The old trout my charming hostess, your benevolent employer and collector of writers' foreskins, Peg, told me that a raccoon would disturb my sleep rummaging through the dustbin - the trash pail?- whatever you call it here - if I did not press the lid *firmly down* every night. And that is why I have not placed my empties in the - in the - bin, call it a bin, then - tonight. For had I done so, Peg, it would have been too full to press the lid *firmly down*. I am only anticipating your reproaches, Peg, and seeking to deflect them. I am not an inconsiderate man. Apart from those empties - I agree their number is not small - I have no more disturbed my delightful environment than a raccoon has disturbed me... I have also been careful not to leave any bits of carbon paper about, although why your employer's Abyssinian cats should raven after carbon paper I cannot imagine. But clearly the beasts prefer it to *pate de fois gras.* Spelt 'grass', pronounced 'grah'. Grass, one could understand. Grass is good for the little short gut. But perversity extends throughout the animal kingdom, Peg. Does it not. My mum had a moggie that loved lemon jelly... I'm not a bad sort, really. A man can love his own children *and* another man's wife simultaneously. He can, Peg. Believe me. And why shouldn't he? Darwin, the dear old innocent, believed that females are strictly monogamous. As human females were *presumed* to be in his England. So he didn't even consider the question as to why female birds should copulate with more than one male. Sperm competition has far-reaching evolutionary consequences. But not even Darwin could think of everything. Many a man will cheerfully undertake the lifelong slog of keeping his family. Why must his family demand that thereafter for ever and ever he keep himself out

of every crack but the matrimonial one? Still, they do, they do...
The coon is blue, Peg... Once in a blue coon... Uncle Tom Coon...
Coon Power (I trust you are not black, Peg)... Once in a coon's age.
And pray, what *is* that, exactly? One of your native turns of phrase,
I believe. 'A coon's age'. An indeterminate thing, like the women
here. (I am not speaking of you,Peg)... The women here, surely they
are of the coon's age. And the coon's habits... small, climbing,
carnivorous mammals of North America, active largely at night in
the dreams of their miserable husbands... distinguishing marks
include long dextrous fingers, numerous rings, eyes masked like a
bandit's. And although their name is a corruption from one of your
Native American languages - arath? Arathkune? No, I have
forgotten. Their name is a corruption, but the animals are said to be
conspicuously clean... Well, Peg, would you like to know who came
to Florence's dinner last night, each one as clean as a coon? Each
one of them Famous, apparently, if not each one a Writer. Such
celebrities as Posy Smarm, the TV presenter from Atlanta. Black
hair with a silver pinstripe and a lovely pair of - lungs. The
scandalous poetess Demarara Bangcroft, she of the fringe. Or is she
from the fringe? Hecate Vendor Vandahl, the former Nemesis, now
a much-feared critic. Wolf Footsore-Sidekick, philosopher and
gentleman farmer, author of *I and Sow.* Marianne Litotes Huffing,
translator of Etruscan poetry and, perhaps surprisingly, author of
The Ablative Case, the historical thriller topping the best seller lists
for ever and ever. According to the blurb - sorry, according to the
jacket copy, Mrs Huffing being very particular about her dignity, -
according to the jacket copy the book is the story of a family fraught
with tragic affluence. Florence, your esteemed employer, says she
just loves it; it's the story of her life. It may well be. What do you
or I know of tragic affluence, Peg? In America happiness is
compulsory. Have I mentioned this? Florence paired me off with
Honeysuckle Grossman, the Famous Massachusetts Attorney, who
told me she has practiced law and homosexuality in Boston for
fifteen years. She suggested that I was suffering from tongue-in-
cheek disease. I explained that I had just had a tooth out. She
clearly did not believe this. Ours was the table next to the door the
waiters used. Seated with us were the two editors of rival literary
magazines. Florence can be a bit mischievous... There are no
Famous Editors, of course. Both seemed equally awful, as are, no
doubt, their magazines, which are called *Catheter* and *Trocar.* All

piss and wind. One suspects that the smaller the magazine the bigger the editorial ego. The first thing the woman editor said - no, brayed - was that the bloke's magazine has been re-launched more times than the space shuttle Columbia, which says something for her prescience, at least. The bloke, a chap called Wiley Blemish, cheerfully explained to me that Arbutus (that's the woman editor: Arbutus Shenshu Firkin) is always a little raucous just before she checks into hospital for her annual autopsy. That set the tone for the evening at our table, Peg. The Algonquin it was not. But very North American nevertheless. I thought.

The Playwright stops and staring into space, tongues the gap in his gum again. He really has had a tooth out.

Good of Florence to send him to her own dentist for the extraction. Good of her to pick up the bill; it was for thousands. Where the painful truth had been was a palpable absence and a gap a meter wide, moist and smooth as sea water. The Playwright lets his tongue slick through the gap. He turns on the lamp, goes to the Venetian mirror, pulls at the corner of his mouth with his little finger, turning his head aside and lifting his chin. Gap doesn't show, really (pulls out the finger and grins like a skull) under normal smiling conditions. Good. That's all right then. Shut your pudding, Purge, and forget about your amputation.

Immediately his tongue returns to the irresistible gap, smooth and plump as the flesh of a lemon. His gaze lights upon the bedside Bible. He picks it up, hefts it. Unexpectedly thoughtful of Florence to provide her guests with the all-time universal best seller: The Complete Works of God. The Playwright holds the Bible up to his eyes to read the spine: Father, Son and Holy Ghost-writer. Eat your heart out, Mrs Huffing. [He switches his note-taker on.] Or was it you, Peg, who put this in here? Have you been born again, Peg? For me, once suffices. An amusing book, this, Peg. Especially if you shut your eyes, open randomly [The Playwright shuts his eyes and opens the Bible] and put your finger on a passage. I did that the other day, Peg. Not a passage in a book. It was a passage in Florence, actually. Let's try it with a book this time... Ah, we've got Jacob, son of Isaac, here on my desert island. You wouldn't know about that British Institution, would you, Peg. America has no desert islands. And no Shakespeare. Quantities of Bibles, though. Believe me, Peg, Jacob was a fortunate man, a lucky man. His trials came to an end in fatness and beauty. These days cirrhosis does as well as anything to bring about a suitable conclusion... In which, as my name would mean nothing to you - I come from Another Country, Peg, and thither today I return. On Concorde. Thanks to Florence - allow me simply to sign myself

> Yours in fellowship
> Part of The Human Predicament

While the Playwright has been dictating the moon has risen, the full staring moon. The Playwright drops the note-taker into the suitcase and finishes the Coors. He is considering where on the ziggurat to place the tin when there is a splash as something falls or dives into the pool. He turns out the lamp and goes to the open shutter. The sounds of vigorous swimming come nearer. After a moment a head appears in the window.

FLORENCE: Hi! Saw your light. Need a towel. Can I come in?

(Florence is short and cubic, with a chin as round as a baby's heel.)

PLAYWRIGHT: Um. It's... it's late, Florence. Well, early, in fact.

FLORENCE: Couldn't get to sleep. Thought you must be awake too. Not a soul around.

PLAYWRIGHT: I'm um... packing, Florence.

FEMALE VOICE [off.] Who are you talking to, darling?

The fluting coloratura has come from the dark bathroom.

What is his wife doing here? She's supposed to be in England. Unmistakable, that finicking RP of hers, shrieking up and down the scale, not once descending even to C prime. The Playwright cannot stand another note of it. He has fallen for the American female baritone now, the ear-scraping, gland-maddening, vowel-mammocking, gloriously declassed barbaric yawp.

FLORENCE: Long as you're up I might as well come in. Why not?

PLAYWRIGHT: Why not. Of course. Yes. Why not. Let me introduce you to my wife. Florence Green - my wife, Nessa.

Nessa is the woman we have seen earlier lying on the chaise. Nessa offers Florence a bath sheet.

PLAYWRIGHT: Now, if you will excuse me, I shall just go out and lie face down in the pool while you get to know one another better.

NESSA: All right, love. See you in a bit.

FLORENCE: Nessa. Name of that Scottish loch monster, isn't it?

The Playwright stops short of the water, groans, lies down on his back. Looks up. The tops of the cypresses are whirling in tight little circles like a stripper's tassels. The starry sky looks down like a spider's eye. Dizzily he closes his lids and waits for the spider to bite.

The exposed white throat of a young female appears in his imagination, her head thrown back in passionate abandon or helpless subjugation. It does not matter which. Here is the jugular, here is the carotid, here is the windpipe, the spinal cord. So many vulnerabilities here. This lovely isthmus, this slender conduit between the body and its brain. The word 'dreddour' appears to him. He turns over and pulls himself onto his hands and knees, his head hanging. The word 'strealing' enters his mind. A real word? Or a neologism he has constructed - out of streaming, perhaps, and reeling. Something to do with rope.

In the guest house Florence Green, wrapped in the bath sheet, extends her hand.

FLORENCE: How do you do, *Nessa*.

NESSA: Florence, how lovely to meet you. Have you slept with my husband yet?

FLORENCE: Sorry?

NESSA: No, no. *I* am sorry. I ought to have put the question another way. After all, the *Chatterley* trial was seven *years* ago. Has my husband fucked you yet?

FLORENCE: ?!?

NESSA: Never mind, love. He will. Look. I'm simply trying to find some common ground. Common ground generally turns out to be Reggie. (Nessa's speech has got faster and faster, her voice larking in the stratosphere). He's very highly sexed. He considers it a form of genius. Prodigious endowment on a Mozartian scale. Of course, the woman is no more than the necessary instrument of his virtuosity, like Mozart's piano. She may feel better or worse for his performance on her, but the performance is certainly not given to make her feel better or worse. Or anything, really. Anyway, these days a faithful spouse cuts a ridiculous figure. No one respects that sort of thing. Everyone's quite openly in contempt of it. A man's intentions towards a woman are always ultimately invasive. Every event in life follows from invasion. Afterwards, a man may say: 'Well, come along with me then, you old dung beetle.' Or maybe just, 'I'll be off now, luv.' Or he simply disappears without a ta-ra. (Nessa's voice levels and drops an octave and a half.) I don't know why I should take any notice of what he does, really. One knows from one's own experience how little the woman matters to a man once he's got what he came for. One loses one's 'fascinating powers' and consequently one is deserted, as wives must expect to be when they lose their physical charms. I suppose it was having someone's attention that one really feels deprived of, when a man moves on, screwing his way to the grave. Or having the *semblance* of attention. We are fools to wait. To wait and wonder did I please him? Was I everything he wanted? Will he come back? *When* will he come back?'

FLORENCE: Self-sacrifice is the worst form of self-indulgence. (She sits down in the ebony chair. Nessa flatters herself that Florence has been carried away in her torrent of words. Whereas Florence is pretending that 99.9% of people have nothing to say that she wants to hear. Nessa sits on the divan, pressing and patting the kilim with the palms of her hands as she gallops torrentially on.)

NESSA: Sometimes, especially at first, there can seem to be tenderness. Sometimes even something more than lust in the way he looks at you. Though not in your case, I should think. Even lust must have come hard in your case. But to come to the point (Nessa's voice sinks another octave and takes on a tone of straightforward menace) Those who betray my trust had best beware. I shall confront and confound them.

(Nessa gives Florence a hard stare but Florence is lighting a cheroot. Nessa's voice, insanely animated, leaps back into its highest register). My stars have promised me success. That is why I am here. Truthfulness is almost as socially unacceptable as fidelity. Nevertheless I shall risk it. Six weeks ago Reggie's horoscope promised him that with Saturn in Aquarius he would reap financial rewards abroad. He said to me: 'Florence Green is the richest woman in America. I must go to America.' Consider *yourself* - it's *Mrs* Green, isn't it? Well, Mrs Green, I should think you do just about everything very badly indeed. I would even say that you do not benefit from the almost automatic increments in skill that sheer repetition brings about. It would surprise me to discover that you have ever got better at doing anything, however regularly you attempt it. I notice that you are left-handed. You can ruin dinner for everyone at the table by constantly clashing elbows with the person on your left. How his *petits pois* roll down his tie! How the slopped claret crimsons the damask! How sorry you always are! How sorry everyone is! Everyone united for once in that shared sorriness without which sharp differences of opinion might creep out of certain mouths and cross the napery to nip particular guests in their certitudes...

FLORENCE: My goodness. Now I see what Purge meant when he said his wife was articulate.

NESSA: My motto - I Look In As Well As Out - I am tolerably pleased with. Men have a special loathing for the internal life in women, though they tolerate the internal life wonderfully in themselves. Men cannot use a woman's internal life for their own benefit and this makes them quite furious. They cannot make her light shine on them and they want it. They want her light. All of it. Shining on *them*.

FLORENCE: But this is not news, darling. This has a beard on it. What can you tell me that's news?

NESSA: The season is very advanced here in America. Yesterday in our Yorkshire garden the white croci were just up - each one like a severed finger freshly bandaged and not yet soaked in blood... For once the wind was elsewhere. The sky dripped calmly like newly-hung-out laundry. Intermittently an ivy leaf flinched at a blow from a drop of rain. I was able to open the windows for the first time in months. Out in the street cars sizzled by. It was cool, sleepy, soothing to hear them from inside the house. Yes, if I could live my life over I would live it to suit myself.

FLORENCE: [Out of the side of her mouth] Says her wet little internal life, pecking at its petrified shell... Go on, then, Nessie. I'm getting used to listening. Tell me, since you seem to know, what do women *really* want these days?

NESSA: [Abandoning her hysterical coloratura]. Justice. A world without violence. A system of economy that doesn't deprive and deform human life...

FLORENCE: I don't believe it. May be what *you* want. But a world full of gentle, peaceful, impoverished females with nothing to do but hunt and gather and be nice to each other? (Florence sticks out her brown tongue) Yuk.

NESSA: What do we do *now* but hunt and gather? And I haven't been very nice to *you*, have I?

FLORENCE: What the hell do you think a man's life *is*?

NESSA: It's starting all over with a new bird in another port on a full wallet as often as he wants to.

FLORENCE: You know that's not true.

NESSA: Many of us think it is.

FLORENCE: Quote you something, Nessa. "The tears of the unicorn are found everywhere in the world, but the unicorn itself nowhere."

NESSA: What is *that* supposed to mean?

FLORENCE: In this context it means if women had the choice they'd do what they've always done. Take power. Only broader power, more openly exercised. Don't pretend you haven't enjoyed it on your domestic pedestal. Taken care of - in every sense. Looked after.

NESSA: Put paid to. Kept in my place.

FLORENCE: Never could understand all those Russian women - duchesses and princesses - who devoted themselves to the Revolution. The hottest Reds of all were the titled daughters. Revolting against Daddy, I expect. In spades. And what did they get for their trouble? A bigger, better Daddy than before. The State they made devoured them. (Nessa's eyes are shining. Even though she seems excited her voice has settled to earth like a brown bird on the nest.)

NESSA: Florence, a noble victim is a priest of justice. Let me tell you something. One day, without ever having had any practice, I began to think. I conceived of gravid space - into which, I was pleased to discover, I could immediately introduce a Rilke's unicorn: a creature "fed not with grain, but only with the possibility of being". As you say: nowhere to be found - *yet*. Of course, almost immediately Zeus and his horrible daughter Athena poked their long Greek noses in. That pair interested me. After all, what had happened? The old man had put his mind to it and conceived a female god. Unmothered Athena. Rationality incarnate. One of the few recorded cases of male virgin birth. And the event was a disaster for women. Athena was loyal only to the male. No sense of sisterhood. Not one whit. Look what she did to the Harpies, poor souls. Physical criticism has never been the same, even in the autonomic twitchings of these 20th century armies of night-flying women. Boiler suits and bovver boots can never replace those lost wings.

FLORENCE: [Quoting] "The Alukah's two daughters - 'Give, give' - Sheol and the Womb."

NESSA: But just imagine an un*fathered* Athena, loyal only to the *mother*! Magnificent!

FLORENCE: Listen, darling, good feminism is *for* women - not *against* men. Like philosphy: right in what it asserts; wrong in what it denies. Leibnitz, darling. "No important change in ethics was ever accomplished without an internal change in our intellectual emphases, loyalties, affections and convictions." The proof, darling, that feminism has not yet touched these foundations of conduct, lies in the fact that philosophy and religion have not yet heard of it.

Nessa gets up from the divan, runs over to the ziggurat and with a well-aimed kick demolishes it.

EXTERIOR. THE POOL. MID-MORNING.

The Playwright wakes up in brilliant sunshine. His tongue is burning. *S'fume, s'fume c'est* is in his mind. Too many cigarettes yesterday. If it smokes, it smokes. *J'adore les mots francaises.* The meaningless phrase 'bemis point' lodges like a demented rat in his brain's maze. He feels that he has spent his weeks here daily lifting that sun in his arms, carrying it across the sky and dropping it over the opposite point on the horizon. Otherwise, without his efforts, time would never have moved on. Now that same sun is volleying back and forth across the blue sky like a yellow tennis ball. The Playwright's eyes helplessly follow its transits, his head whipping from side to side. Any minute now his neck will crack and his head will roll away.

Point of view: the Playwright. Where is he?

The apparition of a severed thumb with a thorn stuck in it appears in the air inches from his face. It hovers. It regards him. It is a hummingbird. It is gone.

He remembers - seems to remember - that the last thing he remembers is the presence of his wife. She had got into the guest house somehow in the middle of the night and Florence had turned up too and he'd left them together to tear him limb from limb, probably.

He wishes to weep.

Yes. Now he remembers. He had come out here intending to drown himself.

So why isn't he dead?

He realizes now that Florence Green, the richest woman in America, is squatting beside him, looking down at him. Or he assumes she is. You don't really see Florence's eyes - just the intricately reticulated pouches under them magnified enormously in her spectacle lenses.

He imagines himself saying

PLAYWRIGHT: [Voice-over.] Florence, I want to look into your yee-yees.

Florence Green, gross, hairy, lovable - the woman her detractors describe as a genetic spelling mistake. No wonder her favourite Famous Writer is Marcel Proust, who said: Let's leave beautiful women to men without imaginations.

Another angle. The Playwright looks up at Florence. Florence looks down at the Playwright. If this were a scene in *The Ablative Case* she would realize now that:

PLAYWRIGHT: [Voice-over.] Beneath his deep tan he is tired. The full light of the sun is catching him on the side of his face and she would notice the network of small wrinkles around his eyes. She would feel a maternal tug which she would conceal with a bright, brisk smile.

Behind that fictitious smile lies an interesting question. At least, it interests Florence. Under what circumstances can one imagine a *man* feeling tender towards a tired woman with the sun on her face and a network of small wrinkles around her eyes? A prune-faced woman makes a man feel nothing but aversion. It would not occur to him to bring her a cup of tea, let alone a glass of gin. He would never suggest she ought to take a little break from the housework. Have a nice day off. He'd probably want to know why there are no clean shirts. Florence Green lumbers to her feet.

FLORENCE: Missed your plane.

The Playwright groans.

FLORENCE: 'S all right. Ticket's not been wasted. Your wife's used it. Left you a message.

Florence fetches a folded sheet of paper from somewhere under her muu-muu.

Close shot: a sheet of stationery headed: The Famous Writers School. Westport, Conn.

> *Reggie, darling, you've been written out of the script; Ma Perkins doesn't need you anymore. Please leave the studio immediately. Take all your personal props with you. Don't come back to England. You have passed the be-missed point. Nessa.*

The be-missed point?

PLAYWRIGHT: The *bemis point!* [Groans.]

The Playwright is too awash in revelation to hear Florence Green say that the maid's complaining about the state of the guest house.

FLORENCE: Got ten minutes to be off the set. You'll need 'em all to walk to my perimeter wall. Better skedaddle.

At first Florence thinks she'll just leave that sticking to the wall and she waddles away in the direction of Fetor, George's Russian manservant, who is approaching with an injection of symbolic gin. But Florence stops and turns around like a sixteen-inch gun turret until she is facing the Playwright again.

Long shot.

FLORENCE: Boy, [Cackle of laughter.] your hinie's in a *real* crack now!

EXTERIOR. THE SOUTH TERRACE OF FLORENCE'S MANSION. MID-MORNING.

Medium shot: Florence lying on a chaise-longue under the pallid wisteria racemes. Her eyes are shut, allowing the sunlight to print a vision in blood on the insides of her eyelids. Florence's visions are always of hot new products no one else has got on the market. She has only to describe what she sees to George Green and he has the thing in production while the competition is still sitting in the bathtub trying to think of the word for eureka. Florence is envisioning a sinkable hardwood coffin suitable for burials at sea. Sea burial is free - if one can find out where it is permitted. That's the difficult bit. But never mind. With all the little wars everywhere the planet is running short of cemetery space. It's a niche market with almost infinite growth potential.

INTERIOR. THE GYMNASIUM IN THE GREEN MANSION. EVENING.

The gymnasium is arranged for sumo wrestling. George and Florence are dressed for their match. Fetor is oiling George's back.

FLORENCE: Basically, George, it's your standard $5000 coffin.

You drill a few holes in it. Have to put a band around the body with its telephone number in case it's ever trawled up again. Just a legal requirement. No problem.

George Green with his grape-pip eyes immediately sees the commercial advantage in Florence's vision.

GEORGE: Flo, I'll say it again - you're a god-damned genius. Know what I'm gonna do? I'm gonna order you a customized sinkable coffin. You'll have the first one off the production line. You wait.

FLORENCE: Yessir, you old dung beetle. [Pats his arm fondly.] Do just that. No hurry. No hurry at all.

George and Florence, standing opposite one another at the perimeter of the wrestling floor, bow gravely.

ENDS.

75

John Upton

The Ailment

Patrick finished working in the factory at six o'clock. His shift should have ended at two but he had worked over. He knew his parents would be pleased by this and besides, his mother was entertaining a nun this evening in the tenement and he did not wish to spend all night making polite conversation. His father would be out until late working on the large church in the village. The factory was in the centre of the city, in the industrial area, a collage of bricks and rusting railings, broken sky lights and silent dusty places turned dark by the autumn rain. Patrick walked along ———— street past the ———— pub with its tiled exterior and stained glass windows, a cathedral to the whiskey and beer. An air vent blew the warm smell of stout onto the darkening street and Patrick, who suddenly felt cold, stopped outside its dark oak doors.

A small man, rotund in appearance and wearing a long blue mackintosh, pushed past him and into the pub. He let the door swing back and Patrick had to put his palm up smartly to prevent it from hitting him in the face. The wood on his flesh made a harsh smacking sound like his father's leather belt on his arms or arse. Patrick pushed open the door and entered the bar.

The room was rectangular, the bar itself taking up one corner of the pub in an L shape. It was dark in here and the atmosphere was truly reverential. The chatting of the two bar men never rose above a whisper. They both wore white shirts and black ties. In the corner furthest from the bar, under a window adorned with the brewery's coat of arms, a priest sat, a whiskey held in both hands. He stared blindly into space and his black clothes sank into invisibility against the dark seat cover, leaving only his face, luminously pale like a spot-lighted porcelain bust in the museum. His features showed the marks of a compassion born out of great failing. From a door behind the bar, a dark-suited man appeared. He was wearing a trilby and shook hands with the two bar men. He shrugged his shoulders and gave them both a small white flower. Then he turned round and walked out again. The two looked at each other in puzzlement, eventually pinning the flowers to their ties. The priest had put down his glass and shakily made his way to the bar. Patrick followed him up.
- Yes please, said the bar man. Patrick ordered a pint of stout.
- It's quiet, he said to the barman who operated the pump directly in

front of him.

- Like a fucking undertaker's. Patrick paid for his drink and sat at a table in one corner. Presently the cleric returned to his table with another whiskey. As if he had been suddenly magicked into the place, Patrick became aware of the man who had pushed past him into the pub. He sat at a table pressed against the wall, drinking a glass of clear liquid. He caught Patrick's eye and came over to his table. He had a quiet, lisping voice and he viewed Patrick coyly, his head tilted downwards, his eyes occasionally flicking over Patrick's face before being cast down again.

- You're a young man to be in a pub like this, he said. Patrick noticed he wore a large ring on his left hand. He twisted it around his knuckle joint as he spoke.

- Ay well I just fancied a drink, you know. Patrick took a swig of his pint.

- I'm sorry. My name's Joseph McReady, said the man, holding his hand out.

- Patrick Furey. He took the hand which, immediately on contact with Patrick's palm, was withdrawn.

- I work in the government offices, the man said. There was a playful note in his voice and his eyes became bolder, pausing for an instant to look into Patrick's eyes before they once again stared into his glass.

- I suppose a lad like you will be off to see his girl on a Friday night like this.

- I don't have one, said Patrick. Joseph McReady leaned forward.

- Don't you? But you're a fine looking garson.

- Did you see the football last week? said Patrick. He finished off his pint and put it down aggressively on the dark wooden table. The noise made the priest and the bar men stare at them.

- O no. I prefer reading. I do a lot of that, said Joseph McReady and he sipped off the last of his drink.

- Excuse me for asking, said Patrick, but what is that drink? Joseph McReady leaned forward conspiratorially once again.

- It's gin and tonic. My friend Tommy, he's that bar man there - he pointed - keeps a secret store for me. I can't stomach whiskey or beer. It's my ailments you see. He leaned back, arched his eyebrows and said

- Another Patrick? For old time's sake as they say in the pictures. Patrick nodded and the small shuffling man in the mackintosh made his way over to Tommy. Patrick's head fizzed slightly. Joseph

McReady came back with the drinks.

- Thankyou very much, said Patrick.

- O don't be so polite, said the civil servant, playfully smacking Patrick's hand. He sat down. Patrick glanced out of the window. It was almost dark now and a street lamp shone brightly outside.

- So what do you do Patrick? I'm curious.

- I'm a runner in a factory.

- You're a friendly chap Patrick, said Joseph McReady and tapped his hand again.

- And so are you, said Patrick as the porter slipped easily down his receptive gullet. A small driblet fell from his mouth and before he had time to lift a finger to wipe it away himself, Joseph McReady had cleaned up his chin with his handkerchief as if he were a baby.

- Thankyou, said Patrick.

- Don't even mention it. Joseph McReady began to make small circular movements with his glass on the table. For several minutes he did this without speaking or looking up at Patrick. Then he spoke.

- You know Patrick, you're a young man, you would take it better. The circular motions of the glass grew more expansive, proscribing almost the whole table as Joseph McReady's free hand clenched and unclenched down at his side. His leg accidentally touched Patrick's under the table. Patrick got up and walked from the pub.

- You're a friendly chap, Joseph McReady said to the glass. The old priest in the corner was slouched in his seat, a whiskey still in his hands. He began to mumble an indistinguishable prayer as Patrick walked past him, a relic of a past that had some meaning, some content.

Not A Pushover Quiz

Answers to Panurge 19 Quiz.

1. A Thousand Acres by Jane Smiley.
2. Reading Turgenev by William Trevor.
3. Mother Sugar is Anna Wulf's therapist in Doris Lessing's The Golden Notebook

Panurge 20 Quiz. Only one question. Who wrote 'The House of Ulloa'? First correct answer wins £20 Book Token. Deadline 16.5.94.

James Waddington

A Small Window On Gomorra

My quack thinks I'm a sadist. Not so. I keep my distance from the great Marquis, in temperament as well as time. But I had to get rid of her, that particular girl.

She wanted me to look at photos of the little farm, her doltish brothers, Rose the cat. She tried to give me a present of childhood treasure, one of those garish plastic windmills on a stick which she had bought "with me own money, at the fair, in Sligo."

There was no hard feeling on my part, no bitterness as far as one can tell on hers. She was upset, of course, but young girls cry easily, and I'm sure within a week she was running around the midden with Rose the cat and the clodhopping Michael, Seamus and the rest, laughter on her lips and only the fading shadow of a trouble in her little breast.

Or am I too pessimistic? Could there be any hope that, while she may have come in the spirit of one of the more self-mutilating saints, she should have returned with an infective splinter of enlightenment lodged in the large, but largely empty, organ of her mind?

I could consider how it might have been, how it might be - not the least amusing way of passing a morning, now I am forced to rise so early. My cigars, a glass of brandy, a good fire burning; the girl's successor, fine plump Sadie with the brain of an ox, to bring me coffee when I need it and stand there saying "Will that be all, Sórh, will that be all, Sórh," but not moving when, idly with one hand beneath her skirt, I do things which make the dew glisten on her upper lip.

The other would have leapt, skin flicking, like a foal that feels the switch laid gently to its side. How did she come to change so? I could consider. Vain speculation, no more.

*

Three nubile adolescents are sitting in a crowded café in downtown Sligo. (Imagine downtown Sligo for yourself - I have no idea.)

The girls are dressed, so they would think, 'smart', in garments with inscriptions of which they themselves do not know the significance. If you say, "Why do you have the words Dirty Harry scrawled across your delicious little bosom?" the reply will be, "Well, sure it's after being Dirty Harry, don't you see?"

They are Kathleen, Mary and Bridget. Mary is working up to be a

79

Bride of Christ.

"The fact remains," Bridget is saying, "London is a dreadful wicked place where they have bookshops with pictures of people doing things it would make you sick to look at and turn your hair grey in an instant, and them not taking a blind bit of notice as if it was the most natural thing in the world." One understands that there are no such bookshops in Sligo. She's probably talking about Smiths.

"What kind of things would those be?" asks Mary. Her excuse is that she must understand before she can condemn.

"Like MacAllister's bull with the great bollocks on it?" breathes Kathleen so softly that the youths at the next table barely catch her words, yet they shift their spotty buttocks in discomfort.

"Look would you just watch the gob," says Mary, "otherwise Father Kelly'll have me in the hair shirt and ashes for another fortnight." She giggles.

"Much worse than MacCallister's bull." Bridget wants to keep the conversation serious.

"Oh tell us, tell us please," pleads Kathleen. She puts out her tongue and pants. The boys at the next table keep their eyes fixed on the red check plastic table cloth.

"Well, you know the picture books at school in the cupboard Mrs MacLaverty was always the maniac for keeping under lock and key, you know the picture with all them people with no clothes on, the one with the strange birds and the globes of glass. You know the man with the daffodil up his bum...."

"In his bottom, if you don't mind," says Mary. "Well?"

"Well!" says Bridget, and doesn't know how to go on.

"I tried it once," says Kathleen.

"You never," says Mary, staring at her with wide blue eyes and a vigorous, healthy complexion. "You're as good as telling the devil to come and get you now. What possessed you to do such a thing? What a terrible risk you would be taking with your mortal soul. Was it worth it for a few brief moments of.... What was it like?"

"Well it wouldn't be going up at all. A daffodil stalk's awful bendy."

"And what did your confessor say?"

"He said it was. He said it's a terrible bendy thing a daffodil stalk. He gave me ten 'Hail Marys' and told me to be careful in future because the juice is the terror for being alkaline."

Mary turns away, re-packing her mind neatly. She tightens the straps, and then speaks:

"Anyway, Bridey dear, what was the point you were making?"

"That in London it would be very easy to fall pregnant without you scarcely knowing how it happened."

"Why would a girl who is determined to keep herself unspotted be any more likely to fall pregnant in London than in Lochmaleish?"

"Because Jennifer, and Edna and Cousin Bridey and Mary Madden and Eileen, none of them fell pregnant at all in Lochmaleish, and every one of them was up the spout when they hadn't been in London six months."

"They must have fallen to temptation then."

"My point precisely. And my further point is," and Bridey waits until the other two, eyes shining and cheeks glowing, have an ear each close to her coral lips before she continues, "my further point is, the future's not ours to see, *che sera sera*, and would it not be the sensible idea if we thought about precautions now, while we have all our faculties about us."

"But it's illegal," says Mary loudly, sitting upright in her chair and drawing the glances of several of the clientele.

"Wisht girl. What I'm thinking," Bridget continued, "is this. If a girl is to fall - and she is, I'm afraid, she is - what's the least sinful way of going about it, the one that wouldn't be upsetting the Blessed Virgin too much at all?"

Mary knows that a wicked trap can be baited with an accident of virtue.

"Is that not a wee bit presumptuous, to be bringing the Holy Mother into it? Should we not be leaving the whole question to them as are qualified, and not be meddling in what doesn't concern us?"

"But," asks Bridey, "will them as are qualified be there to give us the answers when we're in the grip of the overpowering temptation? I'm sure you know what I'm talking about, don't you Kathleen?"

"Oh I do," breathes Kathleen between parted lips, plunging her hands between her knees and rubbing the palms together.

"What is certain," continues Bridey, "is that one is always sorry after."

"A bit," sighs Kathleen.

"Are you not always sorry after, Mary?"

"After what?" Mary's blue eyes shine like mirrors. Her mouth has a sweet hard smile.

"She knows," says Bridey to Kathleen. "Look, suppose I was to fall victim to temptation in London, I'm going to be sorry. I know that. What I want is to be no more sorry than I have to. For instance, is it right I should bring a little babe into the world, conceived out of wedlock, poor and fatherless?"

"You should not!"

"Then she'd have to be taking the precautions, isn't it so?" says Kathleen.

"The precautions," says Mary emphatically, and then, after sharp 'sh's from the other two, repeating it more quietly, "the precautions is not doing it in the first place."

"Sure I know that, but that's a counsel of perfection."

"If I don't do it in the first place for much longer," says Kathleen, "I think I'll go into convulsions."

"So it's the precautions it'll have to be. And that's where you can help Mary. If you have to sin, you'd be foolish not to be going for the least wicked. Of the precautions, Mary, which would be the least wicked, would you say?"

"The Church allows the rhythm method within wedlock."

"The Church is a blithering con then," says Kathleen. "Me Aunty Elizabeth and me Uncle Mick use the rhythm method and they have the nine already and only been married twelve years."

"Now," Bridey continues soberly, "of the effective precautions there's the two different approaches. There's the physical barrier, and there's the hormonal intervention. Now is it the truth, Mary, that once the fella has his willy up you, the most virtuous thing you can do is just let him hump away till he comes? Is that not so?"

Kathleen moans.

"You're in mortal terror of hell fire even thinking such a thing," says Mary.

"I'm only thinking about it," says Bridey, "like you'd puzzle out your homework - which I couldn't say for sure is the case with Kathleen here."

"It's mortal sin," says Mary.

"But that's my point. If it's mortal sin for him to have his willy in there in the first place, can it make it any worse for him to be having a johnny on it? And would that be more sinful than the tablets?"

"Holy Mary Mother of God, I can't be listening to this any

longer. Do you think you can choose between the badness of sin? Sin's not like that."

"Have some sense, Mary girl, of course it is. What would be the point of having mortal sin and venial sin at all, what would be the point of different penances for different sins if they were all the same?"

Mary looks hot and cross.

"She's got a point," says Kathleen.

Mary tries the hard sweet smile again but the lips tremble. She frowns instead, but can think of nothing to say.

"I know it's difficult," says Bridey.

"Difficult. You're talking as if it was a horse race. Would I be better going for a winner, or would I be better putting a bit each way?"

"I think you're beginning to follow me," says Bridey. "I mean if I'm not tempted, then we're laughing, but if I'm swept off my feet, surely to God it's best I fall as soft as I can."

"I wouldn't know where to begin."

"Well let's set about it with a bit of organisation. Here's a page out of me diary. Let's write them all down, then we'll put them in order. Precautions; physical barrier. Precautions; hormonal intervention. Oh and there's the Intercourse itself, we mustn't be forgetting that."

"You can't have precautions without the intercourse," says Kathleen. "A fella would look a right dickhead sat all by himself with a johnny on his plonker, reading the newspaper."

"Could we not at least keep the language a little bit decent," says Mary.

"That's a thing," says Bridey, "are the tablets a sin until the moment of intercourse? If not, at what precise point does the sin commence? Is it with 'the introduction of the very tip of the glans between the outer lips of the vagina', is it with 'full penetration so the hairs of the pubes meet', or is it 'at the moment of ejaculation of seminal fluid into the upper reaches of the vagina, against the neck of the cervix'?"

"Will you shut your gob," says Kathleen, "or I'll be having the convulsions now. What about if he whips his cock out just before he shoots off?"

"That's the point I was making. Would that be even worse than leaving it in?"

"No, no," says Kathleen, "I mean as a precaution."

"Och, I'm with you. Precautions; physical barrier. Precautions; hormonal intervention. Precautions; if he whips his cock out just before he shoots off."

"Oh dear," says Mary, as of one who has tried and tried and of whom no more can be expected. "What else?"

"Unnatural acts," says Kathleen.

"Like French kissing?" says Mary. She can but hope.

"Like cocksucking," says Kathleen.

"Holy Mother save my soul."

"And daffodils."

"Och we'll have no time for the flower arranging," says Bridey, "but the other ought to go down. Even if it is no more enjoyable than it sounds, and wouldn't you think it would have to be, there's all sorts. What if he slips it between your tits? What if he tickles your lug with it?"

"Will you shut it?" says Kathleen, "or I'll have to be taking a short walk." And, by Jove, if the actual girl had spoken as these do now, and not tried to interest me in blurred snapshots of her cat Rose, she might not be back in Galway today. But no matter. I strike the bell. Sadie will soon be here with the coffee.

"May the good Lord preserve you and keep you from your wicked, wicked thoughts," says Mary.

"I wonder where the sin is exactly," muses Kathleen.

"Is it not obvious? I never even knew it was possible to think such thoughts, let alone say them aloud. Oh Holy Mother..."

"No, I mean the sin in the precautions. With a married couple, say a married couple with six children, where would be the harm...?"

And here we leave them to go through the fascinating conundrums of Catholic theology. After an hour or so more of attentive discussion, Bridey and Kathleen at least will have convinced themselves that there is nothing peculiarly or overwhelmingly wrong with 'the precautions'. It's a conclusion that well-adjusted catholic couples come to quite naturally after their third or fourth child, without all this ridiculous argument.

*

"But it's mórdher, is it not mhórdher," the young woman protested when, after the disturbed few weeks which led to her unexpected departure from Lochmaleish and, under my roof, six months of violence to everything she held sacred, she came to me not with more photographs of farmyard chums, but the news that she hadn't had 'the chorse' for two months and felt herself to be with child. I think despite what she had been through she saw herself on a donkey, in something blue and voluminous but becoming, heading for a stable.

When I say violence, I don't of course mean anything physical; but her beliefs were badly bruised.

I talked to her. I explained how everything was, if not for the best, at least not for the worst. I wonder how it ended. Mere vanity.

*

The same café in Sligo - or another very like it.

"Was it terrible, the abortion?" said one.

"The termination. It was, indeed it was terrible, it's like losing your heart, it's like grieving waking and sleeping and not being able to grieve enough because you've lost the bits that help the grief to heal itself," - or something to that effect.

"And have you confessed?" said the third.

"I have not, not yet. I haven't the strength a while. Is it not a terrible sin?"

"It's the worst," said the third, "it's mhórdher."

"So I thought. But we talked a bit, him and me, and he was ever so understanding in the way you'd never expect. Do you know what I think now? Sure the wec soul only flies away to limbo, without the faintest notion that it even exists. Now what is the soul, could you tell me?"

"Sure the soul's the spirit," said the first after a weighty pause, "it's the bit that goes on for ever when the body has returned to dust."

"Does the soul know of its own existence?"

"These are terrible hard questions you're asking," says the third.

"Does the soul exist in its own consciousness, or in the consciousness of God?"

"How would I know?" says the third.

"Och Jesus and Mary, do you think you exist or do you not?"

The third shrugs.

"Have a guess, yes or no."

"How would you tell?"

"Are you serious? OK, forget it. Just get a hold of this. If I exist only in God's consciousness, then I'm either something like a stone, or I'm part of God - and that's contrary to the Catholic faith to say I'm part of God. And I know I'm not a stone."

"How do you know you're not a stone?" asks the first, who

85

recognises this for a philosophical discussion but can't get the drift.

"Well, do I look like a stone?"

"You do not."

"Have some wit then. Honest to God. Where was I? The point I was working round to is, if I don't exist in my own consciousness, I don't exist at all."

"What about the stone?"

"What about it?"

"Does it exist in its own whoda?"

"Well what do you think?" The second girl is getting exasperated.

"I would think that it didn't. But it exists, all the same. Something doesn't have to exist in its own whoda to exist."

The second is entirely nonplussed. Then she sees. "But a stone is a thing. You can see it, you can touch it. It's thingy." She is struggling again, but not for long. "Take away the stone from a stone, and what have you left?"

The first shrugs. "And that," says the second, "is the condition of the soul without self-consciousness."

"Could you not put it a bit simpler," says the third, "for the distressed of brain."

"Souls in limbo do not exist. Therefore, theologically speaking, no crime has been committed. Abortion," she rose and curtsied," is not murder. Q," she conducted each letter archly, finger tip to thumb, her blue eyes shining like mirrors, her mouth in a sweet hard smile, "E, bloody D."

Old women mumbling their tired fig rolls looked horrified. The girl sat down.

"Well, in that case," said Bridey, "where will we be putting it at all in the list of sins? Wait, I have it here," and she drew out of her handbag the page of the diary, grubby now with addenda and consultation.

"It was bad was it, the termination?" asked Kathleen.

"The worst."

"Worse than unnatural practices?"

"Much worse."

"Its own punishment, could you say?" asked Bridey, pen ready.

"You could."

"Then if the wee soul comes to no harm, it's hardly a sin would you think." She put the list back in her bag and dropped the pen in after it. "I don't think we'll even be bothering to write it down at all."

*

"Are you truly sorry?" asked Father Kelly through the grille.
"Oh I am, I am."
"Sure you were always a good girl. We sent you into the world for a space because we detected a questioning spirit. Satan found you out, Satan made you fall, but perhaps it was God's will. You have no doubts now, do you child?"
"None, Father."
"I knew you would come back, my child. Before, you were not ready to leave the world, but I detect a change in you, a new certainty. Do not let it go too long. Come to us when Jesus calls you. How do you think you will serve, my child? In the world, with care and sacrifice, or will you leave the world for a life of prayer?"
"In all humility, it was the study of theology I had in mind, Father."

*

Vanity, mere vanity, but ... bitter in years, I still have hope.

TEN YEARS OF PANURGE 1984-1994

Celebratory readings in the N.E. and N.W.

Morden Towers, Newcastle on Tyne 8 p.m. Friday 15th April 1994
JAMES WADDINGTON & NORAH HILL
plus birthday balloons, quizzes etc. Ring Connie Pickard for more details. Tel. 091-477-4430.

Wheyrigg Hall, Wigton, Cumbria, courtesy of Solway Arts.
7.30 p.m. Friday 6th May 1994.
JUNE OLDHAM & WILLIAM PALMER.
Ring Panurge for more details. Tel 06977-41087.

Christine Hauch

The Sarum Twins

It was a year so topsy-turvy, so scarifying in its shocks and cruelties
as to make the toe-nails crack. Spring came in February. It tempted
the bluebells up through the earth before they were ready and fretted
the pregnant ewes under their too hot coats. On Lady Day it lifted
my mother's skirts to the lecherous intentions of a passing mercenary on
his way home from who knows what butchery. There will always be
wars enough to go round for men who hanker to fight in them.

The day after my conception.

*(Our conception, surely, the case for 'my' in the phrase 'my
mother's skirts' being arguable.)*

The day after our conception, however, the promise of summer
was abruptly withdrawn. Chilblains sprouted on knee-backs and
knuckles, icicles tapered from the well-head. Our grandparents
watched our mother vomiting and bewailed the loss of her purity
and the waste of the food she had eaten.

When warmth finally returned in the middle of June it was too
late to restore a balance to the seasons. Trees that had uncurled their
fingers early in March found them frost-bitten in April. Seven
weeks of dusty heat dried the stream-beds and scored a tracery of
cracks across the fields; then followed another seven of ceaseless
rain. The people of our village muttered about devils and spirits, but
despite their prayers and ritual sacrifices what crops had survived
rotted on the stem.

All this she and I were told much later.

Floating heads down alongside each other, I and my sister, who is
also I *(yes, I who am she, but so far and no further)*, we sucked our
thumbs through drought and downpour. For as long as we were fed by
the cord of life, we could give our mouths to comfort all day long.

*(This entire account of the time before our birth is, I should add,
a matter on my sister's part less of poetic licence than of gratifying
the imagination. However, the writing of this story is her decision
and I may interject but not prevent it. That much we have agreed.
For the present.)*

After such an ominous gestation our birth was as normal as such
things can be. The midwife would have drowned us like kittens, but
our mother heard our mewing through her pain and clung to us. She
never spoke about our early childhood. I can only suppose that we

ate and defecated, grew hair and teeth, as infants do. We crawled not at all, and walking came late. It must have seemed that we were to be denied that erectness which sets humankind apart from the beasts of field and forest. We have had to find our own way to acquire humanity.

I and my sister, who are one person, were kept well hidden from neighbours and gossips. As far as our mother was able, she made us invisible. My grandparents were convinced we were the work of the evil one and a curse on the family. I would never blame them for that. She who is I and I who am she have between us two heads, four arms, four legs, four breasts, two hearts, two livers, two wombs, one vagina, one anus, and no buttocks. Tied back to back by a malign creator, we are trapped together for life and death *(and in the Life Everlasting, though she refuses to believe in its existence, despite my prayers)*. We are the Sarum twins. You may have read about us in the literature. We have been examined by men of science and expatiated upon in monographs. Before Phineas Taylor Barnum thought to add spice to his greatest show on earth by exhibiting Eng who is also Chang, the Chinese brothers born in Bangkok, thereby making all conjoined siblings Siamese no matter where they had been born, there was a short time when Wiltshire might have claimed the honour of providing the label. To commemorate the diocese of our birth, there were British doctors ready to describe our condition as Sarum syndrome. But our fame, such as it is, cannot compete with the spangles and flourish of Mr Barnum's set pieces.

We are not unique, or so we have been told, but we are unquestionably rare. We are also unlike almost all women of our time and station in one other important respect: we have received an education. However I may weep for my outward shape, I shall never cease to be glad that my mind has been trained.

(With that, at least, I can wholeheartedly concur.)

At first we found it disturbing to be treated as specimens for examination, even if interest on the part of others has seldom given way to unkindness. But children can become inured to much. Indeed, as we acquired the ability to read and write, we began to make our own notes on those who came to view us. It has been a simple exercise to develop a secret coded written language, a Sarumish. Although he knows that we can read, the bishop still believes that our writing is gibberish.

(I regret that we continue to deceive him on this point. However,

there is no denying that were I to tell him the truth he could not be trusted to keep it to himself. And, while there are times when my sense of spiritual proximity to the bishop, or George, as he has asked me to call him, outweighs my loyalty to her, the fact remains that I am bound to her by the most extreme form of consanguinity. Moreover, she has left me in no doubt that disclosure of our cipher to George, or to anybody, would result in a physical response by her of such frenzy that I should have to fear for the life of my child.)

Besides, no fools we, since our mother has relinquished her claims to us, it has become clear that our very survival depends on the fact that we are known to people of reputation who will feed and clothe us, even if we are to remain in captivity. Given who we are, we do not harbour many illusions about the freedom available to us. A cage in the circus is probably the best we could look forward to. Our only hope of anonymity would be to return to the house of our grandparents; but there is no guarantee of our safety in such a step. Were there to be another summer like the one before our birth, the villagers might come looking for a sacrificial victim, or two, to placate the wrath of nature. *(We have quarrelled so fiercely over this point that I shall not unduly delay her narrative by iterating here all my arguments on the subject. I shall say merely that her love of fanciful hyperbole must by now be apparent to all.)*

We cannot remember when we first became aware of our otherness. I would say that the initial experience of such things has little meaning in any case, that their effect is cumulative. She would try to recapture the original sensation. That is how we are, general and particular. I the broad sweep of things, she the finicky. *(I the fineness, she the unruly.)* I the wayward child, she the prim and priggish miss. *(She the mischief-maker, I the prudent keeper of the peace.)*

We agree, at least, that it is the bishop who has done most to bring home to us our plural singularity.

It never worried my mother that we were not baptised. She had not been able to disguise the signs of our impending arrival; and, since scandal flies round village kitchens fast as dragonflies, she would have expected the news to reach the old rector. At the due time he would be sure to come in search of new lambs for the flock. When he ignored our arrival she assumed that our unusual nature had been made known to him and that he, too, had dismissed us as the spawn of Lucifer.

'I'd not let him near my children, in any case,' she'd have said. 'The last time I prayed to his god was when I found I was expecting them. He did nothing for me then, he'd do no more now.'

(The attribution of such ungodliness to my mother is not to be borne. And I give warning that I shall find some means to put an end to this account unless these provocations cease. She may threaten damage to the unborn, but she knows that I am not without an arsenal of my own. There are many ways in which I could make her life much less comfortable without myself incurring undue suffering.)

In fact, there were no such excommunicatory motives behind the rector's neglect of us. He was a squeamish thing, who had taken to the study of toadstools as soon as his wife started coughing, and was out in the woods with his specimen basket when the consumption finally claimed her. The village midwife, while she had little enough respect for him, knew that, as long as he rather than another continued to dispense morality in the parish, it would be easier to help her patients out of difficulties, and no questions asked. So she had no wish to see him go, and fearing the sight of us would tip him into the grave, she told him we had been a phantom pregnancy. If he never scented the least whiff of gossip about us after that it was probably because the midwife had suggested to her customers that it would be better so.

When I-she were beginning to master the awkwardness of walking at around the age of 7 or 8, a new god-man came to the parish. *(The meaning is clear, I suppose, though I could wish for a more respectful title. I hope also that it will be clear to any reader that her portrait of the old rector is simply more of her tarradiddle. Since my censure usually leads to her committing yet further outrages, I am endeavouring to control my natural revulsion at her flagrant falsehoods.)*

The old rector had died, and not from eating a misidentified fungus, but from the same blight that had shrivelled his wife. For the first time in forty years a different voice was promising eternal salvation from the pulpit, and with startling vigour. Desperate for new souls, he was. Somebody told him about us, although little enough, and he came to offer us an afterlife. I laugh about it now. The years of contact with educated minds have given me a more refined sense of humour. Imagine the knotty problems we must have posed for him. How many souls do we have? What is St Peter to do with us at the pearly gates? One entry ticket to paradise, or two? For paradise must be our destination if there is any justice.

To give the young rector his due, he never treated us as if we were a deformity, more perhaps an aberration, a cause for wonder at the diversity of his god's creation. After his first tactful visit, eyes carefully trained at a point between our two heads, he bade us goodbye at the cottage door and we did not see him again for several months. We were not to know that we had become a topic of conversation at the episcopal dinner-table. Our spiritual shepherd had attended the university with the bishop's son and was a frequent guest at the larger houses in the cathedral close. The bishop himself had his curiosity whetted and offered, as a favour to his son's friend, to grace our parish with his presence in order to take the next confirmation service.

After admitting a small group of girls into full membership of the Anglican communion, the bishop postponed his return home for long enough to make a short tour of the neighbourhood. He admired the view from the top of Gibbet Hill and waved a ringed hand at a scattering of stone-picking children who scarcely looked up as he passed. The arrival of his carriage at the end of our lane brought us out of the house to see what had happened. The only time any vehicle stopped there was when they brought my grandfather home drunk from the ale-house, but that was Saturday-night business, and this was Sunday afternoon.

(It is difficult for me to say exactly how, difficult to select the precise word or phrase that offends, but there is something sardonic here. The facts are probably more or less accurate, but the manner of their telling sneers.)

The bishop beckoned us towards him, and as we began our scuttling crab-like progress along the track he took out a pair of wire-framed spectacles and looped the ends round his ears. A trick of the light made the discs of glass look opaque and my sister, who is not always me, took fright. She tried to turn back while I would have carried on. Equally determined, we both tugged the other in the direction we wanted to go. The bishop found us a startling sight. He ran towards us, then changed his mind and stood, panting from his burst of exercise, at a distance of about thirty feet.

He held out a gingerly hand in front of him, as town people do when they are suddenly confronted by cattle and need to make a gesture of propitiation and good will. She, glimpsing the movement, took it for a threat and made an extra effort to run away. We fell over.

I was very angry and caught her a satisfying slap across the fleshiest part of her right leg. She tried to hit me back, and we were soon too absorbed in our awkward attempts to hurt ourself to notice that the bishop had come closer, close enough indeed to bend over and try to stop us.

His intervention united us in a common hostility towards this stranger who had effectively laid us low by his approach. But small children, even in pairs, have few tools of aggression to deploy against fully grown men. She-I scrambled to our feet and fled homewards, yelling and screaming for the largest weapon in our armoury, our mother.

An angry woman, our mother, with cause enough to be so, goodness knows, she never let her indignation run amok, but marshalled all the forces of it to deliver perhaps a single sentence of such concentrated and unanswerable scorn that the recipient would retire defeated after the first salvo. Mother saw the bishop off. She wasted little time on the young rector, too, when he came a week later to offer her money to allow us to be taken away by important people who might, as he put it, be able to do something for us.

"And what sort of a something would that be?" she asked. "A rosy future, is it? Fame and fortune? Or a satin-lined box for my daughters to live in while the public pay to gawp at them?"

My grandfather could see no harm in the suggestion. The sum of money mentioned by the rector represented a good few months of drunken Saturday nights. He and mother argued about it for several days, and for the first time I heard ourself alluded to as a sport of nature, an entry in the human family album of curiosities, albeit not in those terms. However, as I said, that's my recollection. I don't speak for her, my sister, though there are plenty have thought I do. *(Only, I might add, because she opens her mouth at times when I find it more prudent to keep mine closed. She accuses me of playing the hypocrite, of allowing her to voice my less agreeable thoughts while myself maintaining through silence the appearance of untainted virtue. I have not consciously sought to make her my scapegoat, but honesty compels me to admit that her outspokenness has spared me the necessity to expose my own occasional dissentience to general view. She has a choice. Since she has decided to play the dog, why should I bark?)*

Two years passed before we were taken. There had been a grudging agreement that my mother should stay under her parents' roof - which was not theirs at all but belonged to Farmer Sedgely - so that she could care for us; but as soon as we were old enough to be left at home occupied in some useful task, she was forced out to work on the land.

As we sat on the doorstep in the April sunshine picking out the best of last year's peas to be sowed, the bishop's carriage again drew up at the end of the lane. This time it was our grandfather who descended from it and beckoned. As a special treat for being good girls we were to be given a ride. And good girls that we were, we climbed in without a fuss and waved grandpa good-bye. On our jolting journey through the countryside we were allowed to survey the scenery, but once the outskirts of the city were reached the bishop moved us to the floor, where our only view was of his booted calves.

Wrapped in a rug, to avoid frightening the servants, we were carried through a side door in the bishop's palace, past the portraits of his predecessors lining the stair-well, and up to the loft. There two dormer windows, with a low colonnade edging the parapet beyond them, admitted light and the astonishing sight of the cathedral, a stone leviathan basking in a sea of grass. We had never imagined there could be anything so immense and assumed that our privileged view of this wonder was part of our reward for goodness. For some time we stood at the window, in silence. She and I only talk to each other when we disagree, and not always then. It is a waste of breath to speak out loud to her alone when all I am doing is echoing her thoughts.

Shortly afterwards the bishop himself brought us white bread and butter, two glasses of milk and two small sweet cakes covered in a chocolate coating that looked like eggshell but melted on our fingers. Even she began to doubt that anything we had done could merit prizes on this scale. And my-her suspicions were justified. It was not for what we had done, but for what we were that a double bed had been set up there under the roof and a lock put on the door, to which only the bishop had a key.

He was not an unfeeling gaoler, however. He did his best to reassure us that our sleeping in the bed was part of some pre-arranged plan of which our mother had approved. It seemed plausible. We had grown accustomed to spending nights without her. Farmer Sedgely had recruited her labours in his kitchen the previous Christmas, when a large house-party and an epidemic among his household staff had necessitated drafting in extra workers. His appreciation of her beauty had led to further occasional invitations, both to scour the pots for a penny, and to perform additional services for the promise of his protection. If Mrs Sedgely knew, she turned a blind eye, grateful no doubt that the risks attendant upon a further confinement were to be foisted on to some other victim.

(Lest there should be any who could imagine this idle and calumnious speculation to be proven truth, I have no choice now but to interrupt. Our grandfather's drinking habits are unfortunately too much a matter of general knowledge to deny, which is why I made no comment earlier, although it is not necessary to draw attention to them. But her transcription of rude gossip concerning mother and Farmer Sedgely is the last straw. My dear sister, in her no doubt admirable efforts to paint the lives of hard-working country people in their real colours, has a tendency to dwell upon squalor. I shall impute no evil motives to her. But the blamelessness of the end does not always exonerate the means. Whatever her intentions, her wilful disregard for the basic tenets of good behaviour and for the sensibilities of those to whom she owes respect and love is no longer endurable.)

Mrs Sedgely always treated our mother well.

A down quilt is a considerable improvement on a blanket of uncertain origin and several layers of sacking. Under the elegant episcopal roof we slept the sleep of fear-free innocence until the bishop woke us with breakfast, warm water to wash in, and clean clothes. He withdrew, saying that he would come back when the cathedral bells started ringing for matins. The clean clothes were finer than anything worn in our family, but did not fit. And yet the problem was not so much that they had been made for two separate people. We could have contrived some semblance of decency had they not been much too small.

I have no doubt that the bishop had done his best to prepare the two men with whom he returned for the sight of us, but there are phenomena for which words are inadequate. The way in which we are joined has necessarily entailed our appearing to lean away from each other since we first learned to sit or stand. But the bodices with which we had now been provided were so small that we were only able to fasten them by rounding our shoulders still further, as though each were shrinking in horror from the other. Even the bishop, who must by then have grown accustomed to our general outline, was taken aback.

"Gentlemen," he said, endeavouring to regain his composure by an observance of the conventions. "May I present to you the Misses Dibden, Mary-Anne and Mary-Jane."

The taller of the two visitors introduced himself as Dr Stillwater, physician and surgeon. He expressed himself delighted to make our acquaintance and went immediately to the window to admire the view, as he said. The other man was more voluble.

"I am Charles Wicks," he said, and stared at us, unabashed. "I have heard so much about you. As a man of science I have always taken a particular interest in the variety of the human condition. You will perhaps be generous enough to afford me the opportunity to further my investigations into the daughters of Eve."

(She cannot possibly recall so precisely what he said.)

He baffled us. Indeed, most of the people who came to see us during the first months of our life here spoke to us in language which might as well have been Polish or Pushtu for all the sense we could make of it. But, as I have said, the bishop has been no Barnum. Although he brought his friends and, later, a wider circle of spectators to visit the living whims of Dame Nature in his vivarium under the eaves, he also supplied us with schooling and books and eventually gave us access to his library. That he should have conducted such experiments on our cognitive faculties is not perhaps so surprising. Whatever his other failings, his curiosity may be accounted a moral strength and his kindness a blessing. Even under the present circumstances, when most people would not have condemned him if he had let us loose to fend for ourselves, he has cared for her, if less for me, with as much solicitude as a doting grandfather.

(I feel a weakness in her, at last. And how just it is that it should be a recognition of George's goodness that is undermining her misanthropy. With the help of his Blessed Redeemer, God made Man, I shall persevere in my efforts to feel compassion for her who rails so against her fate. It is she who has brought me to my present condition, whether I would or no. But now that I have been granted this chance to fulfil my purpose as a woman I owe her some gratitude.)

With the freedom to choose our own reading matter, admittedly from within the limits of the bishop's collection, I found intellectual independence from her.

(And I, thanks be to God, from her.)

Travelling with Aeneas and Gulliver, with Falstaff and Candide, I was able for the first time to leave her behind.

(She drifts. And as her firmness of purpose wanes, so mine waxes. I will no longer confine myself to comment. I shall emerge from my parenthetical existence. This story shall be mine.)

*

Yet, how should I best tell it? If I return to our birth, amending her account in the interests of veracity, it will seem small-minded. She has brought us to the bishop's palace, and it is here that our true lives began. For we have been given the best possible gift, one not to be measured against riches, noble birth or beauty: the knowledge of the Love of God. In His Wisdom He has created us. Every vessel, however misshapen, may receive His Body and Blood.

The strict chronology of events is unnecessary. In due season we reached womanhood. Precisely when matters little. Since there is no record of our birth in the parish register nobody can be sure of our exact age. Although we were not forewarned of the ways in which our maturity would become visible (being almost entirely divorced from the company of our own sex from the day we were abducted to the time of our first bleeding) *my faith in the benevolence of Providence was by then sufficient to allay her fears* (and the bishop, noticing certain undeniable symptoms, arranged that we should have an older female servant to attend us).

Despite George's assurances of my innocence, I cannot help reproaching myself that I did not do more to quell the spirit of perversity in her or to discover the paths along which it was taking her. The books she read did not interest me. Her silences and fits of abstraction I took to be similar in nature to my own: a time given to the proper contemplation of higher things. Since there is no deviousness in my own nature I sought no other motives in her behaviour than would have influenced my conduct.

(Ha!)

Although we have never been out in the world, I have had no cause to resent our enclosed existence. The dangerous notions she plays with, equality, self-determination, liberation, are will-o'-the-wispish. Seduced by their false allure, she has threatened to sink us both. But an all-merciful Father has seen fit to allow that some good may come of her errors.

(Overt persecution would be preferable to this regretfulness for my misdemeanours. Her condescension saps my resistance.)

It is natural enough for a woman to seek the joys of motherhood. I had simply assumed that we had been chosen for a different life and had put all such ideas from me. But not she. For how long she had entertained her vile schemes I shall never know since she has solemnly sworn the most impious oaths never to speak of them. It may be that motherhood was not her aim at all, but that she was seeking to arouse in a man, any man, that emotion which leads rightfully to wedlock.

(I have been foolish, I admit it, but not so naive as to believe in the possibility of a sensual attraction towards me. Of course I wanted to bear a child, a creature in my image who could yet be free of her.)

During the weeks between a late Easter and Ascension Day George was called away to attend his dying father. He had never left us for more than a week since bringing us to the close. But Eliza, our servant, had always proved equal to the task of caring for us during these short absences, and he had no reason to doubt but that she would do so on this sad occasion also. As the days lengthened, the afternoons we spent reading in the library stretched further into the evening. Eliza came later and later to fetch us - we never went up or down the stairs without an escort for fear we might fall; and one evening, it being too dark to read, we waited for her by the open window, leaning side by side on the sill to relish the scents of the garden.

A young man appeared from near the stables which stand at the end of the east wall. She waved to him. Perhaps she smiled. Since I must stand with my back to her I cannot know. He walked towards us, hesitantly as it appeared.

(And no wonder. What monster must have he been led to expect?)

He came close enough to see our faces clearly, said his 'good evening' and walked back to the stables. I dismissed the episode from my mind. But the next afternoon she, under pretext of difficulty with small print, insisted that we sit right by the window so that she could watch for him. He did not come. She fretted. I asked what was disturbing her. She said it was the heat.

For three days we sat by the window that she might benefit from the light, the breeze, the delightful perfume of the wistaria, and at last her patience was rewarded. The young man returned. This time he walked straight up to us. She asked his name. He muttered a reply.

(Hugh. His name is Hugh.)

When Eliza came for us he was still standing there. She told him to be off to where he belonged, but she smiled at him, indulgently. "The coachman's nephew, young charmer he is. You'll need to watch yourselves with that one, my Marys." And she laughed.

(It was a laugh directed at us, or so I felt it to be.)

Once more he came to see her, earlier than before, so that there was less chance of his being found with us. He moved round us until he was facing her. I could scarcely make out his continued presence without turning my neck until it hurt. They talked together so quietly that I could not hear their words, mouthing like fish over their love-play.

(Jealous, ah yes. How she betrays herself. Does she imagine I was after billing and cooing? All I ever wanted was my child.)

He did not return. She no longer asked to sit near the window. She complained of headaches and asked me to read to her. She tired of my voice and suggested that we conduct an experiment. She had been reading, she said, of the work of a Mesmerist newly established in London. According to his theories, it was possible for one person to relieve pain in another through animal magnetism. We were both to be blindfolded that we might concentrate on transmitting the necessary influences between us, and then I was to wish her headache away.

Against my better judgement I agreed that she should tie her sash around my head. I thought only to humour her in her migraine. She knotted it so tightly that I cried out, but before I could protest further I found myself tipped forward. I shall not describe in any detail the horrors of what followed. When she allowed me to breathe again and released the blindfold we were alone in the room with our ruptured maidenhead.

(And now my child moves inside us, but it dances to the rhythm of her heartbeat. Too impetuous, too desperate fully to consider the consequences of what I longed to do, I had made no allowances for the blind thrust of male seed. Spurning my welcoming womb, it entered hers who would have rejected it. And now in the weeks of waiting my barren emptiness continues to weep the red tears of its loss month by month as though nothing had happened, while she grows fat and contented around my future. How should I not 'rail against fate', as she puts it, when I have sacrificed so much in order to achieve so little.)

Because her monthly bleeding continued, it was not immediately apparent that I was to have a child. When my body swelled and Dr Stillwater was summoned to examine me, there was talk of a dropsy, or worse. It was not until I finally determined to break my vow of secrecy and disclose the nightmare that had befallen me in the library that the true nature of my condition was diagnosed. My shame upon learning of it is hardly to be imagined. And yet, with George's help, decency will triumph. Although I was unable to name the father of my child, not having seen him, my suspicions as to his identity were confirmed by her eventual confession.

(A confession extracted from me under the severest moral torture. I was given a choice: to see all the menservants in the bishop's household brought before the law accused of attacking us, and thus under threat of hanging or transportation, or to name the one man who might then be coerced into marrying her and so give the child a name.)

I am to be wed next month. Tomorrow the banns will be read for the first time. It is understood that this marriage is being solemnised for the sole purpose of providing my child with a legitimate birth. My husband will continue to groom the horses. She and I will continue to live under George's protection. Our apartments will be extended to include a nursery.

(You may think me powerless now, but while there is breath in our body I can curse your stony-hearted piety. For the moment you have appropriated our story, but the ending is still to be written. And who can say how matters will turn out? The child kicks impatiently. Will it wait until you have exchanged your unmeaning vows with Hugh? Were I to implore your god for anything, it would be for the patience to bide my time.)

She is silent. Once I might have tried to penetrate her thoughts, but they no longer interest me. I have my own concerns. I pray God that He will see me safely delivered in the hour of my greatest need, and that I may be given the strength to raise my child as a true Christian. Soon George will sit beside me, and together we shall recite the words of the Magnificat. 'My soul doth magnify the Lord and my spirit doth rejoice in God my saviour... he hath shewd

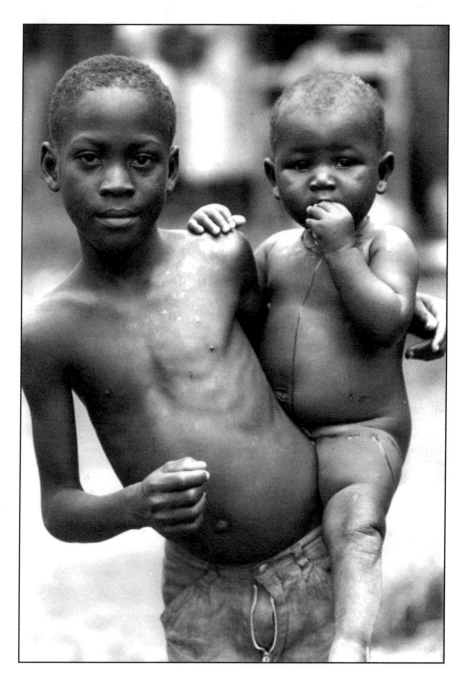

Children of Haitian sugar workers.   *Philip Wolmuth*

strength with his arm: he hath scattered the proud in the imagination of their hearts...'

Feel our child, sister. Even you cannot ignore it. It will be born.

LETTERS

The Hard Life

I've been writing for four years, due to unemployment, no other career, old age, too much intelligence on one occasion, (would you believe), not a female etc. etc. Expenditure on writing vastly exceeds income. Ach well, it keeps me off the street corner.

Brent Hodgson,
Ayr

WPs and the Bible

These days everyone is telling me that WPs produce sanitised writing. Such texts it seems are always over-written and de-risked, for as William Burroughs assures us, rewriting is censorship after all. Lorna Tracy praises her old fashioned electric typewriter. Behind this point of view is Romantic metaphysics, that original inspiration should not be tinkered with, a slap in the face of the gods of creativity.

I have before me a book that's been rewritten, redacted, amalgamated, translated and destroyed etc. for over 2000 years, and yet still sells much much better than *Naked Lunch.* Censorship never did the Bible much harm.

The point is not whether you rewrite or how much you do, but to make it look as if you haven't.

Robert Loughrey,
Brighton

Why Mags Fold

I was amused to learn that my story was the most disliked in Panurge 15/16. I did find it incredible that a group of writers at a fiction workshop should need to be 'forced' to read an anthology of contemporary stories. What did they expect as set texts? Dickens? Surely this is part of the answer to your own question about why so many magazines fold.

David Rose,
Ashford,
Middx.

Raffles

Thank you for the Raffle Prize. Life looks up. Last time I won anything better than a bar of chocolate in a raffle was 30 years ago when I worked in Brighton. I won a re-style, set and manicure in the town's leading ladies' hairdressers. I was as bald then as I am now, and didn't even have a beard, as I have now, and nary a hair on my head either! Life was hard.

R.E. Benn,
Umberleigh,
Devon.

Panurges 18 and 19

I thought Joel Lane, Sandra Anderson, Bill Leahy, Justin D'Ath and June Oldham were all extremely well written and entertaining. Wilson Fuchs was brilliant (*thank you very much, Ed.*). I thought Dilys Rose's story was thought-provoking with strong dialogue and a devastating elegiac ending. I like the way Brian Howell gets under his characters' skin and so under the reader's and the way he manages almost imperceptibly to subvert reality.

R. Stone's and C. Wastling's stories did nothing for me and Matthew Kramer's failed miserably. Peter Lewis's publishing piece was timely and provoking. Long live the small press.

Mike O'Driscoll,
Swansea.

Richard Bowden

Seven Questions About Her

As sleek as a deer, she soaps herself in the bath. A radio plays in another room, the melodies hanging out in the air with the scent and steam of her wash. It is getting late. I glance down at my watch, and am irritated to find that I have left it by the bed. Looking over her crumpled sheets, designed and coloured (*Harlequinade*) to her own exact, expensive tastes, I spy it on the cabinet. It is lying upon her silk scarf, next to the crystal glass containing a single red rose. As I walk across her bedroom to collect the watch, my toes sink into the rich carpet and nudge against a pair of her outrageous shoes. I slip the watch on over my wrist, and without thinking fondle her scarf. A pillow of the large bed still carries the impression of her head from the night before, and I drape the delicate material like a veil over her side. Across the amber coverings it is exquisite, perfect, delicate. My fingers linger over the quilt, stroking the stitching, smoothing out ruffles, folding back where her arising has untidied. She is singing softly to herself as the radio plays. It is an operatic fragment, a cadence or two from an aria by Puccini. Her voice is languorous, cultivated, as perfumed as the bathroom she washes herself in.

I leave the bed, pull on my shoes and socks, and walk to the door. She has fallen silent, as if she is expecting me to say something, anything, after last night. Her bathroom tiles are blue, and droplets of water are forming over the patterns and rolling down towards the enamel. Her gown is on the white chair. A copy of her favourite novel, Josquin's *Pas d'Artifice* is scrolled in one distended pocket as it has been each time that I have seen it. In the clean brightness of the bathroom, her dark body is a surprise. Her back is turned from me. I watch the brown curves of her shoulders, gleaming in the steam, with fascination. In the luxury of the bathwater they are moving slowly and the water laps around her skin. Is she crying?

*

Ashamed, we meet under the trees. Here the foliage complements her dress. The fabric has been torn by the brambles, and I know that she will buy another. She is breathing heavily, out of breath after stumbling towards me through the tangled shrubbery. It has been a warm summer this year and the undergrowth is luxuriant. We say little to each other. Despite the roar of the traffic a few hundred yards away, here amongst the trees it is quiet, and I listen to the slow swish of the branches in the canopy above. Her hair has a shower of tiny leaves on it. I pluck one or two out, and let them flutter into the grass, the small shapes soon lost amongst its untidy growth. I notice that she has kicked off her shoes, or has lost them on the way over to meet me. Although her dress is torn, she makes no effort to cover herself up, and I catch a glimpse of the tiny hairs on her upper arm, standing erect in the cool air.

I am wearing white, for outside of the shade of the trees the day has been hot. I imagine the grass stains that will spread across my trousers and my shirt as our meeting progresses, the fresh loam of the forest that I will carry back home with me after we part, mingled with a hint of her perfume. My gaze returns to her dress. It is fascinating. Chosen by her husband, brought from the *De La Roche Salon* in Paris, it seems a symbol of their marriage, an import of the fading relationship carried deep into our wood. I pull the tear of material on her arm wider and she throws back her head, her perfect teeth catching in the sunlight breaking through the trees. Is she happy?

*

He is always aggressive after the opera. I do not know why he goes, except that the brute accompanies his wife. Tonight the same sad events, repeated so often before my furtive eyes, drive me close to tears with rage and frustration. The opera building is beautiful, with long marble colonnades terminating in exquisite stucco work, elegant steps and passageways, with cool marble craftsmanship throughout. Gilded frames fill the grand spaces, the nineteenth century studies hung from painted chains. Many of the splendid dresses worn by the women present are reflected in the polished wooden panels of the auditorium, and the perfumes of the rich and famous fill the air. Gowns of all colours flutter up and down the antique floors like butterflies. And amidst all the finery and the resplendent decor his fury smoulders, burning like a fuse. I fear that no one can sense it except for the two most intimately bound up with his passions.

I am dressed impeccably, with dinner jacket, ruffled white shirt and silk tie. My manners are perfect as I answer the occasional solicitations of slight acquaintances with an incline of my head. I do not know the Massenet that is performed this evening, and have only attended to be near her. The work (*Manon des Rouges*) is pleasant, but grows immeasurably in stature by the fact that I know that she is listening to it as well. During the grand aria of the first act I dare to look at their box. It is empty. In the interval I make a surreptitious search of the old building, past the flushed faces of the music lovers and their paramours as they drink champagne, my gaze skirting the silken hangings and delicate mantel-clocks, seeking the missing couple. Finally, standing perplexed and despondent on the entrance steps, I spot them in a taxi. The evening has turned to drizzle, and parked cars in the busy street have become spattered with fine drops of rain. I can see their argument progressing through the windows of the cab as it waits to turn into Boulevard Phillipe, her face pale in the orange lights of the street. Like players in some play of their own, they are acting out a familiar scene. As the car turns away from me, I think that he slaps her and that she slumps back sullenly into the interior. I imagine her features growing swollen and red from the blow. Can she understand such pain?

*

Her passions are unbounded. I know many of her obsessions by heart and in many cases am a slave to them. She prefers silk to cotton, so I spend a small fortune on hand-made shirts bought on the Rue Mignon. She adores cognac, and my apartment swells with a collection of bottles. Her favourite perfume is the obscure fragrance *Chez Danson*, and so I have opened an account with the small supplier in the Old Quarter. I study so many of her enthusiasms to make them my own that she occasionally chides me for being ridiculous.

Today she tells me that she can not see me again. At first I think that she is joking, or that I have misheard, and start to smile. I know her penchant for teasing of this kind, and am used to it. We have drunk some of her best cognac together, her rooms full of the smell of the drink mixed with her perfume. Her scent is in my hair and in the bed as we lie together. Although it is the middle of the day we have drawn the curtains, making love in the dark, and so I cannot see her face. I pass my fingers over her fluttering lashes and her lips, but she is not smiling. I am still naked, suddenly feel cold, and think of my blue nightshirt hanging on the back of my door, across the other side of the city. The chorus of *Rigoletto* falls quiet and her favourite recording comes to an end. In the silence I sense her fingers stroking the sheets, as if to calm the fabric. When she touches me like that I tremble. Can she feel pity?

*

You, Monsieur, work in a pigsty. I did not know what to expect when I snatched the name and address of your office from her

105

handbag. She had gone to the bathroom, leaving it on a chair by the bed. Picking it up, I noticed that it was made exclusively by *Maison Ricardin*, as are her gloves. I longed to handle such an expensive item and the rich leather was smooth and cool beneath my touch. On impulse I unfastened the gold clasp and slipped my fingers inside, quickly finding your wife's purse, tucked amongst the luxurious clutter of cosmetics. She carried your business card, and I crumpled it into a pocket. I lingered on her lipstick, remembering the times I have watched her apply make-up leaning elegantly over the dressing table, and how merely the reflection of her lips and her teeth would arouse me.

13 Rue Bresard, 4.29 p.m., and I have found you. A miserable district. A building that is provincial, and poor. The streets are unswept, and the workers in your company must shuffle like the lost to their positions. The facade of the company *Romberg & Co* is dilapidated and water-stained. Your floor and the exact whereabouts of your office are unknown to me, and I have no desire to enter the foyer to examine the index of personnel. I know that you must be important, as the sums which you spend on her are enormous, but your workplace repels me. In a small café across the road I order two croissants and a cognac, and watch from over the street. When you emerge into the late afternoon and step towards your motor, your suit is an expensive blue pinstripe, perfectly tailored. You do not have a coat or your usual Homberg, but it is not cold. The car park is across the road. I slip into an alley as you pass, then follow you to your white Jaguar. As you move I sense the power in you that she finds so irresistible, something of your easy brutality. I had intended to confront you this afternoon, but now find myself unable to, so intimidating is your presence. The car keys are deep in your left pocket. You open the door and slide in, and I watch, discomfited. As you drive off I think again of my hands in your wife's handbag, and her lips in the mirror. Is she waiting for you?

*

She telephones, and it is torment. She tells of that evening, of her husband, and of the opera. They have not been out. Instead he has kept her by him, away from the live music of the stage, alone in their apartment. Undressed, he is like a bear; undressed, she is like a branch. As she whispers the details, I sense his presence, in her next room perhaps, his hairy bulk depressing the bed. I do not know whether to believe her story, and that she has found the return to his caresses pleasurable, or whether I am confused. She is breathless, excited, outraged. He has found a new will to love her, manipulating her body with music, their grotesque engagement punctuated by Verdi, Puccini, and Berg. As singer replaced singer, act followed act. The music drove him to passions that terrified her one moment, aroused her the next. None of his brutality mattered; he was overwhelming, his deliberate movements symphonic. No doubt he has marked her again, but now she does not care. She admits to phoning me without dressing, fresh from his embraces, and I close my eyes, cradling the receiver beneath my chin. Her voice is husky with secrets we have shared already, but I listen to her confession. I can smell cognac and *Chez Danson*. She says that he saw me, and I laugh. He is not jealous; he is too certain of her for that. Neither is he dangerous to me; no matter how he abuses her in the bedroom the aggression rarely extends outwards to others. Instead he has reclaimed her, as the incoming tide reclaims a beach, and like a beach she has vanished from sight.

Today her copy of *Pas d'Artifice* arrived in the mail. Unscrolled, and packed flat, it refused to lie down and curls up in the litter of my table. After speaking to her, I find her handwriting on page 278. It is a brief note, almost a formal condolence. She writes in thin red ink; it could be her nail colouring. Applied with a delicate brush, much of the lettering is indistinct and obscure. Bitterly I imagine her constructing the prose while he works upon her like a dog, something which I have always refused to do, even when with her in the forest. As I read and re-read her words I can almost hear their laughter, and the panting slobbery that passes for his pleasure. Can she love like that?

This evening I drink more cognac than is good for me, sitting among the discarded sleeves of opera sets playing duets, quartets and recitatives at random. I reduce her book to scrap paper, stripping out the pages and distorting the spine, screwing the Gauguin cover into a tight ball. My flat seems empty now that I have lost her. The etchings and paintings on the walls, many bought at her insistence, are suddenly poor and pointless. Even Watteau depresses me, and eventually I turn *Le Jardin d'Ariadne* to the wall. I do not eat, but feel no hunger. Finally I pull on my grey overcoat and leave my rooms to wander aimlessly into the night. It has just rained, and will rain again. The first chill of autumn is upon the city, and a few leaves have fallen from the trees. Some drunks are gathered outside of the patisserie at the end of the street, jostling and peering into the window. They make me nervous, and I cross over to the other side of the road to the Metro. On impulse I buy a ticket and travel across the city, not knowing where I am going until I arrive; then I stagger up out of the carriage, out of the station towards the ornate building by the park. The posters proclaim her name. She is singing tonight, and neither her rejection of me, nor my profound misery, can erase the fact, nor make the attraction of a performance by her any less. I have no ticket, for she would normally send me one, but still the opera house has drawn me like a magnet. It is late, the adoring crowds are inside, and the house is full. I linger outside, straining to hear the notes of the piece, and her voice raised to the gods. For once I do not care or notice what she is singing. Instead I think of the elaborate costumes she wears, shining in the stage lights, her lips, her pure white throat vibrating with melody; and then of his thick fingers, gripping the front of the box as she articulates her music, his eyes ablaze. I am again struck by the strange equation that marks their relationship. Perhaps it gives her art its strength. It is as if his wife's every cadence on stage must be balanced by her cries from their bed. How have I lost her?

*

The last time I see them they are leaving the opera through the stage entrance. It is late and the audience have long since left the building. Her performance, I gather from their excited voices, has been another triumph. I have to stand some time, and am cold and wet in the worsening weather. I know that he has her, but I still wait for them, as an impatient critic would wait for a last act. They finally emerge under an umbrella, his arm round her waist, pulling at her clothes. They intend to walk home through the park. I suspect that tonight he has taken her in her dressing room, perhaps coupling among the bouquets she has gathered from admirers. Her face is flushed and excited, and she has removed all of her theatrical make-up. Away from the stage, she pretends nothing. Just as they pass into the trees, she throws her head back on his shoulder, as if to sing out to the dark sky. From a long way off, the thunder growls an answer.

Clare Portman

On The Edge In A Home-Made Jumper

I call them the dump-dwellers. They come mostly at the end of the day, when the light is fading so that their faces will be hidden by the shadows, as they stoop and shift and root among the piles of rubbish. They huddle in shapeless coats and disguise their individuality behind glasses and inside hats, but we recognise each other after years of hauling trolleys and wheelbarrows over the same artificial mountains. We never speak, because that would somehow encroach upon our anonymity and our rights as scavengers.

Because, of course, I am the greatest dump-dweller of them all. My home stands poised on the edge of the tip, drawing nearer and nearer to its final judgement. It wasn't always so. The house was someone else's once, and some distance away. But the tip moves. It shifts and spreads like a giant amoeba, mindlessly growing, creeping away from its origins, and now it has reached the house which I have taken for my own. I can sit in my lounge all day, watching and waiting until there is no-one around, and then I go out and make my voyages of discovery. I fill my house with my treasures and the only person to see them is PC Watson, who visits me once a month to check if I'm still here. No one else comes. I have no relatives, none of my old pupils had affection for me and I have never had any friends.

"Still here then, Ursula?" says PC Watson. He is a large and solid man and far too laboured for any intellectual exchange of thoughts.

"No," I say because foolish questions deserve foolish answers.

He looks around my lovely house. "The Council would give you a nice flat."

Comments like that don't deserve an answer at all.

"You've got some new curtains, I see."

"Found them on the tip," I say.

I remember the day, actually, because it was one of the best finds I have ever made. It was a secret, misty morning, when the sun rises unwillingly over the mounds of the tip, only grudgingly letting its rays seep through the half-light to outline silhouettes of other people's discarded possessions. You can't see the cars arriving with their loads until the people creep out, slowly like the sun, distastefully, believing they are in a twentieth century Golgotha,

Haitian sugar workers near Tamayo

Philip Wolmuth

unaware that they stand on the edge of an Aladdin's Cave.

I was up early that day because my dreams had not been comfortable. I had been at school again. "Miss Tucker," the girls of the Lower Fifth were chanting. "We haven't done our history homework." They were all shouting, as if by saying it louder, it would justify their lack of effort. I tried to reason with them, to tell them that there were lessons for us all today in the arrogant way in which Palmerston dealt with the Chinese in the Opium War. I wanted them to understand that not all British history is admirable. But their mouths seemed to expand as I watched and the shouting became more and more raucous until I felt I couldn't bear it any longer. I put my hands over my eyes and pretended I wasn't really there at all. And then I wasn't because I had woken up in bed, still sweating at the thought of teaching all those dreadful girls again.

I heard their voices from my lounge while I was having breakfast.

"Do hurry up, Anthony." Her voice was cultured and cold. "It's awfully chilly."

But Anthony was much nicer than she was. I slipped through the blanket that hung where the side wall should have been, and crept up the side of the dump, so that I could just see him, standing on the edge, looking round with an awed fascination that I instantly recognised. He was a born dump-dweller, that one. If he hadn't had the misfortune to be born with brains and middle-class parents, if he didn't earn so much money that he could live in a detached house with fitted kitchen, central heating and shower room *en suite* to the main bedroom, he could have been there alongside the others, alongside me, hunting through other people's cast-offs with the same delight that I felt.

"What an extraordinary place," he said quietly, and nobody could hear him except me.

She - the monster who would clearly never understand him - started hooting the horn.

He paused, took another look around - I thought for a moment he saw me watching over the mountain of rubbish - and then he gently placed his black plastic dustbin bag alongside all the others. It was neatly tied at the top, like a parcel ready for the post office, ready to send to their friends in New York, or the South of France.

"Coming," he called pleasantly, with no malice in his voice. I liked him. I knew there was going to be something good in his bag.

"I told them that we would be there by nine," she said petulantly.

111

He got into his car, a blue Volvo, another impediment to his true destiny - started the engine and drove away.

*

Going to bed is like setting off on a mystery tour, never quite knowing which distant lands and worlds I will visit while asleep. They are waiting for me, these places, and as I burrow into my quilt, transformed from two old eiderdowns of genuine goose down that I found many years ago on the tip, my mind tingles with anticipation. Where will I go tonight? What people will I meet from the past, whom I have nearly forgotten, who will become real again in my dreams? Sometimes they are nightmares, but I accept the terms of the lottery, and that heightens the tight-rope of anticipation when I go to bed.

Sometimes it is right back to my childhood. My school days. Not happy times, really, but now that I look back at them, I am filled with a sense of sadness that I quite enjoy in a sentimental kind of way. I had a friend once, for a short time, called Cecilia. Only everyone called her Cecil.

"Why do you wear those strange jumpers?" said Cecil. "They are cheating a bit for school uniform, don't you think?"

I did think so, but the choice was not mine. It never had been mine. "My mother gets my nanny to knit them for me," I said.

"You mean a real nanny, or a grandma?"

"A real nanny," I said with shame. Cecil thought I was showing off. Nobody else had a nanny, and of course, in time, I would learn to keep quiet about my strange background. About my mother, who was born the wrong sex, into the wrong age, and spent most of her time in Africa, pretending to be an explorer, while the other mothers were cooking nutritious stews for their children, plaiting their hair in the morning, and testing their Latin verbs. My mother didn't even have the good taste to be famous. She never discovered anything of any value. If she arrived at somewhere significant, she was always ten years too late - long after the world's curiosity had moved on.

She died in the war. It was a matter of great grievance to her that she wasn't allowed to be a pilot. So she was killed by a stray bomb on her way home from a fundraising committee meeting. I'm sure she did it out of spite. Just to show them that she would have been more use as a pilot. Since she got herself killed anyway, she might just as well have done it in a Spitfire and contributed to the war effort.

Cecil often questioned me about my family because she thought we were rather odd, I think.

"What about your dad? What does he do?"

Do? What did he do? I wasn't actually quite sure. Sometimes he was there, and sometimes he wasn't. His explanations were always vague. "Just taking a few days' break in Tahiti," he would say, and disappear for the next three months.

Then he would breeze in one day, bursting through the front door with an impeccable instinct for an entrance and confess that he had forgotten to buy me a present, so would I like to go on a shopping spree with him?

I didn't mind the shopping sprees, except that he never bought what I wanted, things like proper school uniform jumpers - he thought that was boring - so we bought mounds of beautiful dresses that I never wore and party shoes that sat in the bottom of my wardrobe, growing daily more reproachful and mouldy because I was never invited to anyone's party.

"He's an entrepreneur," I told Cecil. I thought I was pretty safe with that one, because even I wasn't entirely sure what it meant, and I was cleverer than Cecil. She certainly didn't have a clue, and didn't like to say so. Truthfully, I hadn't quite made up my mind if he was a spy, or if he went off to prison periodically. I never did find out. He disappeared one day when I was fifteen, and I have never heard of him since.

Even now, I wonder sometimes if he will just turn up on my doorstep one day.

"Hello, Ursula," he will say. "I forgot to buy you a present. Shall we go on the tip, and see what we can find?"

Cecil didn't stay my friend for long, because she made it up with her real best friend who had temporarily fallen out with her. I realise that was the only reason she played with me. Still, I can look back at that period of my life with fond memories, and remember that it felt good at the time. My dreams of Cecil's friendship are always comfortable dreams.

*

The quality of the material in those curtains was impressive. I hauled the bag home without even looking inside because I knew it was going to be good. And I was right. Yards and yards of heavy quality material, shades of shimmering pinks, woven tightly; Sanderson, probably. I knew why Anthony had lingered over them, why he had tied the bag so lovingly. He had not wanted to abandon them, but his wife had, of course, wanted a change of colour in her lounge.

A little grubby, it was true. But a trip to the launderette is money well spent. The regulars know me down there, and they chat to me sometimes. They look at my thick stockings and my hat, with the crooked felt red rose on the side, that came from the tip, and they smile affectionately. "Poor old Ursula," they say to each other. "She's harmless."

And they don't know about my History degree, or my thirty-eight years at Hentlesham Ladies' College where I taught generations of privileged young ladies with lots of money and no brains.

I hung the curtains in my lounge, and they matched the standard lamp I had salvaged, and the table cloth I had woven from the dozens of ties that had come from the tip over the years. I was proud of that table cloth. It was artistic, it was original, and it was a symbol of success - it demonstrated self-sufficiency and my personal satisfaction with my life on the edge of the tip.

*

I was out there every day on the tip. I loved it in the grip of ten degrees of frost with its mounds frozen into rigid shapes and I loved it in a heatwave, when the air above it shimmered like a magical mirage of hidden delights. And the smell. I have lived with the smell for so long it is part of me, a deep ripeness of decay that develops into mysterious alien growth. Like cheese, like mushrooms, like mould. Penicillin protects the body against germs. The tip protects me against the world. Such beautiful things people throw away because they are changing the decor, or they have bought something new and they no longer have the room or the right colour scheme for the old. Such waste. Why don't they take them to jumble sales, or Oxfam shops, or advertise them in the Under-a-Tenner sections in the local free newspaper? Don't they realise some people would like their rejects?

*

I have been so contented here near the tip. It has been the only time of my life when I have been able to go to bed and think, I am really happy. Which is why I was not pleased at the arrival of Mr Shuttleworth on my doorstep.

I was in the kitchen when he first came and I had watched him pick his way through the piles of rubbish that had begun to spread past my house and round to the front. The dump was on the move.

114

I liked to think of it piling up round my house, burying me totally in the end, so that I could die with my only source of pleasure wrapped around me in a warm embrace of friendship.

He was a small man, and he wore a trilby. If I see a man who wears a trilby, I know that I would not like to know him. And he had a very large nose. I spotted this, even while he was a long way off. A nose that twitched and smelled things out, that was sensitive to the things going on around him. I did not like his nose either, because I knew that it spelt trouble for me.

He came and knocked on my door with his knuckles, and I hoped he would not knock any harder because the door was not fixed, just leaning against the doorpost. He could not see me in the kitchen, because I was sheltered behind the cream antique lace that I had once found mixed up in a bag of exhausted Marks and Spencer's underwear.

"Miss Tucker!" he called, and I froze.

Stay still, I said to myself. He cannot see you. He doesn't know you're in.

But he did seem to know that I was in.

"Miss Tucker!" he called again, and I could have sworn that his eyes were looking directly into mine. I dared not move in case he caught sight of the movement through the lace curtains.

After several tense seconds he left and I relaxed, wiggling my shoulders to ease the stiffness in my back. Salesmen do not come to me here. Nobody tries to sell double glazing that will last for a hundred years to a house that has a side wall missing, that is about to be united with the predator on its doorstep. This was no salesman. This was a man who knew my name and it frightened me.

I finished making my porridge and bananas, my midday ritual - nobody turned the water off when they declared the house unfit for human habitation, so with my little camping gas stove I can be quite civilised - and I took it into the lounge where I could sit and look at the tip while I ate.

Then I stiffened again in panic. The strange little man had come round the back and was even now finding his way down the little path I had burrowed through the rubbish. I didn't really know what to do. I stood there with the bowl of porridge in my hand, wondering whether I would pass for a statue, unable to decide if I could just pretend he wasn't there at all. He had only to come round the side to find the blanket that hung over the missing wall.

I could see his nose twitching, like a true bloodhound's. Was he a spy? Thoughts of my father here. Had he returned from his non-existence? "Shall we go shopping, Ursula? I'll treat you to a new dress from the tip -"

"Miss Tucker!" he called again.

I decided that I would have to respond. I put the porridge down carefully on my woven table-cloth, and looked at him aggressively through the window. "What do you want?" I called sharply.

He smiled and I instantly regretted my decision to talk to him. "I have a proposition to put to you."

"I'm too old for propositions," I said.

"I wonder if I could come in."

I hesitated. "Why should you?"

"I would like to talk to you."

I let him in. Well, I don't often speak to people - only PC Watson and he is boring. "Take your hat off if you're coming," I said. Nobody in a trilby comes into my lounge.

"My name is Henry Shuttleworth," he said, seated in the chair that I had re-covered with a large piece of velvet that had originally been theatre curtains - shades of Scarlett O'Hara. He had somehow contrived to make himself comfortable, with his small neat leather shoes pointing inwards towards each other and his knees balanced supportively together. He needed a cup of tea to complete the image, but I wasn't going to offer him one. That would be acknowledgement of the fact that I didn't really mind him being there.

"Well?" I said. "Get to the point."

His face creased into a patchwork of leathery segments and I knew he was pleased by my directness.

"I work for the Social Services -"

I was furious with myself for not recognising his job, although it wasn't entirely my fault. He was the wrong age-group. His hair was too short, he didn't wear jeans and he had a trilby. "Go away," I said. "Leave me alone."

He started again. "The Council are willing to offer you a nice flat," he said.

I said nothing.

"With central heating and a fitted kitchen."

He reminded me of Anthony's wife. Anthony of the refined curtains and the blue Volvo.

"The thing is, the Council are planning to close down the tip. They want to flatten it and landscape it."

I sat very still and looked out of the window at my tip. It looked bleak and unloved suddenly, as if it knew that the guardian of its lasting welfare were to perform the extreme act of treachery. Could I desert my old friend? The place that had brought me tranquility, the only place that had taken me to itself and allowed me to develop in the way that I wanted to develop. If a place can be your mother, then this tip was my mother, and my father, the security and sense of belonging that I had never found from my parents or my intolerant nanny.

"But why should I want to move into a flat?" I said eventually, looking him straight in the eye, challenging him.

The smile was still there, but it was beginning to be slightly forced as he realised that I was not as pleased as he had anticipated. "I'm sure you will appreciate the benefits of electricity and running water -" he said carefully.

"No," I said. I didn't tell him I already had running water.

The smile faded. He was not a very good Social Worker. He should have been able to persuade me with subtle psychology, only he didn't seem to be able to understand my position.

"I like living here," I said.

I suddenly felt rather sorry for him. He was shuffling about uncomfortably in his chair as if he suspected there were fleas in it. I decided that I shouldn't tell him that the chair had come from the tip.

"It's all right," I said. "I don't have a cat."

He now looked totally bewildered, and I realised that I hadn't explained properly. "There aren't any fleas in that chair."

He still didn't understand.

*

My dreams again. The wonder of the human brain, that once it is programmed, nothing can wipe it, even if you can't summon it all at the touch of a button. All those past events, lying dormant somewhere in your mind, waiting, watching for the right moment to reappear. It's a bit like the tip. A mass of forgotten relics, tokens of somebody's memory, some of it just rubbish, some of it valuable treasure. One person's reject is another's miraculous find. Yesterday's nightmare is tomorrow's nostalgia.

My mother this time. The only way I could remember her face was in my dreams. I had photographs of her in her exploring gear, all in the wrong century, of course. She should have been a Victorian, and she should have got wherever she was going before anyone else. But the photographs were of another person that I didn't remember. The only reality was in my dreams.

I do remember some brief moments of conversation with her, and the memories are stronger after a dream, although the sensation of floating, meaningless attempts at communication is clearer than the details. Like the day she came to talk to me in my bedroom.

"Why did you shout at Nanny like that?" she said.

I lay in my bed and looked at the ceiling. It needed painting, and I knew that it never would be done until I was old enough to stand on a step-ladder and reach it myself. "Why don't you paint the ceiling?" I said.

She didn't really listen to me, because she was looking at her profile out of the corner of her eye, watching the movement of her hair as she tossed her head, trying to decide whether disciplining her daughter suited her liberated image. "Because she does her best, you know, darling."

"I know," I said, looking at her fresh tanned skin and her bleached blonde hair enviously, although now the face in my mind is quite featureless. Why didn't I inherit any of these desirable qualities? Perhaps I would have had a few more friends if I had looked a bit better.

"The thing is, darling, as you grow older, you can't just go around doing as you please, expecting everything to fall into place around you."

"But you do," I said.

And suddenly she was bored with the conversation. She pecked me lightly on the forehead, avoiding all unnecessary physical contact, and rose abruptly. "Don't do it again. We can't afford to find another nanny."

We could only afford a nanny who hated children and had no more interest in me than in the beetles that wandered so profusely in our unloved kitchen, the beetles that she enjoyed crunching under her cruel feet so much.

"Can you buy me a proper school jumper?" I called as she turned off the light.

"I expect so, darling," she said. "If you want one."

She shut the door behind her, and I knew that I would never have a proper school jumper.

*

Mr Shuttleworth sat more comfortably in my armchair once I had provided him with a cup of tea. I'd felt sorry for him because he was sent on an errand he could never complete. He had adopted a cosy, familiar tone with me, that demonstrated his inability to comprehend my position, rather as if he thought he were dealing with an irrational old lady who could be persuaded.

"There are some new flats nearly finished only ten minutes from here. You could still be close to your friends."

Friends? What do I know of friends?

He was watching me closely to monitor my reaction. I ignored his words.

"I made that lampshade," I said. "I used all the oddments of ribbon I have found and strung them all together. I even made the frame with some abandoned wire."

He looked at me carefully, and took a long sip of tea. Then he wiped his lips methodically with his tongue, followed by a careful inspection with his finger. "You like living by the tip, Miss Tucker?"

I beamed with genuine pleasure. This was a discerning man after all. "Yes, Mr Shuttleworth. I do."

Strangely, now that he had established this fact, he seemed more relaxed. As if he knew he was fighting a battle he couldn't win, so he was not going to continue trying. "What about the smell?" he said curiously.

I wasn't going to tell him I liked the smell. "What smell?"

"The smell of the tip. You can't deny that sometimes it is quite unsavoury."

"I have never noticed," I said.

His nose twitched again. "I have a very sensitive sense of smell," he said. "I can smell things that most people cannot."

I knew this. I was beginning to understand Mr Shuttleworth, and I realised he was not a happy man in his job - he did not really fit in. "Would you like to see the rest of my house?"

I took him upstairs, and he admired the wonderful things I had found. He was impressed, I could see.

"They're not going to like me very much back at the office," he said.

*

My father. Dreams of my father, and clear memories too.

119

"Come on, Ursula. Let's go shopping."

He always had money when he came home. Did he rob banks and go into hiding? Did he work for the Foreign Office, and get paid handsomely? Was he a hit-man? Was I helping him to spend blood money?

But I loved my father. He was the only person I could remember feeling affection for. I would have liked him to be at home all the time. But if he were, perhaps I would tire of him. Maybe it was the glamour of his frequent absences that made me love him so much.

"How's the Latin?" he said.

I grinned. "What are you going to buy me?"

"That's my girl. Get your priorities right. Your mother tells me you're doing rather well at school."

How did my mother tell him that? She was never at home and he was never at home. Did they write to each other? Did they meet in faraway exotic places and discuss my exam results? Or did they leave notes in the bedroom where I couldn't find them?

"I got 89% in History."

"You'll need more than History to succeed in life. How's the Science?"

"Can we buy some school jumpers? I hate the home-knitted ones that nanny makes." I was not very good at Science. It was my only weakness.

He was a tall man, and very strong, so that even when I was fourteen, he could easily lift me off my feet and swing me round as if I were still a toddler. He was always sun-tanned, and sometimes, when he wasn't thinking about it, he spoke with a slight accent that I couldn't place. As if he spent his whole life talking to people in different languages, and he forgot which person he was when he came home.

Was he a real person at all, or was he just a conglomeration of assorted personalities that he used for different occasions? Today I am an American with secrets to sell. Today I am an undercover Nazi pretending to have secrets to sell. Today I am a loving caring father.

I was on the spy theory today. "What do you do for a job, Daddy?"

He smiled, and opened the front door. "Come on. To the shops."

"But what is your job?"

He helped me into the car. "I sell things."

120

"Like what?"

His grin was utterly charming. He was not a spy. He was a con-man. "Oh, this and that."

So we went shopping. Only we didn't buy school jumpers, we bought two coats. One for best and the other for super-best, that I couldn't possibly wear unless I were going to the theatre or entertaining royalty.

But Daddy thought they were perfect. "You look like a little princess," he said, although this was far from true. "Come on, we'll go and buy some cream cakes."

*

Mr Shuttleworth came back.

"Hello," I said, smiling at him, and feeling a certain fondness for him. "Have you come back for some more tea?" I had always known he would return, because we had got on so well together.

"Can I come in?" he said, and I realised that this was not a social call. He wouldn't look at me properly. Those gleaming eyes had lost their lustre, and I could smell the guilt on him.

"Didn't you tell them?" I said crossly, as we walked carefully over my sheepskin rugs that had been accumulated gradually over the years. Ignorant people threw them out because they looked dirty, when I knew that the footprints of a thousand passers-by gave them dignity and depth.

He sat down in the same chair as before, and I didn't offer him a cup of tea. He looked sadly over the tip, as if he had begun to understand my attachment to it. Had it influenced him as well? I felt a little warmth of satisfaction, conflicting with my worries about my home.

He cleared his throat. I waited. "I did tell them, as a matter of fact," he said.

"And?"

He looked far out over the tip, as if he were trying to spot something he had seen the other day, and wanted to confirm. "Did I really see a stuffed monkey out there last time I came?"

"Maybe," I said irritably. "Explain why you have come."

"I did tell them, and they said - "

"Yes?"

"They said you would have to go, because they are going to flatten the tip in two weeks' time."

I looked at him. My only friend has a terminal disease, I thought.

Only two weeks to live. A tip moves and grows and spreads. If it has a beginning, a birth, then it must have a death. "So you laughed at them, and told them I wasn't going?"

He shifted uncomfortably, and I was reminded of the fleas that had never been there. "They said if you weren't out by then, they would have to send the police to remove you."

A coldness had settled over me. I looked out of the window, at my world, my land of milk and honey, my reason for living. This could not be happening to me. It was so unfair. All my life I had been moved around by other people. Nobody had ever said to me, "What would you like to do?" And now, after my retirement, I had come to a place where I did find things I wanted to do, and I found a kind of freedom that had eluded me all my life. I lived here, I hurt no one, I scavenged, and I even had a vague sort of relationship with the dump-dwellers that I had come to recognise and love in my own obscure way.

"I'm not going," I said.

His nose seemed larger than ever, and the rest of him seemed to shrink. He looked like a cartoon figure, distorted completely out of shape, shrivelled with embarrassment and empathy.

"It really would be best if you went voluntarily," he said. "Then you could take all your lovely possessions with you."

But I was adamant. I have never been strong before in my life. I have swayed with the tides of thought of those who wanted to influence me. I have always wanted to please others, not upset them. I would have walked a million miles to avoid hurting someone's feelings, and I would have walked another million miles to try and win a friend. But it had never worked. Not a solitary friend in all the world.

So now, suddenly, I felt filled with an alien strength, the strength to do what I wanted to do. "I'm not going," I said.

"I live on my own too, you know. My wife left me and took my children with her. I have four children, and I haven't seen them in fifteen years."

Fifteen years. My age when my father disappeared for ever, on the eve of war with Germany. Three years before my mother died, leaving me with no money, having spent it all on her wasted explorations of Africa, and her endless fundraising during the war.

"I'm sorry," I heard myself saying. "But I cannot leave this place."

Was it just my imagination, or did he look at me with a new kind of respect? But then again, perhaps I was just seeing the first manifestations of anger in that little unloved face.

*

I dreamt of University last night. A friendly dream. I was popular, and my fellow students were at a dinner party, drinking excessively, telling how they would vote for me when I became the next Prime Minister.

It had not really been like that. They laughed at me there. In the lectures I asked questions; quiet, careful questions, that seemed to me to need asking. And the lecturers understood the more complex thoughts behind the questions. "That is an interesting point, Miss Tucker."

But afterwards my fellow students mocked me, because we were all clever people together, and I was not used to conversing with people who were my intellectual equals. It confused me. It should have stimulated me, but it didn't because I had always lived in a secret world inside my head and I had long since forgotten how to share it with others of like minds.

"Come to a party tonight," said Mary, my reluctant room-mate. "Loosen up a bit."

Loosen up? If I loosened up any more, my skirt would fall down. It was hanging on nothing now. There was no money to spare, and I ate just enough to survive, but no more.

The students sailed past me on their bicycles while I walked, and I saw them all hysterical with mirth as they played by the river, brilliant as the sunshine that rippled over the water. They belonged to a world that I could never enter. They had normal parents who talked to them and a home to go back to in the holidays. I didn't even have a nanny any more. Nothing. Not even the house that I grew up in, because that went when my mother died. And my thoughts were beyond theirs because I could observe them from the outside. I could stand on the edge and watch. They were children. I was never really a child at all.

*

People stopped coming to the tip. There were notices up to say it had closed down and they would have to travel across town to Potter's Green. A death is often followed by a birth, they say, but Potter's Green could be little more than an embryo yet. Mr Shuttleworth came to see me every day now on his way home from

123

work. "Do it for me, Miss Tucker," he would say to me. "The Council have good intentions. They are going to landscape the whole area. There will be trees here one day." I thought of his absent wife and children and his lonely world. But for the first time in my life my problems came first and I was not going to give in without a fight.

"I do understand, Miss Tucker, really I do," he said.

Maybe he did. I had begun to regard him more as an ally than an enemy after all this time. If only he would stop wearing that dreadful trilby. "Take your hat off," I always said to him, "and you can come in and talk to me."

*

He enjoyed the tours of my house, and admired my acquisitions. "You could take them with you," he said feebly.

I glared at him. "I know that. But how will I spend the rest of my days, if I can't go exploring the tip every day, knitting up the wool I have found, cleaning the rugs, renovating the furniture? I would die of boredom."

"Perhaps you could try a hobby like painting, or weaving. You might enjoy something like that."

A hobby! I glared at him. "How could I wake up cheerfully every morning if I couldn't look out over the tip and watch the early morning dumpers? What about my friends, the dump-dwellers? How can I judge the weather if I can't sit in my lounge and see it spread itself over the world that I know?"

I knew my days were numbered from the sadness in Mr Shuttleworth's face, in the way he had shaken my hand, from the twitching of his nose and the dullness of his eyes. "I admire you," he said. "They are all on to me to get you out and I have spoken up for you everywhere. But nobody listens to me any more. I have lost my credibility." He sighed. "But I don't blame you. I admire you."

I was proud. Nobody had ever admired me before. Nobody had ever lost anything because of me.

*

Custer's Last Stand. Ursula's Final Battle. Chests of drawers holding up the front door, wardrobes filling the hole in the side wall. I bring my mattress down, with quilts and blankets to block out the downstairs windows, and then I leave a tiny space in the top corner, so that I can stand on the furniture and see out without them seeing me.

PC Watson stands outside with another policeman called Jim. He is a tall man with big muscles who reminds me of my father. I am not going to let him into my house. This is a man you cannot trust. He says one thing and he means another. He reminds me of my father in more ways than one. I talk to him through my upstairs window.

"You can't move me," I yell. "I won't go."

"Come on, Miss Tucker," says PC Watson. "Don't make this any more unpleasant than it has to be."

"Go away!" I shout.

They stand there for a while in silence, watching the house, the inactivity somehow intensely threatening.

"I could have a heart attack, and then you'd be sorry."

Jim grins and I do not like his grin any more than I like his voice. "Feel free, Miss Tucker. That would save us a lot of trouble."

I am so consumed with hate that I can't look at him any more. I climb down on to the kitchen floor and decide to make myself a cup of tea.

I am reminded of my teaching days, when I had often been besieged by girls who did not respect me. They cheeked me, they threatened my mental stability by their behaviour, but I had survived. I had stuck it out until retirement. The governors had wanted to retire me early, but I had resisted them. You can survive anything if you stick it out long enough. I drink my cup of tea and I decide that the policemen will have gone when I go back to the window.

They haven't. There are four of them now, talking quietly to each other.

"Go away," I shout again, because it makes me feel better.

"Come on out, Miss Tucker," calls PC Watson. "Otherwise we'll have to break the door down."

I sit down on the floor behind the chest of drawers that's propping up the door, and think of my father. Now would be a good time for him to come back into my life.

They begin to push against the front door. They are all strong men and I can feel the drawers beginning to move, sliding me forward on the floor.

"No!" I shriek, jumping to my feet and trying to push it back. I have heard that you gain superhuman strength in critical emergencies. It is not true. I am unable to make any impression on their onslaught.

They come storming in, scattering my precious things around them, destroying my life as carelessly as a child stamps on a sandcastle.

I retreat up the stairs.

"What a dump" I hear one of them say. "How could anyone live here? It's not even safe."

I howl with rage and tear pieces off the banisters, throwing them with all my strength. "It's safer than any of your anti-social high-rise flats!"

But the banisters don't stop them. They just dodge or catch the missiles in their hands and discard them on the floor. They follow me upstairs. "Mind that stair," I hear PC Watson say. "It won't take your weight."

"Go away!" I shout desperately. I run into my bedroom and try to bolt the door. "Stop it!" I shout.

They push the door open before I can lock it. I climb on the bed and back up against the wall. "You won't take me alive," I say.

They come towards me grinning.

I shut my eyes.

*

They have to carry me out. I'm not going to co-operate with them in any way. It takes all four of them, I am proud to say, and I wriggle as much as possible. Once outside they put me on the ground and stand round me so that I can't run back inside again.

"What a dreadful smell," says Jim.

Mr Shuttleworth appears unexpectedly. "I'm sorry," he says. "But I couldn't let you stay there any longer. You could have been hurt when they came to demolish the building."

I am going to scream at him and claw at his face, but something in his expression stops me. He is genuinely upset, I realise, and I am devastated by the knowledge that he really does care. He is not just doing his job. We look at each other, and in the midst of my distress, I feel astonishment. I am not wearing home-made jumpers any more. I have a friend.

*

I lock the door of my flat for the last time. It is not a bad flat - it has been warm during the winter and you could not really call it high-rise. Mr Shuttleworth has visited me regularly. But it is bare and organised, with none of the bright clusters of colours that I like so much.

I hold a large bag with enough bananas and oats for a week and a change of underwear. Inside my hat with the red felt rose on the side, I have folded my cheque-book.

I go down the stairs and outside I smell the air. I head for my tip, but then walk straight past it, because it is flat now. They have laid turf and planted lots of little trees with fences around them to protect them from vandals. The house is gone, the tip is gone. It is like those First World War graves of Flanders, like the fields of poppies.

I keep walking. It is a long way, but I am a fit old lady and my purpose is clearly defined in my head. When I finally see a sign that says 'Potter's Green,' I sniff the air again. There is a suggestion there, a hint that opens up the memory shutters and pours nostalgia into my mind.

I believe in reincarnation.

Brian Howell

The Swing

For the past two weeks as he came home by the short cut through the housing estate, Albert had noticed an unnerving occurrence. The first time he thought that perhaps he had imagined it, that the corner of his eye was active while he concentrated on the steady, predictable footfall of a man who has other things on his mind, of someone who has pushed the intrusive forays of everyday life to the periphery of vision and thought.

But the swing did move. It proceeded through a semi-circular arc like a hand scraping the bottom of a bowl, and the bowl was the inside of his head, encrusted, silted up against the past.

He had started coming this way again not because he was getting tired in his old age but because it meant he was less likely to see the stray dog that had recently started to roam around one of the two exits from the station. Until recently he had avoided this route but now he was forced to take the short cut. The dog was an Alsatian, exactly the kind he despised above all others. To add to this, it had a pendulous growth of tissue dangling from its neck that insisted he find the creature even more repulsive than usual, as if in its globular ball, like an elasticated Adam's apple, it balanced his fate.

He craned his neck away from the swing and thought of Rose, of the present he was going to buy her for their twenty-fifth anniversary.

He had seen a gold necklace with a small ruby in the shape of a pear, or a dew drop; he hadn't quite decided what. He walked to the jeweller's every lunch time and stopped, staring for a good five minutes or so at the display. The shop assistant, a young girl of about eighteen, had caught his eye on a couple of occasions, and now she never failed to look up at the expected hour. His regular vigil over the jewel had taken the form of an obsessive punctuality, and it was rarely that he didn't exchange glances with the girl. But he hadn't yet gone in. He had become a little confused; he wondered if he wasn't prolonging his decision so that he could be sure of another look from the girl.

When he got back, Rose was ready with the food. She didn't seem to have heard him come in; her attention was fettered by the dual demands of the radio and the cake she was baking. He studied her from the back as she drew off the form from the sponge cake, like a mayor unveiling a sculpture.

Over the years her body had rounded out, to be sure, but rather than sap his enthusiasm, it had filled it out; he still liked to hold her from behind and feel his penis grow into the furrow of her buttocks. She didn't usually react much beyond a brief sigh of mock surprise or a non-committal stroke of her hand. This woman, he sometimes thought, was still a mystery. She had been his only sexual partner; she knew the workings of his body and his desires like a watchmaker his favourite clock; she had given him milk when their two sons had sated themselves at her breasts.

He moved up to her, massaging the knotless tendons in her neck; she did not start.

"You knew I was there all the time, didn't you?" he said.

"Of course I did," she replied, her attention still on the cake.

They had played the game many times before, but the words always seemed new.

"I'll never lose my appetite for you," he whispered like an actor in music hall, his voice hinged between a note of threat and promise. He almost said, 'What are we going to do tonight, then?' in a pretence that a pattern did not exist, or that if it did, it could be broken.

Instead he waited, and, over the beef, she said, "How was it today?"

He told her about the office round dance of shuffling files and shifting glances, of the new overqualified temp, of the latest bomb scare, of the variety of sandwiches in the new local café, but he left out the trip past the jeweller's, or any mention of his preoccupation with a present.

After the supper and cake Rose sat down with her knitting in front of the television.

In the night he woke out of a dream. He thought he had screamed but Rose was still sleeping. It was strange, because she was normally hypersensitive to sounds or sudden movements when asleep, sometimes waking even if he blew his nose or coughed.

He tried to remember what the dream had been about, but he could only recall an uncomfortable feeling of being constricted, as if in a straitjacket. Unusually, he had gone to bed in his T-shirt, and he decided this must have been the cause. In his slumber he had worked the shirt off only as far as one arm, and now he was caught in this sweaty wrap.

He got up, realising he had an erection, and stood there awhile, wondering what to do with himself, like a child unwilling to accept the day has ended. He would not disturb Rose now; she needed her sleep. The stiffness soon went, but he still felt as if something in him were unfulfilled.

He sensed now that something was coming back, something he had held in check too long. He dressed quietly and slipped out towards the estate. As he walked, fragments of the dream came back in waves - but it was hardly a dream. It was rather a memory of a childhood event. He had grown up in this area, on the housing estate itself, and his mother had carried on living there until she had died a few years before. From the window of their old flat the playground could be seen. It was because the short cut went past this spot that he normally avoided coming this way.

As he expected, the swing was moving, as if someone had just jumped out and run away across the estate. But it was two in the morning. Would nothing stop this perpetual motion?

He went up to its stationary partner, sat in it, and stared at the swing still moving back and forth a foot away from him. It had been night then too, when he had taken part with Sheila in her game. Sheila had been known as the 'swingboat Sheila'; she lived for this machine, rarely willing to share her time outside school with anyone or anything else. She was patently uninterested in boys.

Albert had tried all the enticements he could think of. Nothing would bring her away from that infernal flying chair, not even his standing there and looking up her knickers. When he was doing his homework, he was held back by the thought of her endlessly in motion, just outside his bedroom window. She was usually still there when he finished, and his mother allowed him to go down and join her.

"Why don't you stop swinging?" he finally had the courage to ask her one evening.

"I have to, silly."

He stared at her, blank-faced.

"Didn't you know?" she continued. "It's the swings that keep the world turning. Each one creates a wave that jerks us a little bit more forward. We learned it in physics today."

"You're lying. That's not what they teach at all."

"Listen," she said with a grandmotherly air of explaining a fact of life to a child, although she was four years younger than him. "Sit here, and just lean back."

He got into the seat.

"Slowly, let yourself float. See how the earth edges away. But it's not us moving. It's the sky being pulled away, like a cover on a table."

He was confused. He was aware of a rectangle of space coming forward and then of his falling back, the dimensions of the image were liquid, expanding like those of a reflection in water or a fairground mirror. On the sides were his hands, but they didn't seem part of him.

"D'you see?" she said.

"No, I don't. I don't understand, anyway."

He felt that he would only know what she was talking about when they were locked into parallel arcs. He put his hand out against the metal bar to slow himself down, but now her swing was going faster. He jumped off and ran home crying.

"See you tomorrow," she shouted perkily after him.

Rose didn't wake when he got back, but turned in her sleep and wrapped her arms around him. For a few moments he felt as if he were going to suffocate, but he didn't want to disturb her.

*

There was only one day till the anniversary. He must buy the present today, he told himself as he came through the barrier of the underground station. He helped a young woman untangle her leather duffel bag where the strap had hitched on the plastic-padded metal protrusions which were like hands cupping buttocks. She cursed the barrier but thanked him.

He was irritable throughout the day, especially with the younger girls in the office. Did they know it was his anniversary? He didn't remember telling them. He felt they were sensitized to his state, to his age; they were motherly, protective, laying down restrictive barriers of glances. Especially Bev, who had once let him place his hand in her lap and roll up her skirt while she stood at the sink where they made tea; everyone had left that evening, but it hadn't gone any further. He had wanted to prove that he wasn't that old, that he still had desire for a young girl like her. Rose, more than anything else, had stopped him pressing on.

Now, though, they were radiating off him like offspring from a parent at different stages in their lives. He made a resolution. He would be more fatherly from this moment on.

At lunch time he went straight into the jeweller's without bothering to stop at the window. The same girl was behind the counter. Her smile braced him like a lover's arms supporting his diaphragm.

She made no allusion to his habitual visits, beyond her knowing smile. It was perhaps only now that he consciously registered her resemblance to Sheila. Sheila who had died so young.

The assistant held the stone up to the light for him awhile, letting the necklace chain hang loosely. He felt dizzy, and touched the back of his neck as if to hold himself up. It was only this action that distracted her and made her stop the necklace's motion. He had wanted to ask her to stop it, but he could only have done so at the risk of seeming neurotic. She asked him if he wanted a glass of water. No, no, he was all right now. He had almost fully recovered by the time she had wrapped up the necklace within its coffin-like box. The ruby, he thought, lay like a dismembered, still-pulsing heart, shading the velvety padding of the box with its own hue of crimson. Only when it was thoroughly covered up did he feel the thing was at rest, sleeping.

In the office, he kept the box in his briefcase, refusing to open it for any of the girls, who had by now revealed that they 'knew'. He absorbed Bev's wounded look like gauze soaking up blood. He couldn't defend himself except by saying he was superstitious about showing other people's presents before they had been given, as if showing them to someone else devalued them. Besides, it was nicely wrapped. Bev kept a distance for the rest of the day, but giggled with the others at the slightest provocation. If only you knew, he thought, if only you knew, and he imagined the ruby now as a live heart inside a special case for transporting it for a transplant. He opened his case again, almost expecting a ridge of crimson to seep out, but the stillness, the anonymity of the contents of his case shocked him more than his imagination.

He was the last one to leave the office, and though everyone said goodbye and wished him good luck, he still felt a whisper of resentment in the air around him. Half an hour later, as he locked up, he summed up his unease philosophically, saying, I've done right by Rose, she's had no reason to complain. She would never guess. No one would.

Before he reached the station, he had intended to go back to his usual route, even if it meant facing the dog. It would be like drawing a veil across the intrusive memory, a fresh start. As he approached the choice of paths - two ends of a tunnel at right angles to another, larger tunnel - he was no longer so certain.

A superstitious habit came back from his childhood. He was suddenly presented with the reasoning that if he took the old route everything would be O.K. for him and Rose. In the manner of someone making a momentous decision, the right decision at the right time, when circumstances drove that person down an irrevocable path, he reasoned further that his greater fear was of the dog, and so took the old path, past the swing. All the time he insisted to himself that he could not be hurt by an apparition, an eidolon.

This time, however, it wasn't a question of the swing moving independently because from the distance he made out the two swings tied together like embracing lovers. Only when he was ten metres or so in front of the twisted chains did he clearly see what he had tried to avoid for so long. There, through the crossed metal strands, like a bird in a trap, extended the girl's neck. The chains were draped around her half-naked form like exotic jewellery, an exaggerated jacket of chain-mail.

He bent down to look at the slumped form, to examine her face, her lapidary features. She had Sheila's hair, Sheila's eyes. He began to cry. The time had come. Before he entered the house, he unwrapped the necklace, and let the smooth links run through his fingers like the cable of a windlass.

Pushover Quiz

Answers to Panurge 19 Quiz.
1. Barnaby Rudge (Grip is his pet crow).
2. Peig Sayers (of Blasket Island fame) wrote An Old Woman's Reflections.
3. Ivo Andric wrote Bosnian Story.

The Winner was **Mary Knight** of Sheffield who got a £20 Book Token. Only one other person got it right.

Panurge 20 Quiz. Only one question. Which giant of 19th Century European letters worked in his country's embassy to Newcastle-on-Tyne? He also wrote **'The Sin of Father Amaro'** *(published by Black Swan)*
First correct answer wins £20 Book Token. Deadline 16.5.94.

Jane Smith

Walking Out

He lives alone now, numbed and bedazzled by the constant raging of the weather and the trees. He watches the rabbits graze his gardens to a stubble while a sparrowhawk haunts the trees: he puts out bread for the birds and stripe-faced badgers come instead. And when the animals hide there are the sunsets and the wind and the relentless procession of the gathering, fading clouds.

When he lived in London he would spend hours each day just looking at the people: he would sit at his window and gaze out at the street below and see people, all day, and in the evenings his friends would come, his children would sit up talking and so the hours would pass. Now all he has to watch is the sky rushing with clouds and the tamarisk throwing itself into the wind. He watches the wind and the sea and the sky just beyond and he thinks that perhaps he could fly: he walks out to the downs behind his house, he watches the air about him thicken and collect into pockets of cloud, he sees the substance of the island all about him and he must wait a while until he can breathe easily again because of the richness of the air.

*

It was a holiday which first brought his parents here: they all came, the three of them, to spend a week away from home, to rest and walk and recover. Right from the start the holiday was a magic time: first the adventure of the ferry ride, and then Yarmouth, the harbour, a sudden brilliance as the sun flashed out from behind a cloud. The harbour wall a thin band of logs stuck end-up in the swelling salt water: the water within a brilliant, pale mercurial blue, densely opaque and glittering: then the line of the wall and beyond, the water still pale and opaque and intensely liquid but greener. It was a hot sunny day in late September, the middle of the afternoon: the town was quiet, hushed in the hot sun: just the clanking of ropes against masts, a soft splashing against the quay. A harbour taxi throttled past, white with a thin blue stripe. He looked around and saw the quiet and the sun: and the Solent lay between them and the mainland and it was a barrier between them and their endless, constant lives. His father drove them to the cottage he had rented for the week and all round them they saw trees and hedges and little stone cottages and the people on the streets were smiling as they walked.

He lived on the island for seven years and when he left to go to

London, to go to university, he said that he would never return: but he did, he went back for holidays, for Christmases and birthdays and then when Gillian would not have him in their house any more, he did not know where else he could go but home, to his parents' house, waiting there for him to return. Now he is here he feels like he never left: and he does not know if he will ever be able to leave again.

*

He can see the lights of Bournemouth strung out like beads across the Solent, the mainland coastline defined by the clusters of lights and the narrowing patches of darkness. From his house high on the cliff top, isolated from the village by acres of heathland and gorse, the stars and the moon show clearly in the sky: the stars look larger here, cleaner, voluptuous chunks of bright white light hanging in the sky. For the first time that he can remember, he is aware of the waxing and the waning of the moon: he watches it racing across the sky, pulling its stars along behind it.

He phones Gillian one evening, although he has promised not to: but the wind and the isolation overwhelm him and once the idea to call her comes to him, he cannot fight it for long.

She says hello and then waits a while and when no-one replies she says hello again, only this time there is an edge to her voice, a hard, suspicious edge. He is surprised: he has never heard her sound like this before.

"Gillian: Gillian, it's me, sorry, I should have said hello... Hello. Are you alright? You sounded peculiar."

"Philip? Why are you phoning? What do you want?"

"I just wanted to say hello... what's wrong, are you alright? You sounded odd."

"Anna has been calling," she says in a careful, flat voice. "She's told me about the baby, that you want to have a baby with her. Please tell her to stop calling me: I don't want to speak to her any more." And again he is silent, he did not think that Anna would call, he did not think that she would say such things to Gillian. And now, he wants to let Gill know that Anna was confused, had not understood him, but all he can say is sorry: that he did not mean it: that Anna will not call again. He wants to tell her that he has not seen Anna for weeks, that he will not ever see her again: but he does not think that she would listen and even if she did, he does not think that she would believe him.

Instead he asks her what she is sewing, what sort of picture, the colours, what it will be when she is finished and she says, flowers, bright pinks and oranges, it's for a footstool. To cover a footstool. He can find nothing more that he can say to her and after a few minutes more of near silence, she asks him not to call again and hangs up her receiver: and he listens to the open line breathing at the end of his phone and he wishes right down into his gut that he could somehow stop this happening. He sits there in the dark for an hour or more, thinking of Gillian, what she will be doing: he pictures her putting down the receiver and standing there with her hand to her throat, then, after some time, wandering off to sit with her sewing while the house settles into silence around her.

Before all this, when they lived with each other still, she would sit in the evenings with her frame before her and stitch tapestries. She sewed pictures, cabbages, flowers, parrots, everything. Over the years that they had been married she had covered acres of canvas, their house was full of her work and he remembered each piece: the one she worked on when they were first married, the chair cover she started after their eldest child was born: each piece a reminder of the time that they had spent together, each piece another milestone in their life together. She sat with one hand above the canvas and one hand below and she stabbed through the canvas with her needle, from one hand to the other: using short lengths of wool so that each length was finished before it was fluffed thin by the wear of the canvas. She would stitch vast pieces, rugs and chairs and wall-hangings, all divided into sections to fit between the struts of her frame. She kept a little pair of scissors hanging at her side and when she finished with each length of wool she would flip the frame over and work the end of the yarn into the backs of the stitches and then snip the tail end off. She cut the end quite close so that it would not poke through the finished piece and once, just once, she snipped a length off too close with the points of her scissors and severed one of the threads of the canvas. At first she said nothing: she flipped the frame over so that she could look at the right side again and there was the broken thread, the ends poking up between her tiny tent stitches, showing like pale ivory bones out of the green and gold wools. As she watched, one of the ends loosened itself and slipped under a stitch: she sighed and left her work and went to wash up. She told him later what she had done and although she mended the broken thread they could always see a little lump there, a thickening in the fabric: a fault.

He wishes he could be home with her now. He wants to sit with her as she watches TV and works at her canvas: he wants to drink tea with her in the mornings. He wants to sleep with her in their wide, soft bed: not even to make love with her, just to lie there dozing and feel her solid warmth against him, to hear her breathing through the night. He does not even have to close his eyes to remember how she feels to sleep with: the memory jumps into his mind at odd moments and he has to stop, wait, try to breathe again when all the time he feels like he is dying.

Making love with Gillian was like breathing. She was as tall as him, and soft: her body was accommodating. He knew exactly the taste of her, the smell: he could have recognised any part of her by just her texture or her scent. He knew how to touch her to make her come: they both knew this about each other. Sex with Anna was frantic: it was like a race, a scramble, it was always a desperate act. They would meet and her mouth would be on him, his hands searching for the buttons on her clothes. Within minutes he would be inside her: they were quick, sudden: silent when they had to be. After making love with Anna he felt excited, exhilarated, younger somehow. She was hard, hard to the touch, hard to refuse. The only thing soft was her hair, short and silky and pale flat blonde. When they made love, her hair would ruffle up and stick out like a baby's: later it would plaster itself to her face in little damp strands, darker, thinner.

Her body was firm: she was younger than him, quite muscular, shorter than he was. When they had been lovers for a while, two, three months, they were lying together and he was rubbing his hand in circles over her belly. He wondered whether she would ever have children: her belly was so taut with muscle that he could not imagine a baby stretching her there. It just seemed too tight. He rubbed her belly and wondered and she asked him what he was thinking of and he said,

"I wondered if you wanted children." She said nothing at first but then she drew him to her and kissed him, and said carefully,

"You already have two: do you really want more?" and he fell into a panic at the depth of her misunderstanding.

"Gillian: I could never leave Gillian, she would never let me go," he said, looking for an excuse, knowing that she would if he wanted it, knowing how Gillian loved him: but he did not know what to tell Anna, naked and lovely before him, he did not know what to say to her, how to explain to Anna that she was too hard for him.

"If you want to leave Gillian, she can't stop you," Anna said after a pause. "She can't hold you if you don't want to stay. Do you want to stay with her?" and although he knew that his answer was yes he could not tell Anna that then. She lay on her back on the bed beside him, naked and bare and she looked at him out of the sides of her blue, blue eyes. He could not tell Anna how he loved Gillian: he could not say he would never leave her, he was too wary of Anna, suddenly anxious that he would not get her out of the house before Gillian returned. So instead of saying to her, "Yes, I want to stay with Gillian," he rolled closer to Anna, naked on his bed, and he buried his face in her shoulder and said to her,

"I want to be inside you," even though they had only just made love and he did not think that he could again so soon. And she laughed at him and said that they did not have enough time for that now, and that she would see what she could do: and she slipped out from his encircling arms and walked away to get dressed.

*

At one end of his parents' house is a long, divided room with views out to sea. When the weather is bad he spends his days there. At night when the room is empty the mice come in and creep about the place, nibbling at the furniture and the curtain hems. After much deliberation he plants mousetraps one evening: all through the night he hears them snapping off like fire crackers and when he inspects them the next morning and finds them loaded with mice he is horrified by the spread of the mouse-blood and the tiny, damaged corpses. The springs have snapped across the ribs of one mouse, the pelvis of another: each one is crumpled and broken. Tips of gleaming bone show through the soft brown skins: blood is clotted all around but their heads are still intact, grinning up at him with open eyes. He bundles up the mice and the traps in newspaper and ties them all in a bag but there is still the blood to remove: he does not know how to lift the spatters of blood from the carpet. He scrubs at the little dark stains with a cloth for a few minutes then leaves them and drives off in his car, dropping the bundle of rubbish on the bonfire as he goes.

All that day the weather worsens. The same thick fog fills the chine when he drives back home: the foghorn on the lighthouse is already sounding out towards the channel, two careful blasts then twenty seconds' silence. After half an hour the wind picks up and drives the fog away: but the rain comes then, a heavy, spattering rain which drives in through the gaps around the windows and drenches the carpets. By three o'clock the sky outside is darkening and an accumulation of thick green clouds hangs low overhead. The wind grows stronger and for the first time that he can remember, he feels the house begin to shudder under the force of the wind: first there is just the rattling of the windows and the doors and then suddenly more than that and the thick stone walls begin to tremble.

He finds the cats and locks them in and he wonders if there is anything else that he can do: his car is inside, the doors are bolted: he can do nothing for the trees except watch them blow about. He switches off his lights and stares out of the window as the storm explodes around him.

An arrow of wind jets in under the door: it pushes under the carpet and lifts it a foot into the air, anchored all around by the furniture. Out in the bay the waves break higher and higher over the lighthouse until the splash of the foam sprays higher than the light itself, spilling over the top of the lighthouse with every third wave.

He sits and watches the storm through the night as it dismantles his house around him: his roof goes first, the tiles slipping off like scales and the timbers snapping under the force of the wind. He hears windows breaking around him but after the first two he does not go to see: they will still be there in the morning. And he hears his two great pine trees go down, one at a time, falling heavily into the arms of the heaving, wind-torn gorse.

When he goes to bed the cats creep in with him, pushing their hot little bodies far down between the sheets and hiding there while the storm continues, for once silent and trembling.

The next morning the wind continues, much reduced, piling up debris in odd corners and scattering leaves through his hallways. All along the house the roof is out, huge great holes as big as beds punched into the tiles and timbers. His furniture is sodden, the carpets squelch as he walks through the rooms. There is no electricity: the water runs slowly from the taps, peaty brown and rancid. The fallen pine trees cross the drive and he cannot get his car out. The cats walk close to him at first, sniffing at the wreckage of the house: then suddenly they are off, scrambling up into the piles of timber which have fallen from the roof, scattering chips of rubble as they go.

The sea is more green than blue and a thin white scum tips each wave. Throughout the day its colour changes: it loses its green and begins to muddy, changing to a thick dun colour but still the white froth caps each flattened wave.

He eats apples and biscuits and finds a box of candles to burn for light: he has no heating so he tries to start a fire in the fireplace of the main hall. But the wood he has is not dry and the smoke it makes will not go up the chimney, it gusts out into the room instead and so he cannot burn a fire. He goes to bed early, huddling up to the cats against the cold.

On the second day after the storm he borrows a chainsaw from the farm and cuts out the centres of the pine trees which block his driveway. He drags the wood away where he can but he leaves most of the trees where they fell, huge sections of wood three feet wide and a hundred long. At least he can drive his car out now and go down to the village: but he does not like to pass through the path cut into the fallen, stretching trees.

He tries to buy a primus stove in the village but there are none, they have all been sold. For the next few days, whenever the coldness of the huge unheated house threatens to overwhelm him, he retreats to the car and runs the engine until hot air surrounds him. The cats do not like to sit in the car with him, no matter how warm it is in there: they scrabble and claw at him as he tries to get all three of them in at once. Just one, the eldest, the heavy brown tabby realises the warmth there and comes in with him: the other two panic and run. So he sits in his car with his fat brown cat purring on his feet as the heat blasts out at them both and he listens to the radio news to hear reports of the storm.

He wonders if Gillian is safe, and the children: he hopes that they have come to no harm. And he hopes that she is thinking of him now. He knows that she cannot call him, for his telephone line is down: but he hopes that she will write, to let him know that they are all safe. He begins to watch out for the postman, who drives up once or twice a week when there is any mail: but nothing comes. After six days of cold his electricity is reconnected but it takes ten more days for his telephone to be put back on line and meanwhile he checks the line constantly, lifting the receiver and listening to the empty noise that waits on the end of the line. He listens to the dead telephone ten, twenty times a day and when it finally is reconnected he keeps returning to check that it is there, listening sadly to the electronic burr on the end of the line instead of the sound of emptiness, like the sea.

He has given up waiting for the post: he waits now to see if Gillian will call. Each time the telephone rings his heart leaps and he hesitates, letting it ring under his hand while he tries to calm his breathing, thinking, is it her? will it be her? Each time he answers, his voice trembles: Hello, he says: hello... and everyone who phones says to him, "Philip? is that you? it didn't sound like you, your voice sounded odd." But Gillian does not call. Instead he speaks to a succession of friends, who call to check on his safety: and builders telephone, roofers and plumbers, everyone trying to help him, build for him, re-tile his roof. And then on the third day Anna calls: slim blonde Anna, her tiny child's voice barely reaching him over the crackling wires.

"Hello, Philip?" she says, almost inaudible: sounding strange, unfamiliar after two months' absence from his life. "Philip? is that you? It's Anna, I'm Anna, can you hear me?" and he is so distanced from her now that he nearly asks, "Anna who?" but he remembers in time and says instead, "Oh, Anna, yes: hello." And there is a long blank silence on the line.

"I wondered how you were," she says eventually. "I thought you might have been hurt, I've been trying to get through to you for days. I wondered how your house is, do you have a lot of damage? Would you like to come and stay with me for a while, if you're lonely there on your own? Or perhaps I could visit you - I've got some time off coming to me, what do you think?" and she carries on talking, trying to cover up his silence with her tiny, chattering voice.

After Anna calls, he puts down the receiver and walks out into the garden. The night is falling around him although the sky is not yet darkened: the wind is changing, coming harder off the sea and cutting lower. The birds are all silent and the trees are beginning to beat against the swelling of the wind. He wonders what he could say to Anna, to stop her calling him, to make her leave Gillian alone. He wishes he had told her before that it was over, that time in his bed, before Gillian found him out.

*

A Saturday morning: the children wait in the kitchen, waiting to go shopping with Gillian and her sister Clare. Gillian is kneeling on the kitchen floor surrounded by heaps of dirty clothes, which she is sorting into groups and stuffing into the machine. Clare sits at the table with the children, drinking tea and eating biscuits. He walks into the kitchen with the sheets from their bed, which he has just stripped.

"Gill, where do you want these?" he says and she points vaguely at the floor behind her.

"Over there will do... I'll wash them later. Did you find anything else?" and he pulls out the little pair of blue silk knickers and says,

"Oh, these, they were stuffed down the head of the bed, they came up with the sheets. Where shall I put them?" and Gill sits there on the floor and frowns at him and says nothing so he says again,

"Where would you like them?" and still she says nothing. She holds out her hand to him and so he steps awkwardly across the piles of laundry on the floor and hands her the knickers and says with a smile,

"Here, you should get some more like these," because they are tiny, sexy, made of silk with little frills around the legs: and she holds them up and looks at them, blue and sleek and silky, and says, in a quiet, puzzled voice,

"But these aren't mine: they're much too small," and he is too slow, he thinks too slowly and he says to her again,

"They were stuffed down the back of the bed, who else would take her knickers off in our bed?" They look at each other and as he speaks he tries to smile but he sees her eyes and he cannot hold her stare: he closes his eyes, just for a second or two and when he opens them again she is trembling, still looking at him. He takes a step forward, whispers her name, says to her,

"Gill, don't, please - " but he cannot say more, he is frozen. She stands up slowly and walks the long way around the table, carefully, avoiding him: and as soon as she is out of the kitchen she begins to run, running up the stairs and into the little bedroom at the side of the house. He waits for her to slam the door but she closes it behind her carefully and then there is silence again. He looks around and the children are still sitting at the table, and Clare sits there too, her face white, her two hands pressed flat onto the table top. She stares at him with her big grey eyes and she is so like Gillian, her look is so much like her sister's that he cannot bear it. He says to her,

"Oh, Clare, I'm sorry: I'm so sorry..." and the children sit and watch as he starts to cry, big, fat tears rolling down his face in a slow, steady stream.

*

One day when he is out walking he sees a fox caught in the top fence. It is caught between two strands of wire and it hangs there, with its front feet scrabbling an inch off the ground. He is a big dog fox, the size of a labrador puppy: he is young and his coat is thick and dense and glossy, black-tipped tan, not the ginger he expected. The fox is held in the wire at the top of the fence by one long slim tapered black foot and as Philip runs up to help him the fox twists and heaves and curls his whole length up and over to the far side of the fence, throwing his body away from Philip, to escape, to be free, and as the fox hurls himself over the fence Philip hears a snap and a noise of wet pressure and the fox's leg breaks and the two parallel bones of his heel come bursting through the skin but still the fox is trapped there, hanging inches from the ground, held swinging on the tendons of his torn foot.

Philip runs back down the hill and calls for help, for anyone to come but there is no-one there: he is alone. He knows he is alone but still he shouts, all the while trying to think of ways to help the fox. He runs into the house and pulls out a big bath towel, hoping to throw it over the fox and hold him still: and then he finds his secateurs, heavy ones on handles two feet long, with a strong weighted head and blades that grip and cut and will take off tree branches three inches thick.

He walks back up the hill towards the fox. He can still see it, looping over the fence, back and forward, tethered to the fence by his one torn foot. He is not fit enough to run all the way back up, his breath comes too short and burning now, so he walks up and throws the big pink towel over the fox and it works like magic and the fox is still and he takes up the secateurs and lifts them up above his shoulder to get a good swing down with them. And just as he lifts the secateurs the fox lifts itself up and shrugs off his towel and loops itself over the fence again, twisting its leg tighter in the wire. Again there is that snap again and another length of bone breaks and now he sees it clearly, four inches of creamy white bone protruding from the bloodied fur and another length showing two inches shorter. The fox twists up and over the fence again, again and each time he twists, his mouth gapes open a little wider. For a second or two between each jump the fox is still and he looks at him. He is plump and softly muscled, his fur is thick and soft, his mouth is pink. His eyes are golden like his fur only darkened and his open mouth looks like he is smiling. Philip cannot kill the fox. Instead he cuts the wire with his secateurs, he cuts the heavy tensioned wire to the side of the fox's trapped foot, leaning on the handles of his long secateurs until the wire snaps and then he moves to the other side of the fox and pulls the end of the wire through, out of the bloodied tangle of the fox's broken foot and the second he is free the fox is running off, running on the broken, splintered bones of his left hind leg, running so fast in an arc away from him towards the sea that Philip cannot believe he is so injured.

Later, at night, when he has set the towel to soak (it is bloodied and grass-stained and it stinks of fox) he remembers how the fox ran away from him. He remembers the fox grinning up at him as it struggled with the fence and its own broken leg: he remembers the fox shooting away the second it was free. He hopes that it will recover, although he knows that it cannot: he hopes that its leg will heal although he knows it will not. He knows that it will probably take days to die and that he should have killed it while he could. And as he sits alone in the wreckage of his parents' house, the night draws in around him and the wind starts to howl through the broken ribs of the roof, and he wishes that he could have stayed in the city, where the foxes ate from the dustbins in the early hours of the morning and vanished by the time daylight came upon the streets.

Panurge 21
William Palmer on Success. Geoffrey Heptonstall on Radio and Short Fiction. Adele Geras (her first story) on Rex's Pictures.

John Rizkalla

The Green Scarab

For a moment when the door wouldn't budge Vanessa panicked. The solicitor in London had handed over the wrong key. Then she remembered how her mother was always going on about seeing to the door and never did. Heard the same voice instruct her to insert the key into the lock, ease it back a notch, and it would turn nicely. Vanessa pushed and the door opened - with a reluctant rasp. The relief! Just as the first snowflakes brushed her hair.

The house had always been funereal, even when her mother spent her summers here, sprouting out of the dank Welsh hillside as inviting as a toadstool. Why her mother should sell the family home in Kent Vanessa had never understood - though she for one had been delighted. Now she lingered on the threshold, pretending to herself she was only doing this to allow much-needed fresh air in. By day every single room had its light halved by a smother of trees. Electric light only succeeded in making the rooms gloomy.

"Oh, mother! I should have visited you more often." Even if out of duty. Too late now. Still, thank God that ordeal was over.

Mother had died in an accident, thousands of miles away on a dig, while on her annual pilgrimage to Ancient Egypt. The letter from the British Embassy in Cairo had added primly (and clearly disapprovingly) that she had wished to be buried in the desert.

"I'll fly out there one day to check the headstone," Vanessa assured the solicitor, trying to make light of yet another duty.

"I'm not sure they have any in a native cemetery," he said.

Meanwhile the isolated bungalow in the Welsh hills was hers, to dispose of as she chose - keep, sell, neglect, if she dared.

She stepped into the hall and carefully placed her overnight bag on the mat, against the wall, as her mother insisted. God, why had she never been pleasant about so trivial a thing! Vanessa shivered as much from the cold outside as from the chill inside. The temptation to rush out, drive down to the village and keep driving until the road returned her to the warmth of her own Kensington flat, was overwhelming. But with a hand as wilful as her mother's, the wind slammed the door behind Vanessa.

"I don't care what you say. I'm only staying a day or two at most," she informed the house in a loud, no-nonsense voice.

Just enough time to clear the place, collect what few items might grab her fancy. What else? Then back non-stop to her executive and absorbing job at the Ministry, sorting out the inconsistencies and shortcomings of other departments. Afterwards it would be up to the lawyers to dispose of the property.

"God, it's freezing!" she said aloud, as much to break the silence as reproach her mother for living in spartan conditions.

In the sitting-room she drew back the curtains. The garden, a patch nibbled off the hillside, was already carpeted with snow, thus obliterating her mother's efforts at cultivation. She turned impatiently to the front window, drew back more heavy curtains. Vanessa needed to make sure her car was waiting by the gate.

She lit the log fire. Mrs Rhys, the help from the village, had thoughtfully left one ready with a box of matches to hand.

"She's a dear! A pity you can't get a word in edgeways..."

Vanessa found it easy and companionable to address herself. The widow Rhys was garrulous, adulating Vanessa's MG sports car as if it were the latest model, instead of ten years old. It had taken great tact to decline her offer of a bed for the night.

"But you can't want to stay up in that house at this time of year. Why, even your Mam drew the line from November to Easter."

"Only because she got sun, free board and lodging, in return for helping out on an archeological dig," Vanessa replied sourly.

"But think of all the fancy souvenirs she brought back with her. To be honest..." Mrs Rhys knew when to put on her sweetest, toothiest smile, "I wouldn't say no to one of her little statues to put on my mantelpiece. Just a lovely memory of your Mam."

"Of course you can!" Vanessa was delighted to be able to repay the widow's hospitality so cheaply. Thinking of the empty house up in the hills she said: "Come up with me and pick out..."

"No, no my dear. You go up there on your own. Get a feel of the place without your Mam. You'll find I've left the house spick and span. Why, if she wanted to, she could walk right in now and pick up her knitting by the fire." Mrs Rhys started to sniffle, embarrassing Vanessa who so far had remained quite dry-eyed.

"Oh, I will miss her. It was hard of her to go so suddenly." Mrs Rhys blew into her handkerchief. No doubt (Vanessa could not stop the mean thought) she was lamenting the loss of a lucrative job too. "Everybody in the village had a good word for her..."

Condolences on the death of dear Mrs Shelley elbowed one another in grey and silver cards across the mantelpiece. Vanessa glanced at the scribbles. She recognized only those who serviced the village. Mrs Rhys had not exaggerated. Unsaid of course but the outpouring of sympathy seemed to imply just how much more appreciated locally Vanessa's mother had been than the daughter.

Well, they hadn't had to grow up at arm's length from her. Vanessa shrugged off what the years had mellowed into an irritant, and went to her mother's bedroom. Nothing had changed. It was still a dimly lit vault, a strongroom, the nastiest in the house.

"My temple," her mother had baptized it from her regal bed.

With its small (only because of deliberately boarded-up) windows, its walls decorated with affected sun-yellow wallpaper of hieroglyph and paraphernalia of ancient gods, its shelves and corners cluttered with clay pots and woodworm statues, it would have gladdened any Pharaoh in his tomb. Except for the dressing-table and wardrobe - her mother's reluctant concession to her own present. Still, these she mostly shrouded in dusty old sheets.

Vanessa's instinct was to burn the lot in a bonfire.

But she was not an efficient civil servant for nothing. She would be patient and sort through them first. Meanwhile rage was permissible and she gave vent to it by tugging angrily at the catches to the windows. A scurry of snowflakes invaded the room. They drifted around bewildered, before dissolving in mid-air. Vanessa's attention however was quickly drawn to the double-bed.

"It's not been made properly," her mind tutted.

A closer look revealed something more disturbing. The bed *had* been made but then ruffled, in the middle, ruffled by someone lying in bed and kicking their legs under the sheets!

It was crazy. But how could Vanessa deny what she saw? She wanted to straighten the bedclothes, tuck them back in. No! She knew she would have to determine how they had come to be ruffled.

Methodically she began to strip down the bed. She noticed nothing until she reached the bottom sheet and her eyes travelled up to the bolster. And there it was about to burrow underneath...

Green, lichen green, hand-sized, delicately engraved with the wings of an insect. And on the finest gold base, the legs, unmistakably those of an Ancient Egyptian scarab.

"This is my life insurance." Her mother was highly emotional about it. The wrinkled hands grasped it in a most repulsive way.

Vanessa knew then that the scarab was worth a mint. The when and how she had stumbled upon it was still vivid in her mind.

147

Her mother had been back a month from Egypt before Vanessa journeyed up for the May Bank Holiday. The next morning she was wakened by fearful groans. She rushed into this same bedroom. In the half light, the sheets thrown on the floor, her mother's heaving figure seemed to be tussling with a nightmare. That was when Vanessa noticed the fat-green blistering creature, toadlike, moving apparently upwards, towards her mother's bared throat. With a cry of disgust Vanessa lunged at the creature.

Two things happened. The thing in her hand was so cold and dead she dropped it. And her mother woke up, then like someone possessed reared up and howled: "Thief! Thief!" Her fist hit out. "Steal it from me, would you? I'll see you first in Hell!"

Vanessa was horrified. She was sure that at that moment her mother was seeing not her own daughter but someone else. Someone she hated and feared. With numbing shock Vanessa watched her mother roll on to the floor and dig frantically into the bed-clothes. She pounced then clutched something to her breasts.

"Too late. It's mine. You can't take it off me. Nobody can."

Vanessa was outraged: "I haven't the least intention. What is it anyway?" she asked contemptuously. "It's not alive, is it?"

"Feel!" Her mother's hand shot out dramatically. It held the perfect stone replica of a very large beetle. "Go on. Hold it."

Vanessa humoured her mother: "It's so cold."

"Naturally. It's a genuine scarab. Over three thousand years old. These insects were sacred in Ancient Egypt. Even today people in the fields avoid killing them."

"Why?" Vanessa was curious in spite of herself.

"The scarab lays its eggs in the droppings of animals, then rolls the dung into a ball before pushing it down a hole."

Trust her mother to be kneeling in shit, peering delightedly at the creature's habits.

"The point, you see, is that the scarab lays its eggs equally in the dead body of any of its own kind," her mother instructed.

"I think I get the picture," Vanessa said indifferently.

"Oh, but that's only the beginning of it. Can't you see how this humble insect expresses so admirably the Ancient Egyptian belief in resurrection? Life emerges from death as miraculously as the young beetle breaks its way out of the ball of dung!"

Vanessa studied the replica in her hand. "Did you know that someone has drilled a little hole at one end?"

"That's so it can be fitted on to a silver necklace..."

"You mean this was once worn..."

"Not worn. Certainly not that one!" snorted her mother. "Notice the legs engraved on the gold base? That type of scarab was only placed round the throat of the deceased in his coffin."

"You mean this was taken off a corpse!" Vanessa would have dropped the stone again, except that her mother had anticipated the effect of her words and cupped it in her hands.

"How did you get it?" Vanessa was more worried than curious.

"Oh, I found it. How else?" Her mother went all coy. "It was lying just under the sand, probably dropped in a hurry by a tomb robber thousands of years ago. Rather lucky, wasn't I?"

"Shouldn't it belong to a museum or antiquities survey?"

"It belongs to whoever found it. And that happens to be me. It could have been anyone at any time. Besides no one saw me."

"That's what usually happens with theft," Vanessa said.

"What you never had, you never missed," her mother snapped. "And I'm quite sure that only if I'm at my wits' end am I ever likely to part with such a precious thing."

In a sly move calculated to catch out Vanessa she added:

"Of course if you feel so bad about it, then you have my permission to return it to the sands of Egypt once I'm dead."

"I might just do that!" Vanessa burst out vehemently. It was said more to vex than do any such thing.

Now suddenly here was this same scarab, to remind her of a moral outrage as dead as her mother. Odd though. Her mother must have been very flustered indeed the morning of her departure to have forgotten the scarab in the bed.

Unless this was a different one. Vanessa picked it up and felt inexplicably certain that it wasn't. Still cold. Though this time it fitted snugly into her hand as if acknowledging a friend. What delicate lines! The eyes, the wings folded back, the biting mouthparts, what perfection of detail! It looked, it felt so sensuous, so right. Vanessa would need no expert to tell her she was in possession of a work of high art and value.

She held it a long while, sliding it from hand to hand. The stone grew warmer, so warm that a snowflake that had floated in from the open window and happening to settle on it, melted.

She put the scarab on the night-table. Extraordinary! It had left an angry mark on each palm. Why hadn't she felt any pain?

She couldn't stop shivering. The temperature was dropping in the room steadily. She closed all the windows. The room tingled, fresh with mountain snow. She removed the blankets to their drawer, made up the bed. Time was going to drag until the second-hand dealer turned up. Was he coming tomorrow or the day after? She had already made up her mind not to haggle over his offer.

She began to wish Mrs Rhys had not been so thorough. All at once she went cold inside. Of course, Mrs Rhys!

"I've left the house spick and span..."

She must have washed the sheets, made up the bed again. So how could she possibly have missed the scarab? Vanessa shivered. Someone had left it there afterwards, having first slept in the bed. That would explain why it had been ruffled.

Vanessa stared at the scarab with that same revulsion she had felt when her mother used to grasp it between her wrinkled hands. Who else had held it? It took Vanessa several minutes to bring herself to touch it again. What startled her this time was not how warm it still was, but how pleasant it felt. It was as if the scarab wanted to reassure, comfort her.

She hurried with the scarab into a dark kitchen. Through the windows she noticed a sky heavy with cloud, portending yet more snow. Indeed everything outside was white. If she hadn't actually registered its old friendly shape she'd have sworn the car had somehow disappeared.

Was it wise of her to stay the night? The answer came from a shrill noise in the hallway. The telephone! She'd forgotten there was one in the house. At last something to thank her mother for. She left the scarab on the kitchen table and rushed to answer.

"Vanessa! It's only me," the lilting voice said with relief.

"Mrs Rhys? Is something wrong?"

"No, no. Of course not. I just wanted to make sure you had found everything to your satisfaction. Rooms tidy and straight."

"They're perfect. Just as I knew they would be. Thank you so much. A bit cold, mind you. It's snowing hard up here."

"Is it now? I did wonder..." Mrs Rhys paused. "You see, it isn't down here, though I do see thick clouds over your way."

"I've lit a fire." Vanessa was still shivering. Its heat had never been able to reach into the hallway.

"There was something I forgot to mention. A letter."

Vanessa glanced at the window recess and saw at once the edges striped with Air Mail red and blue.

"It arrived a week ago. From Egypt."

Vanessa's heart pounded as if an intruder had just got in.

"I hope it's nothing..." faltered Mrs Rhys. "I just wanted to say if the snow is settling you're still most welcome here..."

"Thank you. But I think I'll struggle through with the spare room. As I usually have to," Vanessa said and put down the phone.

The letter had been posted in Cairo a fortnight earlier. For a moment she was afraid it was a last letter from her mother. But the tightly-columned address was positioned down the left handside in spidery, ill-at-ease English handwriting. She ripped open the envelope. Inside was a sheet of pink lined paper. No address, no date. She looked to the signature. None either.

Dear Lady... Lady indeed! Oh, God it was some dragoman, or worse a starry-eyed English-language student her mother had yet again befriended, now begging for a job and somewhere to stay.

Vanessa read on with growing disbelief.

As your most kind mother tells you it is the time for me to arrive. So I am departing from Egypt these days and I will reach you without fail on the 10th of February...

Yesterday. Thank God she'd missed him (such smug assuredness could only have come from a man). Oh God, had she though? Vanessa checked carefully the hallway floor for any note slipped through the letter box. There was none. She felt only a little easier.

It is a great honour to accept your mother's gift. It makes me like her son. Now I am your servant also.

He was no servant. To her credit her mother had disparaged the very notion. So what did he mean? What did he want? Beneath these questions simmered a far more worrying one. How had he known Vanessa would be staying in her mother's house?

She crumpled the letter and threw it into the fire. Then with deliberate steps she walked back to the kitchen. She refused to give way to alarm. Still the words 'As your most kind mother tells you it is the time...' nagged on. Told her what? Time for what? And what was her mother's mysterious gift?

"The green scarab, of course!" The certainty slapped her.

Vanessa pictured the scene. It had happened before. This man had helped her mother out in some way. Eager to reward him she had given him her address, invited him to Wales. God, this time she must have gone senile to have promised him a scarab though.

151

The Green Scarab

"Well, he can't have it. You gave it to me. Remember?"

Vanessa was not sure why she should suddenly feel so possessive about the thing. Except that she did. Maybe it had to do with those expensive trips her mother had undertaken to Egypt - alone. She caught her breath. In her hurry to reach the phone somehow she must have left the scarab right on the edge of the table. It could have fallen off and smashed, unless...

She froze. The idea became a further certainty.

"It's moved. That's what's happened. It's moved."

She watched the scarab, willing her presence to inhibit it. Christ, what would she imagine next? In the hall the grandfather clock chimed six dark times, a reminder that the house was still very much for the living.

Outside dusk was blurring sky and hills. She switched on the light, half expecting it not to come on. When it did she thought it would cut off at any moment. The possibility nagged her into the spare room where she usually slept. Mrs Rhys had cleaned it, aired the sheets, even provided a couple of coat-hangers in the wardrobe. The only valid reason Vanessa could find for leaving was because, unaccountably, she had become afraid of the house.

"Well, I'm not," she shouted as if her mother sat next door.

It was the fault of the green scarab. Finding it in the bed, when it had no business to be anywhere but buried in Egypt, had so played on her mind, Vanessa had endowed it with its own life.

Resolutely she fetched her overnight bag, unpacked what she needed. The folded nightie, a new thriller, the vanity box on the dresser, were echoes of her home in Kensington. Sometimes these felt the only sure things in her life. She felt hungry. The meal came scooped out of her mother's collection of tin cans. She consumed the warmed up concoction, leaning against the sink, staring at the green scarab. But it, of course, never budged.

*

Vanessa put down the half-finished plate. She edged her hand towards the stone. Cold. She moved the scarab to the middle of the table. It was uniquely beautiful. The longer she looked at it, contemplated it, the stronger her feelings of awe, reverence. It dawned on her that she had been entrusted with a magnificent gift. The conviction was shattered by a knock at the door.

Several, loud, imperious knocks. They would not stop.

She was damned if she would answer. But when the house shook with the blows she changed her mind. She pictured the walls collapsing about her. This time she made sure of the scarab, and tucked it in a dresser drawer, under several balls of string.

The blast of cold wind and snow blinded her a moment so that she heard the guttural accented voice before she saw the speaker.

"Madame Shelley..." He was swarthy, a foot taller than her, imposing in his black caftan.

"No! Mrs Shelley is my mother. I'm Vanessa, her daughter."

"I come in."

He did, brushing her aside. She was too dismayed to protest. He exuded such strength she felt like the proverbial chaff in the wind. That he also reeked of cumin and garlic, as bad as anything her mother in her last years had been throwing into her pans, was even more unnerving.

"I close the door. O.K.?"

"You do that." She could not have been more scornful.

"Yesterday I came. There was no one here. I couldn't enter."

"You wrote the letter," she accused. And God knew what else!

The lean face frowned. He had an aquiline nose, thin mouth. He looked ascetic, young too. She couldn't help staring at him.

"It was no good?" His foot nudged the empty envelope dropped on the mat. His eyes though were fixed on the sitting-room. She did not need to turn to know he had noticed the flickering light.

She heard herself say: "I've got a fire going for you..."

Was she mad? She had intended to say quite the opposite. She wanted him off the premises. But she was caught unawares when his teeth began to chatter. He was freezing in that summer caftan, and he looked exhausted. When he tottered her hand flew out to him. What if he fell ill on her? How would she cope on her own?

She helped him into her mother's armchair. He was no weight at all. His eyes brightened but instead of thanking her now he was embarrassingly silent. She built up the fire with more logs.

"I'll fetch some more."

It wasn't easy. Snow had packed up against the kitchen door and she had to force her way out. The snowstorm had come down so swiftly, so unexpectedly. Why had no one, Mrs Rhys, warned her? It took several trips to the shed to stock up. The scullery was littered with logs. Vanessa piled what she could on to her arms and struggled into the sitting-room - then almost dropped them.

The stranger (what *was* his name?) sat cross-legged on the rug.

She couldn't make out what he was intoning. Backward and forward he rocked, blocking access to the fire. She tapped his shoulder. He didn't respond. More roughly she nudged him. At once he relieved her of the logs and stacked them inside the fire. She stared as the flames like a friendly tongue, licked at his hands.

A strangled cry escaped her. This was eerie, more than her frayed nerves could stand. She burst out wildly:

"Who are you? You haven't even given me your name..."

"Call me 'Asal. It means honey in Egypt. You like honey?"

"Why have you come here? We don't know each other. If it's because of my mother, she's dead. Has been for weeks..."

"I know." 'Asal nodded to the fire. "I watched her die."

It was such a shock she dropped into her mother's arm-chair. Her hands wouldn't stop trembling. She had never felt so scared.

She had deliberately avoided finding out how her mother had died, content to accept the Embassy's mention of an accident. She had done it simply to be able the quicker to get on at last with her own life. But now she was going to be forced to ask this stranger for the truth. It would not, she suspected, be pleasant.

"What did happen?" she whispered.

'Asal turned round to fix his startling eyes upon her. He didn't answer at once. When he did it was so upsetting she hardly took in the fact of how dramatically his English had improved.

"She was with a party of Egyptologists from the Exploration Society. They have been engaged for years searching the hills for the tomb of the High Priest Har-em-Kham. Early in the morning they entered a new cave in the cliff face, carrying paraffin lamps. Your mother deviated and lost her footing. She dropped several metres down a narrow shaft. There was a huge sheet of flame from the spilt paraffin. It took her two days to die..."

"Oh God, how awful!" Vanessa covered her eyes.

"Why? She had stumbled upon the entrance to the tomb."

"Stop it!" Vanessa had once thought nothing about her mother would make her break down. But now the manner of her death did.

Then to her surprise and bewilderment 'Asal's arms folded round her. She tensed. But he was warm, instinctively comforting, the nest in which at that moment she needed to go on sobbing.

"It was too difficult with the fall of rocks to pull her out. She's been left there. They have filled up the shaft..." The stranger seemed unaware of how hurtful he was being. "It's meant they've had to dig a different entrance into the tomb."

He released her. But it was the other that had outraged her.

"They should have sealed up the tomb."

"There is no end to the inquisitiveness of the living," 'Asal went on implacably: "In between her screams your mother was able to talk on and off. Perhaps it was delirium but she babbled on about getting to this house. To her life insurance..."

"Life insurance?" Vanessa's heart missed a beat.

"The sacred scarab of the High Priest Har-em-Kham. Her life for the sacred scarab." His eyes drilled into her skull.

She could no more tear herself loose from those eyes than she could have done from his arms. How had she let that happen?

"I don't know what you're talking about," she stammered.

Was he threatening her? She would have to get rid of him. But how? Even if she could bring herself to order him to leave she sensed that he wouldn't, not without the scarab.

What could it possibly be worth to draw a person thousands of miles? Then she realized that wasn't it at all. The green scarab possessed some power she had yet to discover. But she had! She stiffened, remembering, stripped now of any lingering doubt.

The scarab *had* moved to the edge of the table. Just as it had been trying to hide in her mother's bed. Was it even now in the drawer where she had left it in her rush to answer the door? Her heart beat madly. Maybe this stranger whose hands played with fire had already seen into the dresser and found the scarab?

Vanessa jumped to her feet.

"Where are you going?" He made as if to stop her.

But she was too quick for him, as if she must beat him to the kitchen. Her hands ransacked one drawer, then another, every drawer of the dresser. But the green scarab was gone. Gone!

Behind her 'Asal's voice blasted:

"So the sacred scarab has forsaken you..."

"Forsaken? What on earth do you mean?" She spun round.

He was so close she could smell him. The thyme and garlic had turned stale and dusty. But the other smell, the sweat on his body didn't so much upset her as disturb her. She backed against the dresser then when he stretched out his hands, stepped quickly to one side. It wasn't however on her flesh but the pinewood that his nails left a scratch trail. Incredibly, it began to bleed...

She became hysterical: "Go away! I've nothing for you..."

"I can't leave until your own hand gives me the scarab."

"But I don't know where it's gone. I swear you can have it. The moment I find it I'll send it to you. Anywhere. Just go now."

The head, close-shaven she realized, shook slowly.

"But you can't be expecting to stay the night?"

"Will you send me out into the snowstorm?"

Willingly. His smile crushed any such secret wish.

"The house hasn't been lived in for months. If I didn't have to clear up I would never dream of staying here," she lied.

"You can't leave the house either," he pointed out.

"There's nowhere for you to sleep."

"Of course there is. Your mother's room."

"No!" It was impermissible.

He shrugged his shoulders and stalked out of the kitchen. He stood waiting for her in the sitting-room. She no longer cared about the scarab: it was what he intended that worried her most.

"I will guard the fire a while," he announced and flopped down, once again crossing his partially bare legs on the mat.

He remained equally indifferent when she locked her mother's bedroom door, as noisily as she could, and pocketed the key.

Inside her own room she made sure every aperture was secure. Ear pressed to the door, she listened, anticipating whatever might happen. But the snow outside seemed to have muffled every sound inside the house too. They might have been in a cocoon together. The idea overwhelmed her. In a panic she started tugging at the top window. She didn't care how piercing the cold air was. Her fingers wiggled in the three-inch gap, her sole means of escape.

She was too nervous to undress. Or read. She lay on the bed in the clothes she'd travelled down in, determined to stay awake. But in minutes the cold had forced her to snuggle under the covers. Seconds later she was toppling headlong down a shaft of unending darkness. Scores, hundreds of loud whispers urged her to hurry. Trying to pull clear only accelerated her fall. A heavy mass pressed her ever downward. 'Asal was intoning:

"I have been sent to bring you back."

Yet it was not his face that appeared, faded, grew stronger, sharper, then hovered up to her. Though black and eaten by fire, these features were familiar, oozed with a telltale stench.

"Mother! Mother!"

What lips, white as moonlight, there were, parted, hissed:

"Bring me the green scarab. I need it. I need you."
The lips settled on Vanessa's and cauterized her reply.
She woke up screaming. It died abruptly. There was a light in the room. Not from a lamp or bulb. Was it dawn? No, above the packed silver snow, night pressed against the window panes. Then she located the light, a glow that came from behind the door. Her ears plucked out of the silence the padded sound of footsteps. 'Asal was rummaging through the rooms, ferreting for the scarab. In minutes he would enter her room, search her bed, search her.

She sat bolt upright. The frantic beat of her heart would permit nothing more. What could she do if he came in? No question of fighting him. Yet to be just passive... The light brightened as outside the door the steps halted. Could the lock hold?

The handle turned, turned again, further, rattled, shaken by an impatient hand. Vanessa squirmed at the thought, the feel of 'Asal's sweat slipping down her body... A voice wailed, called to Vanessa by name. The solid door blurred, dissolved. In its place loomed a figure shrouded in flames.

Vanessa let out a strangled cry at the sight of her mother lurching into the room. Her hand searched for a weapon and came up with the pillow. The swinging movement carried something heavy with it. The weight dropped on to her lap, squatted glowing up at her with green emerald light. The scarab!

Vanessa stared from one to the other, terrified, voiceless, in mounting disbelief. The figure lumbered ever forward, so blind it bumped into and came to a halt at the foot of the bed. Only for a moment. A black burnt-up hand groped for a way round, forward.

Moved by instinct or sudden understanding, Vanessa picked up the scarab, then nearly dropped it, it was so hot.

"Take it! Take it to whatever hell you've found yourself..."
And she hurled the stone at her mother.
A sheet of fire whooshed over the bed, scorching Vanessa.
"Please God, don't let me be burnt alive..."
As she lost consciousness she heard a long, dying howl, not her own, a howl not of pain but rage, frustrated rage.

*

Daylight. A grey unwashed sky blinked through the icicle eyelashes of the window-panes. Vanessa's only thought was that somehow she was still alive. She explored her face. The skin was unblemished. Gone too were the marks on the palms of her hands. The bedclothes were not singed. The door was solidly back in place. Had her mother really come back? Sent back in a nightmare from hell? No sound came from beyond the door but still Vanessa shivered. It was snowing again, freezing the room. Without giving it a thought she banged the top window shut. The sound echoed through the house. Oh God, 'Asal. Had he left?

She dressed in fresh clothes, slowly, thinking up excuses for the silence that had overtaken the house. And all the time her eyes kept scanning the door, the empty area below and around where the scarab must have fallen, if it hadn't gone through...

Absurd. Yet her search was futile. The scarab was gone. She stood well away from the door and called out. But no one came bursting in, the silence was total. She was alone in the house.

She opened the door cautiously and tiptoed to the sitting-room. It was empty, the fire burnt out. No, she was mistaken. Fear clawed at her throat. Whatever her brain said, her eyes insisted no fire had been lit. The logs were moss-covered, left exactly as the stranger's hands had built them in the flames...

Her eyes darted to her mother's bedroom. The door was ajar. The audacity! A total stranger had ignored Vanessa's feelings and gone ahead and slept in her mother's bed.

She pushed at the door. Like all the others in the house it opened with a prolonged screech. Lying in the bed was a figure.

"Get up! Get out! How dare you!" She clapped her hands.

The figure did not stir.

"You heard me. Get up at once." She advanced on the bed, encouraged by her own clapping. "I want you out of this room. Out of this house. If not, I'll call the police..."

Her anger faltered. The figure was too still. She peered into the half light and gasped. The top sheet covered the figure entirely, even to the head. It was as if he were...

No, that was mad. Why should anything so awful have occurred? How? And who could have come in and covered the face? Unless something *had* happened during the night, something she had done.

The sheet appeared to be held up only by the bulge of the head and the tip of the nose. Vanessa's eyes were glued to that spot. The sheet did not breathe. She knew she had to block out all thought as her hand freed and pulled back the sheet - then dropped it half-way.

What was discernible of the body was ravaged, as if Vanessa had interrupted someone's eating. Yet even that wasn't what made her whimper uncontrollably. It was the head. The head had no face, no recognizable face. Most of the flesh had peeled off, a flap of flesh dangled, revealing beneath scorched twisted muscles that somehow still held in place, the eyeballs. These were the only things left alive. The eyeballs swivelled up at Vanessa. They emitted daggers of light, green light. The baleful stare though was quite unique.

"Where is it? My insurance," it gasped. "The scarab..."

Vanessa fled the room, locked the door. Against it she piled sofa, armchair, table. Only then did she dare slump into a chair, racked with sobs, watching the door. This was her doing. She had hurled the scarab at the figure standing by the bed, caused an explosion, the fire, and inexplicably burnt her mother.

The reek of burnt flesh was spreading from the bedroom into the rest of the house. Its sickening smell was rising off her own sweating body. Then from behind the door the voice gasped again, so loud, so hatefully, the whole house joined in the accusation:

"You're robbing me of my life."

Vanessa fled to the hallway. She picked up the phone but the line was dead. It scarcely mattered. However thick the fall of snow she was determined to brave the mile and a half downhill to Mrs Rhys. Any hardship would be preferable to remaining another second under this cursed roof.

*

This time the front door would not shut. She left it to bang to the whim of the wind. She sank in snow reaching past her calf. At the car she battled with layer upon layer of snow then gave up. She was never going to be able to drive anyway. In her wake the wind was erasing each footprint.

She hurried as fast as she could downhill. Minutes later, just as the coils of smoke from a hundred chimneys in the valley below began to streak the marble sky, she noticed ahead of her, a figure. Like a dead tree trunk it stood motionless, rooted to the ground. Too far to make out the face, but not the black caftan.

The figure raised an arm. Not to acknowledge but to signal. What? She moved to her left. It did the same. To the right as she moved right. She halted undecided but now it started towards her. She backed away, turned too quickly, stumbled, fell headlong into the snow. She struggled to her feet, anxious to keep the figure at a distance. And it was, but nearer, much nearer.

Which way should she go? The figure (she felt now it could only be malevolent) barred her route down to the village. Even if there were any other way (a matter she had never once bothered to ascertain) the snow had made sure it was swallowed up. In this white wilderness her mother's house loomed up tantalizingly.

No, it was impossible to go back in there. Better to climb higher up, past the house. But when she turned in that direction the figure stood there too, arm raised, pointing. She looked back and found it was there too. Wherever she looked the figure stood like some guardian of the horizon.

Why and how, rapidly became of secondary importance? The stranger, all the strangers converging at great strides towards her, were real, growing as if to darken the sky itself. The front door of the house banging only yards away seemed just a respite.

Timely. One figure had reached the car. In the crystal pure air its panting was obscene. She bolted the door. She stayed leaning against it, steeling herself to withstand the hammering, a hundred voices as rasping as any in her nightmare. Nothing happened. Minutes passed. The snow went on burying the house. She peeked through the flap to the letter slot. There was no figure.

Ice cold fear uncoiled inside Vanessa. Maybe there never had been a figure out there, just the stalking of her guilt for that 'thing' lying inside the bedroom. Vanessa trembled, her mouth pressed to the door in an effort to stifle her terror.

What madness had possessed her to go and bolt herself inside the house? At once her fingers were scrambling to undo the harm. She pulled, tugged. In vain. The bolt would not budge. She recoiled at the sight of her hands, all stained with brown red flakes. How could she doubt the fact? Years and years ago someone had closed the house and left this bolt in position to rust.

Something, or someone from years back, pressed against her, embraced her waist, squeezed her breasts, her buttocks. She could not even find the scream to plead with him to let her go.

"Where would you go anyway?"

The sound of the voice from inside the house had the effect of frightening off the molestor. Vanessa swung round to an empty hall. The echo lingered, drew her into the sitting-room. He was there, the stranger 'Asal, arms folded, legs set apart, wearing his original black caftan.

"Who... what are you?" she asked in a dull voice.

"Does that matter?"

"It does. It does." She demanded a moment of sanity. She indicated the door still barricaded by furniture. "Look inside."

"Why should I? I am here now. With you..."

She thought she would faint. She had to dig her nails into her palms until the pain made her sob. 'Asal's voice had slipped into that of her mother's.

"Now you know... So help me. Give me the scarab!"

"I did. I threw it to you."

"Not to me. At me! In anger. In fear. But you can set me free from this dark shaft which is my prison, from this pit which is my grave, if you will only give the scarab back out of love..."

The arms, of blood and sagging flesh, reached out, pleading. But Vanessa had long since learnt to be wary. She drew back, dug her hands into her pockets. And found the scarab...

She could not begin to ask where the scarab had been or why it had come back to her? Except that she was certain that it had chosen to return to her. How else could she explain the sudden relief, the calm she felt? Her mother sounded almost normal.

"Listen, I swore to the gods how much my child loved me. That out of love she would set the scarab of the High Priest Har-em-Kham whom I stole from his tomb, set him free. I promised them. Don't deny me now. Don't leave me in this pit. I need you!"

Not in years, maybe only when Vanessa had been too young to understand, had her mother declared anything like such a truth.

Vanessa doubted this unknown person.

"You're trying to frighten me. I won't be," she insisted.

The stranger hissed impatiently: "Obstinate girl! Very well. Can't you see I am the 'Ka' of the High Priest Har-em-Kham?"

"Ka?"

"His double from the life beyond the grave. His spirit."

"Then why speak in my mother's voice?"

"Because she stole the scarab, and now possesses me. As you or another, and many more may do until the end of time..."

The figure jerked as if to disembody itself.

"Until she surrenders the scarab I am neither woman nor man. I am nothing." The voice wheedled: "Touch me."

Vanessa recoiled.

"Touch me and you will know everything..." it tempted.

And suddenly Vanessa seemed to hear, to see and ache from longings suppressed too well. This stranger was her mother, dead father, desired child, absent brother, absent sister, lover, a slender chain of failed loves...

"No! No! I don't want to remember. I don't want to know."

"You will. And worse. You will know what is to come. Unless you return the scarab. Beware - all who touch it yearn to possess it. Only if you give it back can you bring peace to us all..."

Vanessa drew out the hand in which lay the scarab. It was so real, so solid. It pulsated a green light, asking to be touched, to be held, to be taken back to its own as once long ago.

"I don't want it. I never did," Vanessa said at last.

The sigh of relief echoed in the room.

"And this you do for love of me?" What fear in her voice!

The two had drawn closer, inside a well of light surrounded by deepening darkness. Vanessa felt calm, felt no surprise at all that she should perceive at last a very different mother, the one she had known in dreams: radiant, warm, welcoming.

"What else?" Vanessa closed her eyes, shivered, aching for those arms to reach her. And surrendered the green scarab.

At once another voice carped: "Why did you make me wait?"

Vanessa opened her eyes, alerted too late. She had been tricked. Her mother's features were mutating. Like the voice.

"Behold, I offered you to the gods!" It was said in a hiss of triumph. "The scarab has held me prisoner as now it holds you."

Vanessa stared aghast. Stared at not one eye, but a myriad of them, reflecting her own tiny figure. Stretched over her head, testing her hair, were not human arms, but long, hairy antennae. A giant scarab sat poised to strike.

"Oh God! Let go! Please, let me go!" But only her brain screamed that. The rest of Vanessa was hypnotized, overwhelmed by a desire to submit, to be at one.

The circle of green light tightened. It threatened to crush her. She writhed as a hard probe explored deep inside her, but here too she surrendered. She was dimly conscious of a sudden crunching noise. The scarab's wings, giant wings carefully folded on its back, were beginning after three millennia of sleep to loosen, to span outward, upward, obscuring what light was left.

A deep-throated whirr swelled aloft. Inches away the brute's mandible dropped, emitting a fetid stench. The antennae prodded, smelt, assessed her size and shape, then sucked her in.

*

It was not death. Nor yet ecstasy. Vanessa was having to adjust to a new experience, one in which she could neither move nor speak. She could smell though, something burning and pungent. Incense! It was drifting towards her and its smell acted on her like an opiate. She felt placidly happy, happy to join in the sound of approaching voices, singers, dirge-like chanting.

A sudden lurch threatened to hurl her into the air. In fact she had not moved at all. A young girl whose beauty had been cut from gems glided forward. Black plaited hair hung down one side, her naked breasts peeped over the rim of a tight green tunic. Inside an oval frame of kohl, she kept her eyes severely lowered. She carried something heavy. She stopped before Vanessa, lifted up high then tilted a tray of gleaming silver.

Vanessa gazed into what she knew was a mirror, yet shuddered. Why could she not see herself? Had she become invisible? All she caught was a fleeting vision of a figure in pleated linen robe, with a gold and lapis lazuli necklace, before a cloud of incense blurred the image. A new figure rustled up, exuding a heady aroma of perfume. When the incense cleared, Vanessa discovered that the mirror had closed up. Into it had stolen a long-nailed finger, that began to stroke part of a face, sunken cheeks, the distended nostrils, closed eyelids, before coming to rest tenderly on the line of thin grey lips. When unexpectedly the mirror pulled away, it revealed the whole of the face, drained of colour, the face of a dead man. Vanessa recognized 'Asal.

She had no time to react. A giant hand slipped down to the neck. Simultaneously Vanessa felt the breath being squeezed out of her, caught sight of the gold and lapis lazuli necklace, saw the green scarab. And there at last stumbled upon herself - wedged between its stone antennae as a prayer offering.

She let out a long, searing but utterly puny cry of terror at that and at what happened next. The flames of a thousand torches illuminated her sky, as each in turn passed and dipped towards her. One torch did not. It slipped, hurtled down. A tide of fire engulfed Vanessa. Amid the explosion of anguished screams, the granite sarcophagus lid indented with hieroglyphics was hurriedly lowered, to stifle the flames and bury her in darkness - or until such time as rapacious hands might snaffle her out of eternity.

*

"Mrs Shelley! Mrs Shelley!" More than half a dozen anxious people scrambled on the floor, and hollered down the deep shaft.

Far below Mrs Shelley breathed in the paraffin fumes on her clothes and body. She passed a shaky hand over her face and hair. Except for a film of black smoke they were intact. A hiss like a whirlwind had doused the flames about to devour her.

"Mrs Shelley! Are you all right? Please, answer. Just indicate in some way that you're still alive..."

To think she had doubted the power of the scarab! But it had kept its promise. She had salvaged her life.

"Yes..." Mrs Shelley called back. "Just a little shaken..."

"Oh, thank God. We'll get you out in no time. By the way..." ·

The teamleader hushed the others' excitement, before going on to explain in his own still more excited voice:

"Congratulations, Mrs Shelley. Yours is a most fortunate fall. Thanks to you we shall be spending the winter combing every inch of this area. I do believe you have just found us the way into the tomb of Har-em-Kham..."

However down in the shaft old Mrs Shelley hardly heard him. She had kicked away the paraffin lamp, and now stared in horror at a green scarab that her shoe had just unearthed.

David Rose

Bluff

I wipe my shoes, carefully, slowly, against the spring of the bristles. As I do so, I can feel that the key has been used. It has been taken out and replaced two inches to the left. I go on marking time on the mat, a slow unpartnered waltz.

I open the door with my key, enter, and bang the door deliberately, hearing the echo down the stair-well. But there is no one here.

My wife has gone out, recently, dressed up. Her scent still has the edge on it.

Against the bruise of her scent is another, slightly acid, and reminding me of chrysanthemums. I have traced it now. I spent yesterday afternoon in Harrods. The assistants were helpful; it didn't take long to identify. It's an after-shave called Polo, but with no trace of mint.

I hang up my coat and fold my stick.

I walk through to the kitchen, counting the steps. A dirty cup on the draining-board, still warm, but only one. A slightly tacky smudge of lipstick on the rim.

She has left the kettle filled. There will be instant coffee and sugar in my mug, carefully measured. The dutiful wife.

I check that the whistle is on the spout, then switch on the kettle and go to the bedroom to change my shoes.

A crumple on the carpet. I pick it up - it is a stocking. I drop it into the wicker basket, as my wife would normally do, fastidiously.

The whistle goes. I want to hurry but have to be careful. Strangers - strangers to me - can leave furniture six inches out and still think it is in place.

I choke the shrill and make my coffee. I turn down the thermostat and carry my mug to the living room.

Even with the heating down I feel clammy. The apples in the fruit bowl remind me of death. I open a window and take the damp night air like sea-spray on my cheek.

There was a time when the windowsill housed ornaments - part of her collection of china and dolls. We had to come to an arrangement, so those that weren't broken are now in a trunk. One more sacrifice on the part of my wife.

I wish to God she'd complain once in a while.

My watch pips the hour and I settle back to wait.

I am dragged back to wakefulness by voices. The catechetical murmur of lovers. I strain, but can't be sure - . I slide my tuning fork from its leather case, pring it on my wrist and hold it to my ear. The voices disappear, momentarily. That, at least, is a reassurance.

I want to check the time but my fingers are sweaty, I can't flip the watch-cover. I decide to go to bed anyway.

As I undress, I hear again the voices, laughter. It is the neighbours.

I know that. I know it.

I turn on the television, turn it up loud, get back into bed. I feel the imperative of the sag in the mattress, but resistance is unnecessary.

What throbs is not pain but the sense of unfairness. She doesn't understand my bestowal of immortality; immutability at least.

When my fingers read the braille of her vertebrae, walk the dunes and deltas of her body, I am aware - of course I am aware - of the shifting of the dunes, the obtusing of the curvatures, the slow silting of wrinkles. But there is no connection with the image I carry, have carried, since before the darkness, of the woman I married, surprised into beauty. I withhold the connection, refuse it, for her sake. It seems the least, and the most, I can do for her.

Yet he - if indeed there is a he - cannot avoid the connection, can only see her as she is, coarsening, blurring, with no corrective memory.

Can she really fail to understand this?

But the failure, again, is mine.

I feel myself a tragic figure (yet another strategy, my God, of containment), whose tragedy is not blindness, but the inability to speak. Yet I am, as they say, in my element. A curious phrase, more apt than people realise.

It was frightening at first, of course, painful, as rebirths are. The dark was harsh, viscous, a velvet tourniquet. But it loosened, thinned to the point where I was able to swim in it. Swimming through the ether. I felt I had been liberated into my natural medium, had become amphibious. It was an alchemist's dream: the world made tangible, a world of pure texture.

How to explain that to the sighted, even to her, without it sounding a strategy for warding off pity? Like my half-joke about a moleskin suit.

Yet I wonder if my wife didn't instinctively understand; whether there wasn't a feeling on her part of a letting go, a releasing to its habitat of a creature she had nurtured and tended and thought she had tamed. I can't be sure.

It may be, to change the metaphor, that we could not have remained companion moons, even without the dark; that I was destined to become a planet to her sun, revolving round her in a slowly widening orbit. And though I depend on the regular return, I treasure the outward swing.

Each step of independence lengthened the orbit. Each exploration of the dark makes it harder to surface, much as I would like to, dripping with experience. Words are inadequate; experience isolates. As with the Steinway event.

I had a contract to tune a Steinway grand in Mayfair. The owners have since returned to the Near East and had it shipped out. But for those two years it became (yes) the focal point of my life. After three days of mostly school uprights, Thursday mornings were set aside - hallowed - to the Steinway.

My whole life is one of ritual: a precise counting of steps, an ordained sequence for every task, a set of talismanic cautions. But the Steinway ritual was of and for itself.

It stood, appropriately, on a wooden dais at the far end of the sitting room. I felt I should be wearing vestments. As it was, I took to wearing crepe-soled shoes in deference to the parquet. I would fold my stick and approach as to a bride. Run my fingers over the ebonised mahogany, following the swell. Lift the lid and bend forward to inhale. Take out my tuning fork like a divining rod.

It was not the first visit - I had in fact been going for nearly a year when it happened. I had finished tuning, was doodling with the keys. I ran down the keyboard to the Centre C. I hit the C again, harder. I heard it, felt it, as for the first time. The sound travelled through me, to earth deep in the magma, while above me it spiralled out to the chill interstellar spaces. I felt the overtones as the whorls and folds of my viscera.

Once, as a child, as I walked a field, I was caught in a shaft of afternoon light. I felt singled out, alone, an elect of one.

To describe the Steinway event in these terms is to make it sound mystical - which it wasn't. Nor did it change my life, except to lengthen the ellipse of my orbit.

Yet it may do so, after all; perhaps push me out of orbit

altogether. A few months ago, a phrase entered my head - one of those nonsensical phrases that buzz like blow flies until they drop away. 'The wives of the elect are the lonely.'

*

I insisted on the window cleaner doing the insides as well; to save her stretching. Took out a service contract on the central heating. Encouraged her to dress up when we went to Fortnum's for tea, and took longer than I need in the washroom. Began arriving home later.

Two months ago it began to bear fruit. She changed her perfume - a sample offer from Dickens and Jones, she told me. A sizeable sample, it appears. I have traced that too, and bought her a bottle. A smoothing of the way.

*

There exist in astronomy what are termed Black Holes - imploding stars crushed by their own weight, whose gravity prevents even light from escape.

Then there are Pulsars - collapsing stars, spinning to distraction, emitting a regular pulse, a heartbeat, of radiolight.

*

I turn off the television, listen for a distant car door, a whispered goodnight.

*

I lie here, throbbing; hoping, every so often, she will pick up my pulse.

Panurge 21
Great stories from first-timers **E.H. Solomon** and **Terry Tinthoff**. Involving trickery and trickery respectively. Also hilarious consumer rage from **Philip Sidney Jennings** and an angry chiropodist from **Ivy Bannister**.

Mark Lynch

Medea in Custody

I'll never leave here alive. It's so damp and musty in this subterranean cell I may die of influenza before they kill me. The food, the little I get, is vile. The guards are crude and bawdy, but not to me, I frighten them. I can hear them talking at their table - predictable filth bordering on the adolescent. But they wouldn't know any better. They were actually indentured farm labourers from the Peloponnese but the treasury promoted them to city jobs. Apparently this illusion of advancement eliminates discontent among the peasantry.

They're still not sure what to do with me. Jason is consulting magicians. The Attorney General thinks I should be stoned. The tabloids want to burn me at the stake. The philosophers say they couldn't even begin to pen an apology for me. Imagine - the highbrows and the lowbrows in agreement, thanks to me. A suffragette group in Naupolis has sent me a copy of Frankenstein with the message 'Read this!'. The group are hoping to send their self-tutored lawyer to see me, but three applications have been refused. One of the guards has told me this. He's not sympathetic, just looking for a reaction. He's huge, sweaty, handsome in a rough way. The kind of thug spoiled, urbane women have extra-marital sex with to convince themselves divorce is futile. That they're not cowards after all, the bank account is better than nothing. They can have scum like them. He has 'hate' tattooed on his knuckle. He says it's for fist-fucking the female prisoners. Only females? I say. Come on, this is Greece! He spits in my cell and goes to join his cronies in a card game. I've hurt his feelings.

It has come to this ...they call me a witch, a sorceress. Well, I wish my powers had permitted me to foresee the last few days. Jason, how I loved you the moment I saw you. He came to our provincial Caucasian city of Colchis to resupply the Argos. The Argonauts disembarked for a week of r & r. In every bar and café the Argonauts were fawned. They didn't have to go to the streets behind the agora to pay for sex. They were given it on a plate as though it were a form of hospitality.

My father, Aeetes, The King of Colchis, invited Jason to our palace for dinner. Jason arrived in uniform. I lusted after him certainly but by the week's end I equalled my lust with love. We had sex without inhibition. He shaved my pubes. I look forward to every evening, dinner on the balcony cooled by the Hellenic winds that brought the Argos to Colchis, Jason to me.

Jason, before you met me you were just another rabid social climber. Jason and the Argonauts! Ah! Jason was from white trash stock. His parents could barely afford to feed him! He was farmed out to relatives all over the Thessaly Highlands. Most of these in-laws resented this, what little luxuries they had were eroded by this boy with a gargantuan appetite. Jason had to sing for his supper, he chopped wood, ploughed the fields, every morning he rose with the crowing of the cock. But these relatives were never satisfied. They blocked his education, made him eat in the barn, told him to remember his place. When his cousins were sleeping he borrowed their school books and studied under the stars. By the time he was an adolescent his exceptional strength and beauty were becoming apparent. He earned more money than he had ever seen before. Posing for a Kouros at Trikala Art School, he learned some other things too. He ran away to Iolcos and spent three weeks as the harbour's prized rent boy. He made enough money to go to Athens, where he assumed a new identity. Elocution lessons, head to toe pampering at a gentleman's club, bespoke tailoring. For a season Jason was a star of Athenian society. Dinner party regular, acclaimed watercolourist of Halkidiki in May at a prestigious private gallery. But questions were being asked about his people, his school. Jason told everyone he was a poor scholar and hinted reluctantly at collapsed family investments. Jason had death certificates for his parents faked by a printer. When the man was counting his payment, a marble block smashed his skull. Jason had come too far to be in the pocket of some backstreet shyster. Jason returned to Thessaly, incognito. He visited the regional archives in Trikala posing as a genealogist, with a letter of introduction from an Athenian historian. He was given access to confidential files, but he was only interested in the dull rural documents. The archivists didn't trouble him as he recorded and validated his parents' death certificates.

When Jason returned to Athens after his 'hiking holiday' he was invited to the charity social event , a dinner for Pelias, King of Iolcos. Pelias was an icy man but could be a wit with the right people. As it happened the king was in good form that night and spoke to Jason for over an hour.

During the night Jason's sleep was disturbed by a caller. It was

170

Pelias. This king without an heir saw in Jason the ideal son. He made this proposal: Jason bring me the golden fleece and my throne is yours. Jason had a week to consider.

Iolcos was a third rate kingdom, with only a reserve army. Athenian society howled in derision. Wags urged Jason to sue for slander. But to Jason, Iolcos was a start. The laughter stopped when the challenge was accepted. Jason knew that if he returned with the golden fleece his kingdom's status would be unequalled in Hellas. The Hittites would tremble. The Alexandria Library would despatch a biographer. So impetuous was Jason, that he felt a biographer would be a grimmer enemy than a serpent of the Gods.

On the eve of his departure from Colchis to kill the serpent guarding the golden fleece, I begged him to take me with him. I told him I could help him. He said this was not a job for a woman. Even at that young age I felt the most endearing trait in men was their naivety. But I persisted, begging meekly. Jason, I can help - I can help. "With the cooking?" No, Jason, my magic. You'll need me. He knew what I was capable of but I think it was the physical benefits he was thinking of when he decided to take me.

Just as Jason had seen opportunity in Pelias' proposal, I too saw a different existence for myself, but I would have to fight for it. I had to go with Jason. If he managed to get the fleece by himself he certainly wouldn't return to Colchis with it. And if he failed he wouldn't be going anywhere.

My elopement must have enraged my father. He planned to marry me off to a Parthian prince. He actually dreamed of some trans-Caspian empire. But I knew the scenario would begin to appeal to him once his physician had begged him to calm down (Medea will be back!), he would then be forced to look at my actions rationally, and could afford a grin. I knew this because I am a more intellectually refined version of that man. Medea, niece of Asia Minor's greatest witch Circe, would defeat the serpent. Father knew this and he would be waiting for the returning Medea, minus my virginity but the golden fleece round my pussy would be more interesting to monarchs than any number of hymens. I didn't tell Jason to expect my father, the macho man was a bit of a worrier and even with my formulas he would need all the skill he could muster.

The sail across the Black Sea was calm, the wind never too harsh. When we reached the Crimea we docked for three days. The Argonauts went to the markets in Yalta to buy goats, lambs etc. for their sacrifices to the various cults they hoped would ensure the deliverance of the golden fleece. I shopped for vegetables, salted meats and fish, dried fruits and the herbs I needed for the potions. The harbour fortune tellers were predicting a week of calm weather, so we decided it was time to leave for the Sea of Azov.

The fortune teller's predictions were accurate, capable winds carried us, permitting the Argonauts to save their strength for our dangerous journey back to the Black Sea. We followed a north by northeast route, as legend directed. Just after dawn we saw a horizon of cliffs. As we approached we were astounded at their height. Even more astonishing they were perfectly vertical. It was mid-morning before we reached the cliffs. Properly speaking it was a single cliff, like a wall, like an expertly constructed dam. We had no option but follow the gentle curve of the geology. In little under an hour we found an opening the size of the door of a modest temple. We dropped anchor.

Jason and I used a small canoe to investigate the opening. Like Theseus we used rope to chart our way through this topographical maze. Lysander of Kalamata stood on the tiny platform at the cave opening holding the rope. After about 200 metres we came into a narrow gorge, blue skies overhead. The cave was a tunnel between the sea and the lair of the serpent. From what we could tell the gorge twisted and turned for miles. We had to return the Argos anyway for supplies and weapons but we were disconcerted that no length of rope would stretch to our destination.

That night aboard the Argos I prepared the balms and lotions that would kill the serpent. I put the formulas in terracotta jars and sealed them with wax. I also prepared phials of poison for Jason to coat the tips of his swords. I was reluctant to give him them before we reached the serpent's lair but there was the possibility of encountering something grizzly in the maze. Using vegetable dyes I produced some distemper to mark the walls of the gorge, to guide us back.

The next morning we were nervous, I had never tried my formulas on something as treacherous as a serpent of the underworld and Jason was untested in combat. We had no idea of how long this task would take but we were optimistic and took supplies for a month.

Although the Argonauts cheered when we slipped into the tunnel, they were clearly pensive. We paddled the canoe from sunrise to sunset. There was no current as such but periodic rock formations resulted in rapids. Luckily in the canyons the perfect vertical was rare and we scrambled over escarpments without too much difficulty even carrying the canoe. We managed to discard much of our food because the sunnier parts of the canyon were blessed with apple and pear trees. We also came across hot springs which allowed us to bathe properly. It was a very beautiful and mysterious place. The main canyon curved and wiggled interminably but the smaller gorges, always dead-ends, were ideal for tying up in the evening.

It took eight days for us to travel through the canyon. When we rounded the last corner we came into a semi-circle bay which lost itself on the steppe. Our hearts sank - we simply hadn't considered an overland journey. We didn't feel we could attempt that too. Just as our canoe beached Jason leapt out. As he turned to face me his face lost its colour. The serpent's cave was behind us! We had passed under it coming into the bay. The opening was huge, with a low ridge in front of it; it looked like the stage at Epidaurus.

Since the ridge was so flat it was easy to land and tie up the canoe. We couldn't risk spending the night here in case the beast was nocturnal. We would have to kill the thing now. I got out my deadliest potions. I soaked Jason's sword. Reminding him to avoid raising the sword above his head in case the formulas splashed, I too dipped my sword in the poison.

We went to the cave entrance and sang Bacchanalian hymns. The arrogance of it! The echo was lethal. We heard the roars of the stirring beast. Neither of us had considered the possibility of there being more than one serpent but the noise certainly suggested such a thing. Jason was hurriedly soaking more solution on his sword when the beast appeared. For the first time in my life I felt fear.

The thing can only be described as ...an...upside-down octopus. The serpent was quadripedal with an oval shaped body. Its eight tentacles pointed to the sky - on each a roaring head with a mouth of hungry teeth. Our only advantages were the fact that the beast was slow moving and to injure us it would have to lower its head to our level. The serpent didn't have horns so it would have to come very close. On its first few attacks we were inappropriately positioned to strike. We had no option but to run.

The serpent lunged a single head toward Jason. He used his sword like a spear and managed to hit the creature in the eye. I sprayed another face with my formula. It roared in agony and lost its balance.

Jason managed to wound another head while I was pouring poison over its underbelly. As I was about to run I saw the scales dissolve under my merciless formula. And there it was, the heart. Like some epic oarsman of a battleship the heart pumped to and fro. I didn't hesitate - I delved deep with my sword. Until only the handle was exposed. A torrent of blood soaked me. The serpent didn't even have time to feel the pain. It was totally inanimate. I just looked at it in disbelief and then out of the corner of my eye I see Jason jumping around like a half-wit beheading every tentacle. Eventually he realises the beast is dead and says: "I've killed it!"

We didn't want to stay in this place so we headed for the lair. About 100 paces into the cave along a perfect path we found the golden fleece of the ram of the Gods. It was placed on a circular marble tray, illuminated by a mounted torch that seemed to burn without resource. For our convenience there was a white silk sack waiting there since the dawn of myth for this moment. I held the sack open while Jason used his arm to sweep it up. He looked fulfilled but in a childish almost pathetic way. Once the golden fleece was in the sack, the torch began to fade. Before we left the cave it had died completely. Maybe we should have been frightened but we weren't. Yes, we knew the Gods were watching us but the fact that we were unharmed proved, to me anyway, that we were among their number.

We hadn't noticed that the serpent had smashed the canoe with one of its rear heads. Jason panicked. I put some of my balsam on the sack. If centuries ago Phrixus flew on the ram to the Gods, we would fly to the Argos on its shorn fleece. He was nervous and uncertain but once the sack began to levitate he grabbed it, as if it was a whore. The golden fleece knew where it was going; truth to be told I hadn't considered navigation. I was more interested in that unrepeatable Icarian dream. We flew over the beautiful canyon maze; as the crow flies it was a short distance, only the twists and turns had multiplied our journey. Soon the sea of Azov could be seen, the Argos shimmering in the last of the afternoon sun. The golden fleece landed painlessly - there was delirium on board. In the safety of the hull each of the Argonauts gazed in disbelief at the prize, taking a single strand of golden fleece as an heirloom.

We left the sea of Azov by darkness. It was precarious but we knew we had to reach the open anonymity of the Black Sea to keep our trophy from pillage. The supplies we had left would enable us to reach Thessalonica without stopping.

My brother threw a spanner in the works. My father had a fleet of lackeys patrolling an area 50 miles from the Bosphorus and father had allowed Apsyrtus to go on a scouting mission. A big mistake. When he had seen us on the horizon he ordered the craft to head for the Argos rather than report back to the fleet. Jason was about to have the Argos ram him but I had other ideas. Of course I knew my father would be waiting but I didn't think Apsyrtus would donate himself to me. I loved my brother but by token of his sex he had condemned me to considering kitchen menus and not documents of state. I was not going to allow my father to take the golden fleece and make me a shamed spinster daughter. An example of the folly of feminine ambition.

Oh no, Apsyrtus was going to be our ticket to the Hellespont, because I would be holding a knife at his throat.

My father came to the Argos in a canoe and told me to cut out my foolishness. His very words. He seemed more concerned with the golden fleece than his golden son.

Heirs are startlingly replaceable as far as men are concerned. My father returned to his ship threatening to attack. We knew he would. When he returned to his ship he raised his hand to signal the attack. Then I kissed Apsyrtus on his lips and plunged a dagger into his heart. That way he wouldn't feel the pain of what I was about to do to him. My father would have to retrieve his son's body or face eternal shame ... so I thought I would make it a little bit harder for him. I put my dagger at the corner of Apsyrtus' mouth and ripped as far as I could. I cut off the nose and the ears. And I gouged out his eyes before smashing his skull with a mallet. I threw the bits in the water like a somnambulist suburban housewife throwing stale bread on the lawn for the birds. But then I saw the panic in my father's fleet. Curses awaited them. The gates of Hades opened, two ships collided in disbelief at my actions. Knowing their weapons were useless they deafeningly bombarded me with verbal abuse. They longed to get their hands on me but knew those hands would be better employed collecting the remains of Apsyrtus. By the time I threw the last of him in the sea I had the radiance of a maid of honour throwing confetti. Now the chaos had set my father's fleet aflame. The carnage! It was mine. I had done this ...this. This. Me. Medea. I had destroyed these arrogant men. Omnipotence. Me. Medea. The Sea of Marmara would never forget me. Now I knew the power of my magic and moreover the magic of my power - no more pulling rabbits out of hats at kindergartens. Now my civic duties would take me into an altogether different sphere.

Settlements on the narrow shores must have seen the slaughter, for the news spread like wildfire. Like the plague. Until we sailed into the Aegean we frequently saw crowds on the cliff staring, only staring never waving. The rest of the journey was peaceful, even the sirens thought twice about tangling with Medea.

When we reached Iolcos we were greeted by a vast crowd and a military parade. Pelias led us in a chariot along the corniche.

After this my confidence soared. Three days after our return Jason announced our wedding plans. The wedding was to be in August and when we returned from our honeymoon in Memphis (where we stayed in a villa with a view of the pyramids) Jason would succeed to the throne and I would be his queen. The provincial girl was left behind. Medea was now an urbane woman with a hint of foreign mystery. My exquisite taste, I wore only couture, led to the chroniclers detailing my every move.

The weeks before the wedding were filled with banquets and state dinners. I was more of an attraction, Jason said, than the golden fleece in the Iolcos Institute of Art. After one such evening of revelry I couldn't sleep for excitement and, I admit, self-admiration. I paced around my suite of rooms in the palace. I drank brandy on my balcony but the Meltemi had stopped blowing and it was too sticky to linger. So I planned to read myself to sleep when I heard a metallic noise in the hall. The servants wouldn't dare make a noise. Obviously someone was up to no good. I went to the door and listened. I heard footsteps, but they were getting fainter. I waited a minute then opened my door and there at the end of the hall I saw them, clearly recognising the ungainly gait of Pelias. They were heading for Jason's suite, I was sure. This is why the King, God rest his Soul, insisted we had separate quarters. Not the prude we thought he was. Pelias was going to put my love to the sword - denying him, us, the throne. I went back into my bedroom for my dagger and some of my potions.

As I guessed, Pelias and his bumboys were outside Jason's door. Pelias was talking like something out of a potboiler: "Hermes you take him from the right, Luco you the left. Kythron as soon as he is captive, gouge out his eyes. I don't want him to see me. Being a considerate man I'll spare him the knowledge that his heroics were in vain. We'll let him die with some dignity." But Medea was behind him in the darkness! And just as he began sniggering I said: "Pelias, you won't die with dignity". I plunged my dagger into his spine. He screamed in agony. His boys stood frozen in disbelief, in terror. Jason appeared with his sword. Pelias' three trusted hitmen faced a death beyond their nightmares. They lay on the floor wounded but fully conscious. Using our hands and daggers we ripped out their hearts. Only our laughter was louder than their screams. We were like crazed prospectors who had just discovered gold.

The servants interrupted us. Get back to bed, I told them. We made love in the blood, in the corruption physical and spiritual. At dawn I called the harbour master and told him to send the shark fishermen to the palace to collect some bait.

We were the monarchs of Iolcos. We brought forward our wedding and declared a national holiday. Admittedly the citizens of Iolcos didn't celebrate our wedding as spontaneously as I would have liked, but there was a rally on the stock market.

Our hands-on authority impressed the financial community. Iolcos and Thessaly, which Jason had annexed since he was born there, experienced five years of double digit economic growth. We were now the most talked about couple in the world and we decided to take advantage of this. Jason convened a meeting on the chic island of Hydra. Here he put forward my idea, as his own of course, for the formation of a pan-Hellenic union. The Spartans were instantly keen, a disappointment since Sparta was now little more than an olive oil republic. Jason acted cool, which convinced Argos and Athens to put the idea to their respective senates. Jason also announced we were sending our troops into Thebes, gripped by a rancid civil war. They could have kept on killing each other for all we cared but in geopolitics strategy is everything. The Thebans thanked us by joining by the fold. Argos and Athens were impressed and followed suit. Hellas was ours, almost. The stubborn Corinthians were holding onto their independence like a dog holds on to a bone. Corinth was exploiting its unique geographical location by building, at immense financial cost, a canal and had announced its intention of becoming a free port. All the Levantine merchant fleets had committed themselves to its use, ensuring its success. With the canal the merchants could sail to Calabria without putting themselves at the mercy of the fierce winds and the ruthless Tripoltanian pirates. Clearly, the inclusion of Corinth was vital. King Creon's rebuttal enraged Jason but I knew in this instance we would have to swallow our pride for the sake of our long term ambitions.

Jason visited Corinth over a dozen times in two years. Eventually a treaty of economic union was drafted. Sovereignty was still not negotiable. Still it was progress.

On hearing of this I decided to pay him a visit. Our two sons loved the sea and I took them with me, detouring to see Thira and swim off Naxos. The trip was a delight and it inevitably left me aroused. When we arrived, incognito, we went straight to the embassy compound to see Jason. He was at the Ambassador's residence, having a nap. The aides insisted he was not to be disturbed. Not by his wife? Especially not by his wife they were thinking. You can imagine the nature of this 'nap'. Enraged though I was, there would be no scene in front of the underlings. I had to give Jason his place, even if it was of my making. And anyway, when the cheap nonsense he sought thrills with appeared, I had to banish a laugh. I turned a blind eye to this misdemeanour.

But two days later I discovered the tart was King Creon's daughter, Creusa. I lost control. Even a tabloid astrologer could have foretold my future. Jason had decided to dump me in favour of this slut. Obviously this was the only way he could have Corinth under his belt, and he didn't think twice.

The swine came down to the compound to try to pacify me - not because I was sobbing, oh no, but because I had destroyed a Minoan vase on the head of a permanent secretary. The spiel he gave me! He still loved me! Couldn't I see the logic of his move! Our sons would inherit a pan-Hellenic empire. They would dominate Asia Minor - Egypt, the Levant, ours. Surely you, Medea, of all people can see this? I saw it all too clearly - so brightly it gave me neuralgia. I was to become a glorified babysitter while Jason, the understudy, was to have the odeon of power all to himself. Even in the most intense moments of my fury I kept hearing the Armenian proverb one of our servants in Colchis favoured: 'In a house with two mistresses the floor will not be swept'. This was the reality of the situation and I had to act.

I still can't decide if Jason was actually naive enough to believe our sons would sit on a throne. Creon would only tolerate my boys until Jason's seed had given Creusa a son. Then my sons would have an accident - on a mountain road, diving in shallow lagoons. Something. Jason had helped me beget them yet he had sealed their doom.

The fracas became the talk of Corinth. Creon turned up at the embassy. The guards insisted the ambassador must be here to meet him or protocol would be breached. Creon threatened to have them executed on the spot. Creon and his troops came banging at my door. I opened it - instantly, Medea the Meek was born.

I didn't give him time to speak. Oh, Creon, King of Corinth, please let me see my sons one last time. Just this once, before I leave for Colchis. I'm leaving for a land where I'll be shunned. Memories are all that will accompany me, please permit them to be pleasant. Let them visit me tomorrow, Creon. This is all I ask before going back to my homeland. The ambassador's chariot will return them to you tomorrow night and then I'll leave Corinth. Even with my magic I've always struggled to keep up with Jason, with my own eyes I've witnessed him stretching mortality to its limit. Creusa has chosen wisely. Creon, please? And what did he say?

Medea, you surprise me. Despite everything you know your place.

True, Creon. Look how my breasts sag. The wrinkles - age has claimed me and is calling ever louder. But Jason gets more majestic with age. In every tomb of the unknown soldier, Kouros after Kouros, I see the torso of Jason. What a beautiful couple they will be! Oh, Creon, let me spend a day with his sons, whose destiny is now out of my control. Medea, across the known world I am renowned for my just and thoughtful rule, so I will allow you to have custody of Jason's sons for one day. If you are still in Corinth tomorrow night at the time of the curfew bell you will be put to the sword. And I'll deserve it, Creon. I couldn't resist that. Creon, euthanasia case, threaten me!

My sons arrived from Creon's palace just after dawn. The excitement in their squeals aroused the compound. We had breakfast of yogurt, fruit and banana bread. When I saw their innocent smiles I knew my plan, as grim as it was, would have to be carried out. I wasn't going to allow the viper of fear to devour their insides while some elite palace guard battered their faces beyond recognition. We spent the morning at the gymnasium watching the boxing. At lunchtime we returned to the embassy, where I called a driver to take the boys to Princess Creusa. The night before I had coated one of my finest gowns with a transparent balm of terrifying potency. I packaged the dress beautifully, even quoted Sappho on the gift card!

179

This is for you, Jason's young bride, beautiful guardian of his sons. The little darlings were reluctant to leave me but I coaxed them, telling them how happy this little errand would make me. Leave the package in front of the princess, I told them, let her open it. On no account do either of you touch the gift, on no account. Once she sees the beauty of this gift she will forget you're there. Just bow as normal and retreat, a driver will be waiting to bring you back to Mum for an afternoon of checkers. You would like that?

When they returned they told me that the princess was entranced by my gown. Did you leave before she tried it on? Yes, Mum. I had some lunch ready for them. Drink your milk! I had laced it with a sedative. Within five minutes they were slumped across the table. I moved them to my bedroom and laid them down gently. I kissed and hugged them both. For the last times I ran my hands through their silky hair, desperately trying not to contemplate the manly destinies fate was denying them. I put pillows on their faces. Now all I could see was their beautiful limbs. I put my knees on one side of the mattress, leaned across to the other and put my hands under the bedstead. Once I had a good grip I softly put my weight across them. I stared at the wall, I gritted my teeth. Then they began to kick. Oh, Zeus, take them, please, embrace them, Zeus. I longed to stop that madness, hug them, sing them a lullaby. But I knew I couldn't. At last, the kicking stopped. Their death was even longer than their birth.

I lifted the pillows. Oh, their faces had such beauty. Their eyes were tightly closed, their mouths wide open. They looked just as they always did on those summer evenings when I brought them back from the beaches of Euboea, exhausted after a day's swimming. What beauty! No blood, no bruises. Zeus was glad to have them join the angels.

Then the door! Destiny could be seen on the horizon. A messenger was gasping for breath. Medea, he said, eventually, you must flee! Must? Oh, Medea, don't take that tone, not now. Why? What has happened? You know. You must know. No! Tell me! That gown you sent - the princess cried with joy when she saw it. She ran into her chamber with her attendants. I must try this on immediately! she said. She was back shortly. No-one in the palace had ever known her to dress so quickly. We gasped when we saw her! Radiant? A goddess. Creon arrived, and when he saw her, well, he flushed with pride. And then, oh no, it's unrepeatable. Oh,

Medea, what I've just seen! Tell me. Please, tell me. Creon hugged Creusa. Fair daughter, he said. And then ...as they hugged ...Medea, don't make me! Go on man. The threads of the gown turned into ...snakes! Yes? Yes, snakes. They wrapped themselves round their legs. The biggest snake must have strangled them. The others gnawed at their flesh. Did they scream? Scream, Medea! The yells were like swords! The royal guards couldn't get at the snakes without injuring Creon and Creusa. By the time they realised it would be better to kill them it was too late to spare them their howling death agonies. The royals disappeared under the snakes, like a fish in seaweed. Then the snakes simply vanished before our eyes! There was nothing! It was like a magic trick Medea. A magic trick? No? Go to the kitchen and tell the cook I said you can have a feed.

And now it was Corinth's turn to tremble at the actions of Medea. The servants and diplomats who had spent the day before sneering were in shock. Creon, Creusa and my beautiful sons - all dead. Like navigators of the epics, I have journeyed far from my homeland and made my maps in blood. Philosophers in their symposia shudder at the mention of my name. Philosophers, like explorers, are constrained by natural barriers. The intellect is as restraining as a desert or mountains. But I have explored humiliation and revenge with a zest and zeal that would exasperate Hera.

Jason is once again nothing, but only in my eyes. Corinth sobs with him. I am derided as a determined dockside groupie who didn't let go! Me! My lineage is from the Gods. Yet no jury will belittle itself by hearing my story. The executioners find me too distasteful. Their union wants to import an Albanian. The wardens are amused by this.

The pathetic woman lawyer has sent me a letter of Frankenstein theories! I'm the brains and the monster. Jason is a weakling. Even the Argonauts know this but since Jason was brave enough to marry me, he gets a gold star for valour. It's quite sad, I think.

It's almost a relief to be here. The paranoia, the doubt, the food tasting, the exhaustive enquiries about even the most menial servants - that's all finished. Great love must lead to an end such as this. Jason, I wouldn't live without you. It's as true now as when I said it. Your power, your position, I gave them to you, they are mine. I want them.

I paced the room. Then he came. He ignored me, he ran straight to the bedroom. I heard him sob. He left the bodies for the military police. His face had no future. He had been my husband, now he was my victim. Like many men of his position he saw himself in his sons, and was flattered. Now I know he never grasped their existence, their individuality. Two juvenile bodies lay there, my fingerprints were everywhere. But the facts tell a different story - he killed them. I killed him, no matter how long he lives.

When he came from the bedroom, what did the grieving father say to me? What did I say to him? I don't remember, I truly don't remember. Now... now there's no need to remember. All my life I have seen men do anything, everything just for power. Their motives have been feeble yet the carnage intense. My sons were nothing in that game. To the aristocracy, the civil servants, the financiers, the traders, even the peasants, I am the culprit. I am the monster, acting alone, compulsively in a marital squabble. The men I have spent my life fighting and often didn't know it, have caught me. I thought I had been walking a tightrope, but all the time it was a strand of their web. I have let them have me. I let the military police take me without a struggle. I have always been used to bodyguards so when they led me out of the compound, I didn't feel like a captive. I was accustomed to spectators cheering, but that day an angry crowd shouted abuse.

I am a prisoner, put in this cage. Here I have more freedom than I have ever had. But my liberty won't last. My future is in Hades. There I will spend my death being eternally pursued and tormented by vengeful ghosts.

Peter Lewis

Quartet & Arab Women

Djura: *The Veil of Silence,* hb £14.95
Aïcha Lemsine: *The Chrysalis,* hb £14.95
Sabiha Khemir: *Waiting in the Future for the Past to Come,* hb
£13.95
Hanan al-Shaykh: *Women of Sand and Myrrh,* pb £6.95
all published by Quartet

Does the recent history of British publishing support or undermine
putative charges of 'insular isolationism'? The literary worlds of
many Commonwealth countries are very vocal on this point. The
constant complaint is that while they are expected to know what is
happening in the so-called 'metropolitan centre' (Britain or even
London) and to take notice of it, the metropolitan centre itself shows
little sign of reciprocating. Ironically, the study of 'Commonwealth
Literature' or 'Postcolonial Literatures' or 'New Literatures in
English' is much more widespread in several Continental countries
than in anglophone Britain. The parallel African and Caribbean
Writers Series published by Heinemann since the 1960s are
admirable, but they are geared to the international rather than the
British market.

For many years John Calder and Marion Boyars were the leading
avant-garde publishers in London, first under a joint imprint and
later under separate ones, and they made great efforts to introduce
new writing from abroad, especially Europe, into Britain. Yet when
Calder recently decamped to Paris, it was with a sense of
hopelessness about both the state of literary publishing and the
closed, reactionary intellectual climate in Britain. Apart from
Heinemann's two Series, silver linings may be hard to find. But
despite Calder's pessimism, Quartet Books have been pursuing what
may be called the Calder-Boyars enterprise with considerable
imagination. In 1993, for example, Quartet published fiction and
non-fiction titles translated from a number of European languages,
including Romanian and Swedish as well as French, Spanish and
Russian. In spite of having high reputations in their own countries,
most of these authors are unknown in Britain, although the list does
include Julien Green, translations of whose fiction first appeared

decades ago.

Even more enterprising and unusual, however, has been Quartet's commitment to what it calls the 'Middle East', but which includes most of the Arab world. To judge from translations that have recently appeared, writing in such countries as Morocco and Algeria is flourishing as never before. Yet recognition in this country is barely perceptible. The situation in France is significantly better, partly because of the French colonial connection and its francophone legacy. So far the Arab writers who have attracted attention have been men, but among recent Quartet titles are a group of books by young women from North Africa and the Middle East (specifically the Maghreb and Lebanon), whose primary purpose is to explore and give voice to the experience of women in their cultures, something virtually impossible until fairly recently because of the absence of educational possibilities. None of them is writing feminist polemics exactly, but all share a feminist perspective since a major theme of these books is inevitably the historical and continuing oppression of women in their societies.

Of the four books under consideration, the most outspokenly feminist is the only non-fiction title, *The Veil of Silence* by Djura, the name adopted by a highly successful Algerian singer in France and leader of the group Djurdjura, which performs Berber songs. Written in French (English translation by Dorothy S. Blair, who specializes in writers from the Maghreb) and first published in Paris in 1990, this autobiography is highly selective in that it concentrates on Djura's struggle to emancipate herself from what she calls 'the crushing yoke of an outdated "tradition"'. What provoked Djura into writing the book as an act of exorcism was a violent, even murderous attack in 1987 on her French husband and herself, even though pregnant, by two members of her own family, a brother and niece. Until this traumatic event, Djura had expressed her hopes for better conditions for women, especially from her own Berber background, through her songs, without revealing directly the pain and suffering involved in her own struggle. In the book, however, she abandons such restraint and obliqueness, lifting the veil of silence to reveal the immense pressures on her to conform. Djura's 'crime', after all, was to have successfully liberated herself from ancestral customs rooted in Islamic patriarchy. In telling her own story, Djura is speaking for all those women 'who keep silent out of fear, who seek a decent life while they are forbidden even to exist.'

Djura's early childhood in the Berber village of Ifigha at the foot of the Djurdjura mountains was dominated by the positive figure of her step-grandmother, Setsi (Granny) Fatima, who brought her up since her own parents were extremely disappointed that she was not a boy. This was her first 'crime'. Gender prejudices began at birth. It was through Fatima that Djura acquired her love for Berber festivities and music, the inspiration for her own songs. From the relatively independent and courageous Fatima, described as 'a force of nature', Djura also learned about the secret world of Berber women while living in a state of subjugation to their men. Djura's fairly happy life with Fatima in Algeria was disrupted when she joined her family in France where her brutish father had become one of the many badly paid immigrant workers from North Africa recruited during the 1950s to do the dirty jobs, like West Indians and Asians in Britain.

Living in a Western country, especially during the 1960s, brought out Djura's nascent rebelliousness and she was constantly at odds with her family. In being torn between two cultures, she shared the experience of innumerable postwar immigrants, but for an adolescent girl and then a young woman from an Islamic culture, the stresses were much greater than for her brothers and other male contemporaries. Intent on developing her intellectual and artistic interests in France and on pursuing a career, she was subjected to intense patriarchal demands to do only what her family approved of. She discovered at first hand to what extent women who had suffered under this system were responsible for perpetuating, rather than resisting, it, as though determined to make their daughters endure what they had done. At one stage, Djura was actually imprisoned by her family in an attempt to force her to comply with their wishes. Yet in spite of everything, Djura has not turned her back completely on her cultural heritage but has tried to hang onto the positive elements she identifies within it, especially associated with her memories of Fatima. The aim of the performing troupe Djurdjura is to sing out loud what their mothers would only murmur under their breath.

Djura's highly dramatic life story sometimes reads like a thriller. *The Chrysalis* by another French-language writer from Algeria, Aïcha Lemsine (also translated by Dorothy S. Blair), is a novel but sometimes gives the impression that it is partly or obliquely autobiographical. Originally published by Editions des Femmes in 1976, *The Chrysalis* has helped to secure Lemsine's literary reputation in France, where she was elected Arab Woman of the

Year in 1984 and won the Mediterranean African Literature Prize in 1985. She is well known for her journalism as well as her fiction, and currently works for the *Washington Report* and a number of Algerian newspapers. In *The Veil of Silence* Djura does not employ the symbol of the chrysalis, but what she exposes when lifting the veil is indeed the chrysalis in which women have been imprisoned by Islam and patriarchy. Lemsine's novel concentrates on the attempts by two Algerian women from successive generations in the twentieth century to break out of the chrysalis. The narrative spans several decades, beginning during the interwar years and ending after the anti-colonial war that brought Algeria independence from France.

The historical sweep of *The Chrysalis* allows Lemsine to clarify the rapid social changes in mid-century Algeria by exploring the many differences between the expectations and possibilities of the two generations. Whereas the clash between tradition and modernity in *The Veil of Silence* is precipitated by Djura's move to France, in *The Chrysalis* it is contained within the Islamic culture of Algeria. The central figure in the earlier part of the novel is Khadidja, trapped in an unsatisfactory marriage and subjected to various barbarities taken for granted in village life, especially mistreatment by her mother-in-law. This was still a society in which a girl who lost her virginity before marriage was very likely to be killed by her own family to purge the shame. Despite the patriarchal oppression endemic in her society, Khadidja gradually becomes sufficiently assertive to take a stand against her husband when he plans to take a third wife. Khadidja's struggle against male domination necessarily takes place inside tight boundaries, yet in making her voice heard at all in a society in which women are expected to endure everything silently she bravely asserts her independence against the normal confines. In some respects Khadidja is comparable to Setsi Fatima in *The Veil of Silence*, but Djura says little about her grandmother's early life whereas Lemsine describes Khadidja's life as a young woman, wife and mother in detail.

With the passage of time, the emphasis in *The Chrysalis* shifts to Khadidja's stepdaughter Faïza, who from an early age is intellectually curious and a bookworm, reading English and French classics as well as Marx. Academically brilliant, she benefits from an education usually reserved for boys and eventually studies medicine in Algiers. Such a possibility was unthinkable for women like Khadidja. It would seem that Faïza has emerged fully from the chrysalis and flown off on her own wings. Fate, however, strikes an ugly blow when her fiance is killed before their proposed wedding, leaving Faïza pregnant with their son. In a traditional society this is a scandalous state of affairs, likely to bring shame on her whole family. It is Khadidja, acting out of womanly solidarity with her stepdaughter, who redeems the situation and defies convention. Faïza remains in her home village to practise as a doctor, but like Khadidja she is able to cling to her hard-won independence.

For the English translation of her novel (complete with Glossary), Lemsine has written an informative introduction, 'From Yesterday to Today', which clarifies her aims and describes the initial response to *The Chrysalis*. She conceived it as an *ijtihad*, meaning an 'intellectual effort in the search for truth'. After independence, Algeria became, for Lemsine, a country built on a fundamental contradiction enshrined in its 1976 Constitution. In the spirit of its Marxist revolutionaries it adopted 'egalitarian socialism', but it also adopted Islam as a state religion. Women were simultaneously equal and unequal. The price Lemsine paid for demystifying this paradox in the novel was to have the book banned in Algeria, even though it was warmly received in other Maghrebin countries (Tunisia, Morocco) as well as France. Lemsine makes a fierce attack on the rulers of Algeria since 1962 and the 'so-called left-wing intellectuals' whose complicity in 'disastrous state policies' has, ironically, stimulated the upsurge of Islamic fundamentalism. The main victims throughout have, as usual, been women. Lemsine makes it clear that her quarrel is not with Islam as such, especially its liberal Sunni form, but with a fundamentalism that makes life a 'living hell' for women and a return to virtual slavery.

The most extraordinary feature of Sabiha Khemir's first novel, *Waiting in the Future for the Past to Come*, is that it does not appear in translation from French or Arabic but was written in English. Khemir is Tunisian, but after graduating from the University of Tunis she moved to London to obtain two higher degrees in Islamic Art and Archaeology. Since making an important archaeological discovery in Cairo, she has become an acknowledged authority on Islamic art, but she also works as a book illustrator, mainly for French publishers. In turning to fiction recently, Khemir is moving into the territory Lemsine began to explore nearly twenty years ago, but the approaches of the two novelists are very different. Like *The Chrysalis, Waiting in the Future for the Past to Come* focuses on the experience of Maghrebin women over a substantial period of time - about thirty years in this case - but is decidedly poetic in conception when compared with Lemsine's realistic novel. Whereas Lemsine's narrative is strictly chronological with occasional jumps forward in time, Khemir's is much more fluid as imagination and reality interweave. Her novel aspires to myth in a way that Lemsine's more polemical book does not.

Instead of being a conventional first-person narration, the recollections of the narrator Amina incorporate stories heard and overheard, whether from life or folk culture. Indeed the distinction can be blurred, since in Amina's words:

> I will tell you about reality until I reach the boundaries of credibility, then I will tell you fiction. And I will tell you fiction until I reach the boundaries of imagination, then I will tell you about reality. I will tell you about mysterious realities and real mysteries. I will tell you about the mysteries of realities until I can no longer be credible then I will tell you fiction. I will tell you about real dreams and dreamy realities. I will tell you what I know until what I don't know finds it way out.

From diverse threads Amina weaves a tapestry which at times recalls *The Arabian Nights*, yet there remains a strong core of realism in her account of life in the small Tunisian town of Korba as well as her transition to university in Tunis. Running through the novel is the theme of women's changing experiences and expectations in post-independence Tunisia, and as in *The Chrysalis* there is a collision between tradition and modernity, but there is also a sense of new life emerging from the old without a radical severing of connections with the past. In this way *Waiting in the Future for the Past to Come* is more celebratory than *The Chrysalis.*

The fourth and longest of the books, Hanan al-Shaykh's *Women of Sand and Myrrh*, first came out in English translation (by Catherine Cobham) as a hardback in 1989 and is now available in paperback. Following the success of an earlier work of fiction, *The Story of Zahra* (translated in 1986), *Women of Sand and Myrrh* received plenty of comment in 1989, especially in the USA, including praise from the prominent literary critic, historian of cultural imperialism, and Palestinian intellectual, Edward Said. Marginally the oldest of these four women writers, al-Shaykh grew up in Beirut before studying in Cairo, and subsequently launched herself into a journalistic career, which has made her famous in the Arab world.

Before moving to London, where she now lives, al-Shaykh spent some time on the Arabian Gulf, and it is this experience that lies behind the writing of *Women of Sand and Myrrh*.

The setting is an unnamed Gulf state, which readers will probably equate with Saudi Arabia, although al-Shaykh's refusal to be specific indicates that she is not writing about the condition of women in only one country. The novel is divided into four main sections, each with its own female narrator, the first of whom returns at the end to supply a brief Epilogue. Although these women's paths cross and re-cross, each of them has her own story to tell and they are all very different, coming as they do from a variety of social and cultural backgrounds. For example, the first, Suha, is from Lebanon and has fled from the war there, while the third, Suzanne, is an American whose husband is working temporarily in the Gulf. Tamr and Nur, on the other hand, come from the unnamed state, but both have lived abroad, especially Tamr.

Al-Shaykh is primarily a psychological novelist, exploring the inner lives of her main characters as they try to define themselves through their relationships with women and men, including their husbands, in a social context that inhibits their potential for development and fulfilment. The prevailing ideology is patriarchal, yet in spite of this restrictive and oppressive environment these women struggle towards some form of liberation. Tamr in particular is committed to educational self-advancement. Al-Shaykh is more concerned with sexuality than the writers discussed earlier and brings out the yearnings, tensions and frustrations of her four narrators. Living in a sexually puritanical society, Nur still manages to assert her sensuality and, as in her seduction of Suha into a brief lesbian liaison, is erotically manipulative. In Suzanne's case, her affair with a local man seriously threatens her marriage. Even when exploring the most intimate areas of her characters' lives, al-Shaykh avoids scoring easy feminist points although a powerful feminist consciousness certainly underlies *Women of Sand and Myrrh*.

Without a publishing house in London committed to issuing a substantial number of books in translation, at least three of these four books would almost certainly not be available. In most Continental countries, even large ones like Germany with plenty of writers of their own, books translated from English are in abundant supply. The reverse is not true. To its credit, Quartet has been doing a great deal to rectify this state of affairs, and its advocacy of writers from the Arab world is particularly to be applauded. Very little normally

189

reaches us from these countries, and this is most regrettable when literary activity there is flourishing as never before. Perhaps the next time an Arab writer is awarded the Nobel Prize for Literature, Brits will not look totally mystified and resort to snideries about positive discrimination being exercised in favour of unheard-of second-raters from the Third World.

BRIEF EDITORIAL NOTES

1. Panurge is now *twice* the size but only about 15% dearer! I am getting at least twice as much publishable work as in 1987 and have had to take the obvious practical measure. Blame/thank also the hellish recession in literary fiction publishing and the pitiful number of short fiction outlets in the U.K.

2. We are now a fiction anthology (published by Panurge Publishing) rather than a magazine. **The contents and editorial policy of Panurge remain what they always have been (NEW WRITING BY NEW WRITERS) but this change in designation helps with shop sales, distribution etc.** We still come out every April and October and consider work all the year round. **All fiction is unsolicited** and all articles commissioned as before. The issues now have titles and Panurge 21 (October 1994) will be called *Debatable Lands*.

3. We now have both Development Grant Funding and Franchise Funding from the Arts Council. Our grateful thanks for their generosity and confidence in us. It means we can afford to do double issues for the next year or so at any rate. But please keep on re-subscribing as promptly as possible. You, the subscribers, are our lifeblood, and don't forget that we depend on you first and foremost.

4. Let us know what you think of the new look anthology and indeed about anything to do with Panurge past or present. Have a good summer...

John Murray, Brampton, 1994

Stephanie Hale

Ivy

For some time now, I have been seeing myself in multiples. Like those cut-outs you make at school from folded newspaper. There was once one of me; but this doubled and redoubled and went on multiplying. There are now sixteen of me. I remember their beginning; I cannot fathom their end.

*

The producer was so definite about the task ahead, so sure of its success.

"It's a comedy about the Career Girl," he said. "We'll treat today's issues. Her dilemmas. The conflicts between work and home."

Daragh Smart stared at me with goldfish eyes; the black pupils dilating with excitement and confidence.

"I want it to be representative of how women are," he said. "Not the idealised frosted look. This woman will have brains as well as looks."

I couldn't quite believe my luck; the chance to write for television. I was already looking around the office, wondering how I would fit in; casting sly glances at the staff in the graphics department. There was no rush, no hurry - just a continued quiet tapping, as fingers pecked at keyboards; gently clicking, clucking, like battery hens.

A woman walked towards us, carrying a tray of china. She was immaculate, wearing a cashmere jumper in a muted plum. Her neck was heavy with gold necklaces; her fingers flashed with gems. She was carrying a fat jug of filtered coffee and jangling hand-painted mugs. She poured thick black liquid into our cups, smiling; silent as a Genie. She vanished with the same quiet ease; leaving only the scent of perfume.

"How much control do I have over the script?" I asked.

"Oh, it's negotiable," said Daragh, waving his hands nonchalantly. "We meet every morning to discuss the plot."

The project was a bit of a gamble, but he had been nursing the idea for years. Daragh said he had just been waiting for the right writer to come along; someone with the skill and talent to do it justice. It was just a matter of writing the pilot programme and selling it to the highest bidder. He was aiming for Channel 4; but was prepared to sell it abroad if necessary. However, he was certain of its success. The series would be set in a television newsroom and its heroine would be a reporter. The format would be innovative; actors and actresses would speak over cartoon graphics just like *Roger Rabbit*. It was just the sort of thing he could imagine on late-night television.

"Do you have a partner?" Daragh asked.

"What's the relevance?" I said.

"The last woman we had here left to start a family. It would be nice to think you would be with us for a while."

"No," I said. "No such plans."

When I was offered the job, I took it without hesitation. This was my lucky break; the chance I had been waiting for. I had been writing for newspapers for four years and lived on dreams of script writing. I looked out through the bars of the venetian blinds - on berthing ships in the city docks, on vast crates and cranes, on the black swirl and curl of marbled water - and liked the view.

*

In the week that followed, I started getting nauseous spells. I felt dizzy and tired, and I was sure my back had started to swell. My skin pressed against my clothes, so that I had to wear loose blouses and baggy jumpers. My shoulders ached from the weight of it.

But I wasn't too alarmed. I could see nothing when I looked over my shoulder in the mirror. The doctor seemed unconcerned too. She thought it was psychosomatic; pains induced by the stress and strain of the new job. Once the anxiety had been alleviated, the aches would go, she said. It was just a matter of settling in.

*

Ivy and I took a while getting to know each other. We were both so different and we didn't get off to a very good start. The trouble was mine really. You see, I forgot she had already been invented. Instead, I went off on a tangent imagining dreams, ambitions, quests, for her. When I met the modern career woman, I was quite disappointed. It was the difference between the Ivy in my head and the Ivy on paper.

Take the first scene, for example. Daragh folded back the sketchboard to reveal Ivy in a bleak bedsit. She was half-dressed; sitting by the telephone daubing her face with lipstick. She glanced at her watch, then back to the phone again.

"She's tarting herself up for the office," said Daragh. "But her boyfriend hasn't called. So she hangs around. Waiting and waiting; making herself late."

Over the page, a distraught-looking Ivy dashed into the television studio.

"She reads the breakfast news and makes a complete mess of it," said Daragh. "Make it farcical. Maybe she could read the fire regulations instead of the lead story."

She wasn't the woman I had anticipated. She was scatty, slack, slightly irresponsible. I wasn't even sure I liked her.

But then it wasn't my job to like Ivy. She was only a fictional character after all. I was too excited to get upset anyway. I could not quite believe I was in this beautiful building being paid to write a television script.

I was determined to do a good job; to make Ivy look ridiculous; to generate comic waves and canned laughter. If Daragh's career woman helped me on the road to success, then so be it.

This script was to be my trampoline. As I jumped and bounced and somersaulted with my words, I might just touch the sky. Once I had made my name, I would move on to better things. From that moment, all plots would be mine. I only had to bide my time and wait.

*

Nine days after I started work, I gave birth. My back heaved and shook and quivered; there was a loud ripping. My spine cracked open and a white shape popped out. It was a small, paper-like ball with a squashed head, covered in a thin mucus.

The ball unravelled and slowly found its feet. The head squared into shape. The creature grew legs; unfolded its arms. Then, shaking, faltering, it learned to stand; moving cautiously at first. Gingerly, hesitantly, stretching its limbs; peering with blind eyes.

My back shivered again and two more figures emerged; flopping and floundering on the floor. They were anaemic-looking; bland and flour-coloured. They were attached to my back by a thin umbilical cord and joined to one another by their hands and feet.

I wiped them with a warm towel, rubbing until the circulation came. Then, slowly, colour began to swim under their paper skin, pasting the surface with the shadow of life. They didn't react; just stared without screaming their birth cry. As colour surfaced, I recognised them. They were paper duplicates of me.

*

Ivy didn't grow as quickly as I'd hoped. She took new directions I couldn't anticipate; stubbornly refused to see reason. Perhaps I was just adjusting to the task of script writing. The words were sticky as treacle. They did not flow easily, they had to be coaxed.

Daragh helped me though, tirelessly working over my scripts; explaining Ivy's psyche to me; guiding me when I led her astray.

"No bad language or crude jokes," he said. Or; "Soften it up a little. I don't want her too tough."

It was a struggle though. It was difficult getting into the mind of a woman who threw tantrums when male colleagues replaced her reading the breakfast news. It was impossible to understand her meek obedience when she was with her boyfriend. Her docility within her relationship, and aggression outside of it seemed at odds. Yet slowly, slowly, I started to grasp the principle of script writing. It was just a matter of casting aside my own opinions and knuckling under; working within the limitations of the script, instead of imposing my own opinions on to it. When I learned this lesson, everything else seemed to fall into place.

Daragh seemed patient enough.

"You're getting the hang of it," he said. "The comedy lies in the discrepancy between Ivy's public self and the little girl within."

"I suppose so," I said. "I'm still feeling my way. It's hard to write for Ivy. She doesn't seem very realistic."

"Comedy isn't realism," said Daragh, dropping cigarette ash into his coffee mug.

I jotted this remark down in my notepad and pondered over it. I still had a lot to learn about comedy; a lot to learn about television.

*

There was no rest from my selves; they were relentless. As I arrived home from work one night, I felt a snapping under my skin. There was a bubbling and a blistering. Scissors snipped rapidly; fingers folding origami figures. Paper bent and twisted; then my back split open and more paper embryos emerged. One after another they stepped out. Wet and crumpled at first; then stretching out, shaking themselves, unfolding; drying into their ironed-out human selves.

They tip-toed around in my wake; all eight following me like a giant kite tail. They swirled in free flight, guided by the tension of my string.

*

As soon as my struggles ended with Ivy, I started having problems with her boyfriend Paul. I pictured him as an easy-going type of man; not too pushy and not too backward. A media sales director who was just as comfortable in front of the fire as he was in his executive's chair. He probably wore glasses and talked intensely about literature and fine art.

Daragh forgave my slowness at first; my clumsy first attempts at creating character.

"His audience appeal lies in his toughness," he explained. "Give him guts. I don't want him to appear spineless and wet. Get him shouting or slamming his fist on the table."

The trouble was, I didn't think Paul's problem was his image. He just didn't fit into my plot. To start with, I didn't think Ivy would have been stupid enough to fall for someone like him. For that matter, *he* didn't even seem to be in love with Ivy at all. He made snide remarks when she arrived home late from work and was sarcastic about her cooking. He seemed to spend most of his working day ogling at more homely types; fantasising about the selfless secretaries who ran errands for him.

*

My selves seemed to cause me more and more trouble. They looked harmless enough, swelling and shrinking like a giant accordion, but I was sure they were also playing tricks on me. I was constantly losing my pen, only to find it at the bottom of an old handbag; words scrambled and vanished off my computer disk; my office keys dropped in irretrievable places. I even found coffee spilled on my manuscript, the stain spreading and splitting like an amoeba, blotting out my words.

*

Ivy continually thwarted me. In particular, I had problems with her personal life; her obsession with her biological clock; the man shortage; her craving for a wedding ring.

"Nesting," said Daragh, "is a major theme. It's time for her to start thinking about her eggs and making changes in her life."

"Perhaps she should get a new lover?" I suggested.

I would quite happily have abandoned Paul; leaving him in a knotted plastic bag in the middle of a busy road.

"No, I don't want her sleeping around," said Daragh. "She has to learn to slow down; to make herself more feminine."

"But why?" I asked. "Can't she be the woman who has it all?"

Daragh didn't bother to answer. I realised then, Ivy, the career girl, had no choices. She was not a whole woman, able to simultaneously be a mother, a lover and a journalist. Instead, she was divided - either she was one thing or she was another.

*

"Meet Rupert Winger!" said Daragh, waving his hand languidly. "He's come up from London. He's interested in commissioning 'Ivy'."

"Great!" I said, trying hard to disguise my excitement.

Rupert Winger nodded limply in my general direction. he was reading the latest draft of my script. He was flicking through the pages, marking them with a red pen.

"We might be quite a while," said Daragh. "You may as well make us coffees while you're up."

So I poured Melitta then joined them. They were already cackling in collaboration; discussing potential story lines.

"I just love it, love it, love it," said Rupert Winger. "It's just what we need - an antidote to the stay-at-home housewife in the soaps."

My heart skipped. He wanted to push 'Ivy' for a new programme slot which had fallen vacant. He wanted the script finished as soon as possible.

"This script could make your name young lady," he said, shaking my hand vigorously. "Is there any chance it could be completed in a month's time?"

I nodded. I had planned to take another two months, but I was confident I could complete the script if I worked late in the evenings and on weekends.

"That okay with you?" asked Daragh. "Are you sure you're up to it?"

"Sure," I said. "Course I am."

"Good," said Rupert. "Projects like this separate the men from the boys."

I picked up my manuscript and walked back to my desk. I was gleeful. Here was my opportunity to become a household name. All the weeks of hard work, the struggles, had been worthwhile.

Suddenly, I tripped. My manuscript danced out of my hands and splayed across the floor like litter. Pain shot up my leg as I regained my posture. I scrambled for the sheets of paper, snatching them up quickly to mask my embarrassment. By the time I was sitting at my desk, I realised I had forgotten to number the pages. It would take all afternoon to put the script back in order.

I became suspicious then, and angry. I was quite certain the tail end of my multiple selves had quite deliberately stuck out its feet and tripped me. I was sure it had been done maliciously. I had no proof though. It was just the way they smirked at me.

*

The incident in the office was the last straw. When I returned home I took a bread knife from the drawer. I was sick of having eight selves, their silent presence, their constant haunting. I was sure they were interfering with my work, so I decided to set them free. They would just have to find new homes; another woman to pester.

I grabbed the umbilical cord from behind my back and bent it in two. Then I clasped the knife, sawing, grating through the flesh. But it was no use. The cord just bent the knife blade. Instead, I tried separating their arms and legs. Again, the knife screeched. The skin was as solid and inseparable as rock. The cut-outs were there to stay. Not only that but my back was swelling again.

*

The seconds ticked past on the clock. Everyone in the news studio was waiting. Ivy's co-presenter was on stand-by, glancing hungrily, at his watch. Meanwhile, Ivy was asleep in a double bed, her stockings curled like snakes across the floor; Paul was beside her snoring. Back in the television studio, her male rival watched the clock like a cat, rubbing his hands with glee.

"I'm not sure about this," I said. "It's out of character. I know she's a bit irresponsible, but here she's behaving like an idiotic child. She must know she'll be sacked."

"Character is too restrictive," snapped Daragh. "This is comedy, not drama."

I worked for two hours, but the words wouldn't come. I wasn't concentrating really. Half an eye was on my sixteen selves. There was no telling what they would do next. Meanwhile, Ivy was like a bar of wet soap, skidding across the floor out of my reach. Perhaps I was never cut out to be a comedy writer. My emotions see-sawed. I felt as despondent as I had felt exhilarated the day before. I wondered whether I should have stayed in newspapers.

Daragh peered over my shoulder, spotting the blank sheet of paper. "Struggling eh?" he said. "Don't back out on me now."

I started again with renewed vigour; glaring at my paper selves. I was determined to finish the project without any more interference.

197

They would not get the better of me again.

*

I write late at night, positioning a typewriter on my dressing table now. It is the only place I can work without hindrance. Quite by chance, I discovered that my selves are averse to mirrors. One morning, as I was driving to work, I glanced in my rear-view mirror and realised all sixteen of them had vanished. I was alone; just one woman stared back from the looking glass. They shied away from replication.

Now, I always work with a mirror in front of me. A pocket-size compact will do. I use this as my reference point. Checking frequently; a reminder of who I really am. At least, who I hope I was, before my selves started taking over. I sometimes wonder if I might be another duplicate.

*

I am tired and exhausted; drinking bitter coffees to keep myself awake. Sipping, concentrating, scribbling. Throwing balls of paper away. Most of the spadework is done. I have only to tidy the script; to juggle a few words here and there.

By six o'clock, Ivy is complete. Tomorrow, she will be in Rupert Winger's hands. He can breathe life into her or cut her dead,

Daragh is pleased with me. He takes me out for dinner to celebrate the end of the project.

"Just what I wanted," he said. "Just the right blend of vulnerability and independence. You've done me proud."

"I like the way that the script ends with a cliffhanger," I say. "But does Ivy *really* lose her job?"

"Course not," grins Daragh. "She can sleep with her editor in the next series!"

I go to bed at 3 am. But I lie awake. The floorboards creak. My selves have got out of bed and are pacing the floor. There are thirty-two of them now; all padding. Restless white spirits shifting in the gloom.

*

I arrive early at the docks with my manuscript. It is windy. My selves catch the breeze and tug. They seem to yank me away as I get out of the car. As I reach the door of the building, a gust of wind lifts them up against the building; trapping their tail end in the guttering. I should have known they would try a stunt like this. I reach in my pocket for the mirror, but find I cannot move. My hands

198

are tied to my sides; paper string binds my fingers.
I struggle and suddenly my selves break free. The withering umbilical cord snaps and takes root in the pavement. My multiple selves start to grow; easing themselves up the side of the building. Twisting and twining, slowly at first, their fingers searching óut a path in the cracks. They are growing like poison ivy; tendrils seeking new routes.

Then they start to divide. They split and multiply; sixty four doubling to one hundred and twenty eight. Beautiful leaves wrap around the building. Roots dig deep into the bricks and mortar; searching for food, for moisture. Two hundred and fifty six; five hundred and twelve. The paper plant stretches and yawns. It blocks all entrances, smothers all doors and windows. I cannot enter the building. I can see no way in; no way out. One thousand and twenty four; two thousand and forty eight.

I climb in my car, with my script in my briefcase. The plant is uncontrollable now. Beyond sums and calculations. Too fast; too quick for the human mind. It is evergreen. Poisonous. Stems and leaves twist into tight constricting knots; biting into the brickwork. I drive off, before the company crumbles; before it is sucked dry.

CONTRIBUTORS

FIRST PUBLISHED STORY

Richard Bowden was born in 1958 and works for *The Bookseller*. **Stephanie Hale** was born in 1966 and lives in Norwich. She has worked as a freelance for Anglia TV and the BBC. **Christine Hauch** is in her thirties and has done much translation from French and Danish and also worked as a copy editor. **Mark Lynch** was born 1963 and lives in Arbroath. **Clare Portman** was born 1952 and lives in Birmingham. **Jane Smith** lives on the Isle of Wight and is 31. She runs a knitting kit design business called Just Kidding. **John Upton** lives in Birmingham and is an unemployed Oxford graduate aged 23.

OTHERS

Brian Howell lives in Prague and has been in *Sugar Sleep, Critical Quarterly, The European, Darklands and Panurge*. **Mairead Irish** lives in Waterford, Eire and has published widely in anthologies and magazines. **Kathy Janowitz** was born in the Czech Republic and lives in New York. She has been in *Partisan Review, Lilith* etc. **Peter Lewis** runs Flambard Press and teaches at Durham University. **Patrick McCabe** made his UK debut in Panurge 3. He has published *Carn* and *Butcher Boy* (both with Picador) and was shortlisted for the Booker 1992. Born 1955 he lives in London. **John Rizkalla** published *The Jericho Garden* with Bodley Head in 1988. His stories have been in *London Magazine, Panurge* etc. **David Rose** lives in Middlesex and has been in *Literary Review* and *Panurge*. **Lorna Tracy** is fiction editor of *Stand Magazine* and author of *Amateur Passions*, an acclaimed Virago collection of stories. She comes from Idaho and now lives in Newcastle on Tyne. She was born in 1934. **James Waddington** was born in 1942 and lives in Huddersfield. Winner of a prestigious Yorkshire Playwrights Award last year he has published fiction in *Panurge* and *Sunk Island Review* and *Minerva Book of Stories* and *Heinemann's Best Stories*. He was a prizewinner in the Sunk Island Fiction Competition 1993 and a runner up in the Panurge Tale of Two Cities Competition. **Conrad Williams** is 24 and has been in *Darklands* and *Sugar Sleep*. He recently won a British Fantasy Fiction Award and got first prize for the Littlewood Arc Northern Stories Competition (a previous winner was David Almond). He lives in Warrington. **Philip Wolmuth** lives in London and has regularly had photographs in *Panurge, The Guardian* etc. **Michael Zadoorian** lives in Michigan and has been in *Literary Review USA, Wisconsin Review, North American Review, Paris Transcontinental* and elsewhere. **Richard C. Zimler** was born in 1956. He is an American living in Oporto who teaches journalism there. His fiction has been in *London Magazine, Madison Review* and *Puerto del Sol*. His first novel is published in Portuguese (translated from English) by Quetzal Editores of Lisbon and is represented in the US by Sober Weber of New York. It is called *The Last Kabbalist of Lisbon* and is set among the secret Jews of Lisbon in 1506. He won 2nd Prize in the Sunk Island Fiction Competition 1993.